THE CITY DAIRY

For Margot
The First of the Next Generation

THE CITY DAIRY

A SOCIAL AND FAMILY HISTORY

DAVE JOY

PEN & SWORD HISTORY

AN IMPRINT OF PEN & SWORD BOOKS LTD.
YORKSHIRE – PHILADELPHIA

First published in Great Britain in 2023 by
PEN AND SWORD HISTORY
An imprint of
Pen & Sword Books Ltd
Yorkshire – Philadelphia

Copyright © Dave Joy, 2023

ISBN 978 1 39906 901 4

The right of Dave Joy to be identified as Author of this work has been asserted by him in accordance with the Copyright, Designs and Patents Act 1988.

A CIP catalogue record for this book is available from the British Library.

All rights reserved. No part of this book may be reproduced or transmitted in any form or by any means, electronic or mechanical including photocopying, recording or by any information storage and retrieval system, without permission from the Publisher in writing.

Typeset in Times New Roman 10/12 by SJmagic DESIGN SERVICES, India.
Printed and bound in the UK by CPI Group (UK) Ltd.

Pen & Sword Books Limited incorporates the imprints of Atlas, Archaeology, Aviation, Discovery, Family History, Fiction, History, Maritime, Military, Military Classics, After the Battle, Politics, Select, Transport, True Crime, Air World, Frontline Publishing, Leo Cooper, Remember When, Seaforth Publishing, The Praetorian Press, Wharncliffe Local History, Wharncliffe Transport, Wharncliffe True Crime and White Owl.

For a complete list of Pen & Sword titles please contact
PEN & SWORD BOOKS LIMITED
George House, Units 12 & 13, Beevor Street, Off Pontefract Road,
Barnsley, South Yorkshire, S71 1HN, England
E-mail: enquiries@pen-and-sword.co.uk
Website: www.pen-and-sword.co.uk

or

PEN AND SWORD BOOKS
1950 Lawrence Rd, Havertown, PA 19083, USA
E-mail: uspen-and-sword@casematepublishers.com
Website: www.penandswordbooks.com

Contents

About the Author		viii
Acknowledgements		ix
List of Illustrations		x
Preface		xiv

PART ONE: THE LIFE AND TIMES OF THE CITY DAIRYMAN

Chapter 1	City Dairies – Origins		2
	Farmers Become Dairymen		2
	Railway Milk – All Change!		6
Chapter 2	City Dairies – Operations		11
	The Milkhouse		11
	The Cowhouse or 'Shippon'		13
	Bringing Cows to the City		16
	The Milk Round		18
	Fodder – A Moveable Feast		22
	Muck and Brass		24
	Regulation and Inspection		26
	Trading Partners		30
	Showtime!		31
Chapter 3	Migration		33
	Domestic Migration – City Businesses with Rural Roots		34
	International Migration – The New World		37
	Inward Migration – Welcome to Britain		40
Chapter 4	Rise and Fall of the City Dairy		41
	The 'Hay-day' of the Cowkeeper		41
	The First World War		42
	Between the Wars		44
	The Second World War		50
	The Last Cowkeeper		54
	Open All Hours		57
	No Milk Today		60
	A Legacy of Laughter		61

The City Dairy: A Social and Family History

PART TWO: RESEARCH GUIDE

Chapter 5	Researching Your Dairy Ancestors	64
	Births, Marriages and Deaths	64
	Business Accounts	66
	Census Records *(See Chapter 6)*	67
	County Agricultural Societies	67
	Diaries, Memoirs and Reminiscences	68
	District Cowkeepers' and Dairymen's Associations	70
	Electoral Registers	71
	Family Lore, Myths and Legends	72
	Funeral Cards and Eulogies	73
	Licence Registers	74
	Maps and Satellite Images	75
	Military Records	76
	Newspapers	77
	Oral History and Living Memories	80
	Postcards	80
	Trade Directories	82
	Transport Tickets	84
	Wills and Probate	84
Chapter 6	Census Records	85
	Census Information	85
	Occupation	86
	Occupational Status	88
	Property	89
	Place of Birth	89
	Analysing Census Records	89
	The 1939 England and Wales Register	95
Chapter 7	Literature Review	96
Chapter 8	Blogs and Websites	99
Chapter 9	Tools of the Trade	110
	Vehicles	110
	Milk Bottles and Tops	112
	Bespoke Business Stationery	115
	Hand Tools and Equipment	116
	Competition Trophies	117
	Milk Cans	119
Chapter 10	Buildings and Architecture	121
	The Milkhouse	122
	The Yard	124
	The Cowhouse or Shippon	124

Contents

PART THREE: CASE STUDIES

Chapter 11	The Royal Lancashire Agricultural Society	128
	Archived Records	128
	Annual Journals	129
Chapter 12	Liverpool & District Dairy Farmers' Association	131
	Members' Handbook	131
	Local Licensing	132
	Newspaper Coverage	135
Chapter 13	A Dairy Dynasty	139
	Timeline 1 – The Family of George Nelson and Jane Greenwood	140
	Timeline 2 – The Family of Edward Capstick and Agnes Nelson	144
	Timeline 3 – The Family of John Harper and Dorothy Greenwood	146
	Timeline 4 – The Family of Rowland Harper and Sarah J. Mason	148
	Timeline 5 – The Family of Lawrence Mason and Mary Jackson	150
	Timeline 6 – The Family of John Richardson and Agnes Mason	152
Postscript	Fieldwork: Finding Your Ancestral City Dairy	154
Glossary		155
Appendix A	Key Dates and Events Affecting City Dairymen	158
Appendix B	List of Historical District Cowkeepers' and Dairymen's Associations	162
Appendix C	Rules of The City of Liverpool & District Cowkeepers' Association (1919)	164
Appendix D	The Liverpool & District Cowkeepers' Association Annual Cattle Show	170
Bibliography		178
Index		182

About the Author

Dave Joy BA, MA, is a retired local government executive officer who spends his retirement researching and writing about his family history. He has had two books published to date. The first, *My Family and Other Scousers – A Liverpool Boy's Summer of Adventure in '69* (The History Press, 2014), is a memoir of his childhood days spent at Wellington Dairy – the family-owned, horse-drawn milk business in Garston, Liverpool. His second book, *Liverpool Cowkeepers* (Amberley, 2016), traces the history of the Joy family from their origins as farmers in Yorkshire's Upper Wharfedale Valley, to becoming cowkeepers and then dairymen in south Liverpool.

Dave is a member of The Society of Genealogists, The Society of Authors, Liverpool & SW Lancashire Family History Society, Wharfedale & Airedale Family History Group, The Friends of Raikes Road Burial Ground, Liverpool History Society and The Metcalfe Society.

Since the publication of his books, Dave has become a popular public speaker, much in demand throughout the north-west of England, and has lectured at Liverpool John Moores University and at Lancaster University's Regional Heritage Centre. He has written several articles for the national family history press, as well as for local family history groups and has written two publications for Garston Historical Society. Further information about Dave's research, his programme of illustrated talks and his publication history can be found on his website: **davejoy-author.com**

Acknowledgements

Grateful thanks to the following for their contributions and assistance: Jean Abbey, Meryl Auty, Susanne Barton, Alan Brooks, Stephen Caldwell, Geoff Cannon, Mike Chitty at the Wavertree Society, Stan Cotter, Janet Dalton, Jim Davies, Diane Elphick at Sedbergh & District History Society, William Franks, Bill Frith, Karen Griffiths at the Yorkshire Dales National Park Authority, Angela Hallows, Vera Haydock, Tricia Henton, Mark Hudson, Philip Ingham, Heather Joy, Lancashire County Archives, Liverpool Records Office, Victoria Lyon, Robert Mason, Rosemary McCaffrey, Dave Morton, Ann Osborne, Brian Phythian, Anne Poynter, Tom Pollock, Barbara Price at Garston Historical Society, Kath Robinson, Edith Margaret Royle, Brian Snelson, Sue Smith, Karen Stanley, Janis Stout, Kate Thexton, Roy Thwaite, Andrew Williamson, David Wilson, and the team at Pen & Sword.

And, as always, thanks to Jean, Victoria, Anthony and Heather for their never-ending love, patience and support.

List of Illustrations

1. **Dairy Farms** – When people migrated to the cities, rural dairy farmers struggled to find a market for their liquid milk. Brockbank's Farm, Cumbria. (Courtesy of Jean Abbey)
2. **Backyard Cows** – Cowkeepers kept cows in the backyards of city properties. Simon Metcalfe, Cowkeeper. (Courtesy of Bill Frith)
3. **The Cow Keeper, Golden Lane, London** – Drawing by George J. Scharf, 1825. (Wellcome Collection. Attribution 4.0 International (CC BY 4.0))
4. **Westminster Dairy, The Quadrant, Regent Street, London** – Drawing by George J. Scharf, 1825. (Wellcome Collection. Attribution 4.0 International (CC BY 4.0))
5. **The Dairy Supply Company, London** – A photograph of the former dairy on display in what is now a pizza restaurant. (Author)
6. **Milk Cooler** – From 1872, basic convection coolers became widely adopted in an attempt to prolong the freshness of milk. (Author)
7. **City Milkhouse** – End-terrace properties were those most easily adapted to meet the needs of early dairymen. Bernard Gilpin, Cowkeeper. (Courtesy of Anne Poynter)
8. **Traditional Cowhouse, Yorkshire** – The design of city cowhouses was based on that of traditional 'field barns' in the countryside. (© Yorkshire Dales National Park Authority, 2019)
9. **City Cowhouse, Liverpool** – A typical cowkeeper's shippon and yard in the city centre. Selig Dover, Cowkeeper. (Courtesy of Liverpool Records Office)
10. **Rising Standards** – As standards improved, city shippons were designed to accommodate herds of thirty cattle or more. (Author)
11. **A Good Deal** – Norman Shinkfield swapped cowkeeping for cattle dealing and became very successful. (Courtesy of Susanne Barton)
12. **The Milk Float** – A vehicle designed for milk transportation. Thomas Ranson, Dairyman. (Courtesy of Tom Pollock)
13. **Many Hands** – Three or more generations of a family could be living and working at the city dairy. The Harper family, Chesnut Grove Dairy, Wavertree. (Courtesy of David Wilson)
14. **Grass Cuttings** – It was common practice for city cowkeepers to 'harvest' grass cuttings from municipal parks. The Hogg family at Sefton Park, Liverpool. (Courtesy of Angela Hallows)
15. **Muck and Brass** – Cow muck was stored, temporarily, in a midden until it could be sold to farmers as a natural fertiliser. A. Joy & Sons, Farmers and Cowkeepers, Wellington Dairy, Garston. (Author)

List of Illustrations

16. **Licensed to Sell Milk** – Dairies were licensed by the local authority and were required to display that they were 'Registered for the Sale of Milk'. Edward Hall, Cowkeeper. (Courtesy of Bill Frith)
17. **Licensed to Keep Cows** – Shippons were licensed by the local authority and were required to display the number of cows for which they were licensed. A. Joy & Sons, Wellington Dairy. (Author)
18. **Invalids and Infants** – Many cowkeepers kept a 'special' cow, giving soft-curd milk, suitable for sensitive digestive systems. Edward Mason, Dairyman and Cowkeeper. (Courtesy of Robert Mason)
19. **Jack of all-trades** – Mr I. Rabinowitz was a livestock agent and a wholesale butcher who also ran a city abattoir. (Courtesy of Geoff Cannon)
20. **A Prizewinning Dairy** – Success at agricultural shows was an excellent way for dairymen to promote their business. Fawcett Harper, Farmer and Cowkeeper. (Courtesy of Kath Robinson)
21. **To-ing and Fro-ing** – Relatives from the countryside would come to help out at the dairy and experience city life. William Metcalfe, Cowkeeper. (Courtesy of Kath Robinson)
22. **A Grand Day Out** – Cowkeepers' and dairymen's associations organised extensive programmes of social events for members and their families. (Courtesy of Edith Margaret Royle)
23. **A Dairyman Abroad** – George Eric Wright was a Garston dairyman who emigrated to Australia in 1913. (Author)
24. **War Horse** – During the First World War, thousands of working horses were acquired by the army and used to carry supplies to the front. Richard Harper, Cowkeeper. (Courtesy of Roy Thwaite)
25. **The National Dairymen's Association** – This national association was formed in 1937 to protect the interests of all persons concerned in the retailing of milk. (Author)
26. **From Cow to Customer?** – By the end of the Second World War, the bond that had existed between city cow and customer was no more. (Courtesy of Sue Smith)
27. **End of an Era** – The Liverpool and District Dairy Farmers' Association closed its books on 25 April 1975. (Courtesy of Andrew Williamson)
28. **The Corner Shop** – City dairies survived by evolving into corner shops and convenience stores. (Author)
29. **A Legacy of Laughter** – Bamforth & Co. produced saucy seaside postcards satirising classic comic archetypes, including the milkman. (Author)
30. **Business Accounts** – Messrs T. Sowerby & Sons. Profit and Loss accounts, 1952. (Courtesy of Geoff Cannon)
31. **The County Show** – City cowkeepers were prominent at local agricultural shows, providing a day out for the whole family. J. Hogg & Sons, Cowkeeper. (Courtesy of Janet Dalton)
32. **Daniel Joy's Diary** – Personal diaries can be a rich source of information for the family historian. (Author)

33. **The Professionals** – Many city dairymen were members of local associations. Dairyman William Ingham and fellow professionals. (Courtesy of Philip Ingham)
34. **Funeral Card for Ann Metcalfe** – It was common practice for the bodies of city dairymen and their families to be returned 'home' for burial. (Courtesy of Kath Robinson)
35. **Hold the Front Page!** – City cattle shows provided plenty of prizes, pomp and pageantry for the local press. Tom Hogg, Dairyman. (Courtesy of Angela Hallows)
36. **The Cow with The Iron Tail** – Adding water to milk became a criminal offence. (Courtesy of the artist, Heather Joy)
37. **A Postcard from Home** – Photographic studios turned family photographs into picture postcards. (Courtesy of William Franks)
38. **Bell Stewardson (right), a City Milkmaid from Witherslack** – City dairies recruited workers from rural areas. (Courtesy of Vera Haydock)
39. **London's Milk Supply** – George Barham's former Dairy Supply Company in Coptic Street, London. (Author)
40. **Old Church Street, Chelsea** – A former dairy in Old Church Street, now a residential property. (Author)
41. **King's Road, Chelsea** – A former dairy in King's Road, now a mobile phone shop. (Author)
42. **Delivery Vehicles** – As milk delivery vehicles evolved, many continued to advertise the dairy by displaying name and address information. (a) Joy's (Author); (b) Morton's (courtesy of Dave Morton); (c) Taylor's (courtesy of Kate Thexton); (d) Capstick's (courtesy of Ann Osborne); (e) Greenbank's (courtesy of Ray Smyth); (f) Metcalfe's (courtesy of Karen Stanley)
43. **Fastest in the West?** – Vintage milk delivery vehicles can be found in transport museums. Museum of Liverpool Life. (Author)
44. **Milk Bottles** – Milk bottles were at first embossed (a) and later pyroglazed (b) with the name of the dairy as much to facilitate return for re-use than to promote the business. (Author)
45. **Milk Bottle Tops** – Cardboard 'pogs' (a) and foil seals (b) were often printed or stamped with the name, address and telephone number of the dairy. (Pogs, courtesy of Mark Hudson; Foils, Author)
46. **Business Stationery** – Dairies used a variety of bespoke business stationery. A. Joy & Sons, Farmers and Cowkeepers. (Author)
47. **Dairy Leaflet** – Dairies produced promotional literature targeted at prospective customers. Batty's Dairy, Arundel Avenue, Liverpool. (Courtesy of Brian Snelson)
48. **Museum Pieces** – Hand tools and dairy equipment can be seen on display in agricultural museums across the country. (Author)
49. **Trophies** – Competition trophies can carry name, place and date information. (a) Henry Wolfenden, Dairyman. (Courtesy of Meryl Auty); (b) Charles Blackburn & Sons, Dairyman and Dairy Vessel Manufacturer (Courtesy of Tricia Henton)

List of Illustrations

50. **Milk Cans** – Milk cans were often engraved with the name and address of the dairy, as well as that of the manufacturer. (Author)
51. **Architectural Clues** – There are architectural and signage clues that a building had a previous existence as a city dairy. (Author)
52. **Interior Hygiene** – Easy-to-clean, tiled surfaces are a good clue that the building was once used for the sale of milk. (Author)
53. **Former City Dairy** – The typical layout of a former city dairy included milkhouse, cowhouse and yard, with many features still visible today. 1–3 Neilson Road, Liverpool. Access courtesy of Jim Davies. (Author)
54. **County Archives** – Journals of your local county agricultural society may be found at the county archives. (Author)
55. **Cowkeepers' Association Rules** – Many city dairymen were members of their local cowkeepers' association and had to abide by the association's rules. (Courtesy of Bill Frith)
56. **Cowkeeping Licence** – All city milkhouses and cowhouses were subject to a regime of inspection and licensing. (Courtesy of Sedbergh & District History Society)
57. **'Now Judging'** – Local cowkeepers' associations held their own annual cattle shows. (Courtesy of Roy Thwaite)
58. **Marriage of Fawcett Harper, 1894** – Marriage certificates recording occupations as *Cowkeeper*, illustrate the trend of marriages between cowkeeping families. (Author)
59. **'Cumberland Dairy'** – Thomas James Mason, Cowkeeper and Farmer, was recorded in the 1911 census of Liverpool, living at 2 McBride Street, Garston. (Courtesy of Garston Historical Society)

Preface

My father, Anthony Eric Joy, passed away in 2007. It was his passing that prompted me to write a memoir of my childhood days spent at the family dairy. Dad was born and bred in Garston, in the south of Liverpool, and he represented the fourth generation of Joys who had been farmers, cowkeepers, and then dairymen. In writing a eulogy for his funeral, I was fortunate in being able to call upon my own boyhood memories of spending time at Wellington Dairy, working alongside him.

It was in the days that followed the funeral that my own children asked about the stories I had paraphrased in my eulogy to my father. I then found, for the first time in my life, the one person who knew everything about Wellington Dairy was no longer there for me to ask. It dawned on me that not only was I fortunate in having a loving memory of my father but also a living memory of a way of life that was no more. I had been born just in time to catch the final chapter of that way of life and realised that when I was gone, that memory would be gone too – unless I did something about it. So, I wrote it down. Initially, my intention was to write it for my children and, hopefully, for their children. It was only later that the possibility of having it published materialised.

Once I'd had the good fortune to become a published author, I did what many writers do in order to promote and sell their books: I set up my own website and began giving illustrated talks. It was then that people began sending me information about their own dairy ancestors, along with some priceless old photographs. I researched and added to these family histories, wrote them up as articles and posted them on my website. The response was that I received even more enquiries, from others researching their dairy ancestry and seeking advice and assistance. This prompted me to post more on my website – transcripts of census records, of trade directories and lists of prizewinners at local cattle shows – and to seek out new sources of information about city dairies.

That work has culminated in the writing of this book, which I hope will be of assistance to you in researching your dairy family history and in gaining a better understanding of how your ancestors lived – delivering milk to the doorstep in our biggest and busiest towns and cities – and how they survived by adapting to economic, social and industrial change over a period of some 150 years.

Dave Joy, 2022

PART ONE

The Life and Times of the City Dairyman

Chapter 1

City Dairies – Origins

The word *dairy* (noun) can refer to either a room, a building or a business, involved in at least one of the following activities: the production, the processing, or the sale of milk. As such, dairies typically take the form of either: farm (production), factory (processing) or shop (selling). Although the earliest city dairies were a combination of all of these, they were soon followed by dairies that specialised in the retail sale of milk.

Consequently, if your city-dwelling ancestor gave their occupation as *Dairyman*, they were one of two types: there were those dairymen who kept cows and there were those who didn't. Those dairymen that were also cowkeepers did as it 'says on the tin': they kept cows in the city, they milked these cows on site and then sold that fresh product direct to the customer; they were producer-retailers, and they operated out of a *Milkhouse*. Those dairymen who did not keep their own cows obtained their supply of milk either from farmers on the edge of the city or from wholesale milk suppliers who were transporting milk into the city centres; they were retailers of milk, and they operated out of a *Milk Shop*.

At first glance, this distinction might seem somewhat arbitrary; after all, they were both selling milk and delivering it to the customer in very similar ways. But behind that distinction lay two quite different ways of life – some might even argue, two different philosophies of life – that, for over 100 years, would battle each other for survival in the highly competitive milk market.

Yet, these two breeds of dairymen had their origins in common stock: rural dairy farmers who were eager to sell their liquid milk to a rapidly expanding industrial, urban population with a seemingly insatiable appetite for fresh food.

Farmers Become Dairymen

In the early 1800s, the growth of Britain's major towns and cities was being driven by the Industrial Revolution. In 1801, there were, after London, only five towns of over 50,000 inhabitants – Birmingham, Bristol, Leeds, Liverpool and Manchester – but by 1851 these had been joined by a further seventeen (Mingay, 1989). This situation contrasted sharply with the economic depression being experienced in the more rural areas of the country. The net result of all of this was a mass migration from countryside to city of people searching for work. Between 1801 and 1911, the population of England and Wales not only quadrupled but its distribution also

City Dairies – Origins

Dairy Farms – When people migrated to the cities, rural dairy farmers struggled to find a market for their liquid milk. Brockbank's Farm, Cumbria. (Courtesy of Jean Abbey)

changed – from 80 per cent living in the countryside to 80 per cent living in towns and cities (Burnett, 1999).

Some dairy farmers were fortunate to find themselves in a 'Goldilocks zone' (not too near, not too far) on the edge of a growing town or city. They had a ready market for their produce within striking distance – oftentimes, courtesy of a good horse and trap. For example, such farmer-retailers were able to supply enough milk to meet the demands of the textile towns of east Lancashire and the neighbouring West Riding of Yorkshire (Winstanley, 1996). In London, dairy herds were concentrated in a 'peri-urban belt' fringing the northern limits of the City and Westminster, from Marylebone and St Pancras in the west to Islington, Clerkenwell, Bethnal Green, Hackney and Shoreditch in the east (Almeroth-Williams, 2013).

But the perishability of milk meant it could not be transported on bumpy roads for more than a few miles, and so, to their chagrin, many dairy farmers found themselves isolated from this booming metropolitan market. Still, there was a growing demand for milk in the cities and this could not be ignored. In response, some of the more wily and adventurous farmers took the proverbial bull by the horns and brought their cows into the city, keeping them in their backyards and selling milk, fresh from the cow, to the urban populace. Some of these properties were newly created dairies in the city centres, whilst others were original cowsheds that had continued to operate as dairies once they became enveloped by urban expansion.

Backyard Cows – Cowkeepers kept cows in the backyards of city properties. Simon Metcalfe, Cowkeeper. (Courtesy of Bill Frith)

Whereas, back on the home farm, they were struggling to find a ready market for their milk (much having to be transformed into cheese or butter), in the city these new dairymen struggled to keep up with demand. They were able to sell just about all the liquid milk that they were able to produce on a daily basis; in this way, liquid milk succeeded cheese and butter as the primary produce of the dairy industry. In London, as their cows were considered to be better kept and better fed than those on the suburban farms, urban dairies were judged to provide the best milk (Whetham, 1964).

For the first three decades of the nineteenth century, these cowkeeping dairymen were the main suppliers of milk in most of the country's major towns and cities. The agricultural historian, George Edwin Fussell (1952), described the situation in London at that time:

> Lambeth, Kennington Bridge, the Wash Way, Cold Harbour, Peckham, Camberwell and Newington, with a few in Bermondsey, housed about 600 cows when we were fighting Napoleon. Another 550 were kept in Edgware Road and nearly 4,000 in Tottenham Court Road, Paddington, Gray's Inn Lane and Islington.

Other accounts tell of cows being tethered in St James's Park and milked straight into the customers' vessels, or of milk being distributed by milkmaids carrying the 'loose' milk in buckets suspended from yokes across their shoulders and crying 'Milko!' as they walked the streets.

Bavarian artist George Scharf, who came to this country in 1816, captured the emerging new London in his drawings. Amongst his most famous works are the

City Dairies – Origins

Above: **The Cow Keeper, Golden Lane, London** – Drawing by George J. Scharf, 1825. (Wellcome Collection. Attribution 4.0 International (CC BY 4.0))

Right: **Westminster Dairy, The Quadrant, Regent Street, London** – Drawing by George J. Scharf, 1825. (Wellcome Collection. Attribution 4.0 International (CC BY 4.0))

THE QUADRANT, REGENT ST

drawings of two contrasting dairies, both from 1825. The elegant Westminster Dairy was a brand-new milk shop situated at the bottom of the new Regent Street, in the Quadrant, and was supplying the affluent areas of St James and Mayfair; whilst the cowkeeper's dairy in Golden Lane, was serving a much poorer area. Ironically, despite the difference in affluence, because Westminster Dairy obtained its supplies of milk from the northern and western suburbs of the city, its milk would not have been as fresh or as pure as that being served by the cowkeeper (Johnson, 1991).

However, the cowkeeper's advantageous position in the milk market would change forever with the coming of the railways. And, from the 1830s onwards, that rail network spread rapidly throughout the land.

Railway Milk – All Change!

The Liverpool–Manchester Railway, opened in September 1830, was the world's first inter-city railway. There followed an explosion of interest in all things railway – the country was in the grip of *railway mania*. Within twenty years, the national rail network was virtually complete and almost every major town and city was connected. By the 1850s, numerous railways had reached the fringes of London and major termini were being built at Paddington, Euston, King's Cross, Fenchurch Street, Charing Cross, Waterloo and Victoria. The coming of the railways revolutionised the movement of people and goods around the country and the opportunities it presented for the transportation of milk from country to town were not overlooked:

> Records of the Great Western Railway show that in January 1865, this particular network had carried just under 9,000 gallons of milk. By January 1866 this had gone up to 144,000 gallons; by 1880 'Paddington, Marylebone, Euston and Clapham Junction were the great platform milk markets of the metropolis', and from then on haulage by railway steadily increased until, by 1900, the Great Western Railway alone was carrying about 25 million gallons a year, chiefly from the West Country's 50,000 cows.
>
> (Jenkins, 1970)

In her book, *The Wensleydale Railway*, Christine Hallas (2004) describes how the completion of the Leyburn to Hawes link, in 1878, transformed the economy of the area, providing local dairy farmers with a vital outlet for their liquid milk. By 1894, milk was being sent from Wensleydale, via Northallerton, to Newcastle, Middlesbrough, Hull and Leeds; by 1899, it was also being forwarded to the West Riding and to the large milk depot at Finsbury Park for supply to London. By 1905, the dale was exporting some 500,000 gallons of milk per year via the railways.

To begin with, milk was transported in wooden casks, which were really converted milk churns. But these proved to be impractical and were soon replaced with purpose-built metal containers, though the term 'churn' was retained. Initially, these metal railway milk churns came in a variety of sizes, but in London the trade came to conform to a standard unit of 8 'barn' gallons, or 17 gallons in all. The barn gallon was understood to mean a 2-gallon standard with the odd pint thrown in as a traditional makeweight for spillage and wastage. Farmers who sold their milk by the barn gallon effectively handed, as a gift to the dealer, a quantity of milk reckoned to be around 6 per cent of the total. Although technically illegal, wholesale dealers regarded this odd pint as a prerequisite (Nimmo, 2010). The legality of the barn gallon was raised in the House of Commons on more than one occasion but still became the norm for metal railway churns supplying the London milk trade.

Wholesalers were now able to move milk into the cities in bulk and they began to dominate the milk market. The success of these 'corporate' dairies in utilising the railways in this way is probably best illustrated by the work of George Barham, who in 1864, in London, established the Express Country Milk Supply Company (becoming the Express Dairy Company in 1882); the use of the railways was inherent in the name of the company. His achievements in driving forward the quality, quantity and efficiency of the milk industry were historic and were many. He was knighted in 1904, the first dairyman to be so recognised. When he died, in 1913, his two sons continued the business.

As the London milk market developed, so more dairy companies entered the arena. By 1870, there were eight listed in the Post Office Directory; by 1880, this had increased to fourteen, and by 1890, dairy companies had become common in the London dairy trade. As well as the Express Country Milk Supply Company, also listed were the Amalgamated Dairies Company, the Aylesbury Dairy Company, the Great Western Farm Dairies Company, the Surrey Farm Dairy Company, and Tunks & Tisdall's Holland Park Dairy (Whetham, 1964).

Like George Barham, these new wholesalers were able to supply milk to local dairies for retail. This created a huge opportunity for the non-cowkeeping dairymen, who until that time had been playing second fiddle to their cowkeeping counterparts. Milk from the countryside was now arriving in city railway depots on a daily basis and could be bought on the platform and taken back to the dairy, from where it could be sold direct to the customer.

The dairy farmer sending milk to London in the 1860s consigned his milk to one of several wholesale dealers operating within the railway station:

> On its arrival, the wholesaler's representative received it, and immediately sold it to retailers, who took away what they wanted in their own conveyance, and mainly in their own cans. Most, if not all, of the farmer's cans were emptied without being taken away from the station, and were sent at once to the other side of the line for return. Each [wholesaler] had his regular customers every day. There were about ten dealers, and on arrival about thirty or forty retailers' carts were waiting to take the milk away.
>
> (Fussell, 1966)

The Dairy Supply Company, London – A photograph of the former dairy on display in what is now a pizza restaurant. (Author)

A specially commissioned article in the *Liverpool Weekly Courier* (26 October 1889) somewhat lyrically described the London and North Western Railway Company and its many connections, as providing a 'river of milk' to that city:

> The main stream runs through Cheshire, where it is fed by a thousand rills from all parts of that rich pastoral county; a tributary of considerable and growing importance joins it from North Wales, another from Lancashire; while a tiny rivulet flows all the way from Scotland, in the summer almost ceasing, and in the winter assuming respectable dimensions.

City Dairies – Origins

The article goes on to describe the hustle and bustle that took place at Platform 7 of Lime Street railway station each and every morning with vanload after vanload of milk tankards being shunted alongside the platform, followed by the clanging and clatter of the heavy cans as they were transferred to the waiting shandries for delivery to the retailers, or were placed on the platform to await the demands of occasional buyers and street sellers.

Not all observers welcomed this change. In compiling his *History of the Cries of London*, Charles Hindley (1881) mourned the passing of the romance associated with the traditional milkmaid with her street cries of 'Milk Below!' claiming that the new milk-woman was by then a very 'unpoetical personage'! Instead of milk being delivered by pretty maids, the wholesale vendors would now 'bear it in carts to every part of the town, and distribute to the hundreds of shopkeepers and itinerants, who anxiously await to receive it for re-distribution amongst their own customers.'

The coming of the railways might have brought about the end of cowkeeping dairymen but for the fact that transport by rail did not completely address the issue of perishability; milk, being a living liquid, begins to sour the moment it leaves the cow. Depending on the distance being travelled, Railway Milk could have been in transit for the best part of a day. It was a concern of the farmer that the buyer would reject their milk once it reached the city. To delay the process of souring, farmers attempted to cool their milk prior to dispatch. Cooling could be achieved by standing the full milk churns in water, but from 1872, Lawrence's capillary cooler became widely adopted (Atkins, 2017). This apparatus consisted of a framework of metal tubes through which cold water circulated and over which warm milk was poured. The extent of cooling was therefore subject to the temperature of the water available to the farmer, and during the summer, water from ponds or streams was not particularly cold. However, the obvious benefits of this practice encouraged the wholesalers to set up large cooling depots at the rural railway stations, where milk delivered by farmers could be more thoroughly cooled in bulk, often using water from on-site wells sunk for that purpose.

Despite attempts to cool the milk prior to its journey, in the absence of any effective refrigeration, the souring process could still be well advanced by the time the milk reached the customer. So, a unique selling point for the cowkeeping dairymen was the freshness of their product, and in their competition with non-cowkeeping dairies they 'milked' this fact for all it was worth. Indeed, to underline this difference many were insistent on calling

Milk Cooler – From 1872, basic convection coolers became widely adopted in an attempt to prolong the freshness of milk. (Author)

themselves 'Cowkeepers' – it was a way of saying, 'we keep cows, therefore our milk is guaranteed fresh'.

Another reason why cowkeeping remained an attractive proposition was its profitability. Cowkeepers were producer-retailers, so there were no middle men taking a cut of the profits. Their supply chain was very short (cowkeeper-customer) compared with that of their non-cowkeeping competitors (farmer-wholesaler-dairyman-customer). But, as cows needed seeing-to 365 days a year, keeping cows was demanding in terms of the time and effort of the dairyman. These were key considerations when dairymen decided whether or not to keep cows, for it was more a choice of lifestyle than merely a choice of occupation.

In London, the balance between cowkeeping and non-cowkeeping dairymen was affected by the outbreak of cattle plague (rinderpest) in 1865. The disease was carried by cattle from Russia, brought into Britain via Hull, and 'the ravages of the disease in the London cowhouses was fearful' (Curtler, 1909). As well as the city herds being decimated by the disease, insanitary conditions in the city's cowsheds were blamed for its spread and many of these were closed down. This opened a gap in the market that the milk wholesalers were quick to fill with their Railway Milk, which came from unaffected herds in the countryside. During 1866, some 7 million gallons of milk were brought into London by rail from 220 country stations, in order to replace the supplies lost from the urban dairies affected by cattle plague (Whetham, 1964). Inevitably, this proved to be advantageous to non-cowkeeping dairymen, being retailers of Railway Milk, and for a while gave them the upper hand over their cowkeeping competitors in the capital.

Though the source of their milk set these two types of dairymen apart, the methods for the sale and distribution of their produce were virtually identical: a city dairy with one or more milk rounds, typically delivered using a horse and cart.

Chapter 2

City Dairies – Operations

Setting up a dairy in the city required some degree of financial outlay. Even if the property was being rented rather than purchased it would require fitting out and equipping to make it fit for purpose. Most important of all, if it was to produce its own milk, it needed to be stocked with cows. Acquiring a going concern might have saved on fitting-out costs but then there would have been the cost of 'goodwill' associated with the existing business.

In the absence of any collateral to offer the banks, it was common practice for loans to be secured from family members or even from friends who were confident in a modest return; it was as much an investment in the individual as it was in the business. Another option was to seek a loan from one of the corporate dairies, but this would then tie the prospective dairyman to the wholesaler for his milk supply.

When setting up a dairy in Garston in 1873, my second-great-grandfather, Daniel Joy, borrowed from his cousin, Ralph Bowdin, who ran an inn in Hebden, Yorkshire. This debt was inherited by Daniel's son, Anthony (also a dairyman), and was paid back in 1896 when Ralph's father passed away. The deceased had left a sum of money to Anthony and the outstanding debt was deducted from his share of the estate. Written correspondence from the Bowdin family's solicitors in Skipton, dated 12 May 1896, confirms that the total amount due by then was £15 5s 9d.

To give an indication of the value of such businesses, in 1906, when Richard Taylor decided to give up his farm in Westmorland and seek a dairy business in Liverpool, he was able to secure the franchise of Wolfenden's Model Dairy, St Michael-in-the-Hamlet. The term 'model' was used to describe any dairy designed and fitted with the latest equipment to meet the rigorous public health regulations governing milk production at that time. They were considered to be 'modern' dairies and were often opened up for the public to view. A letter from J. Wolfenden, dated 19 November 1906, confirms receipt of Richard's deposit of £50 to secure the business franchise at a price of £930, 'to cover all effects, when taken over, business to be at same standard as above date' (courtesy of Kate Thexton).

The Milkhouse

Whether or not they kept cows, the basic property requirements of dairymen were similar – cowkeepers just needed more space to accommodate the production side of the business. The term *Milkhouse* refers to a dairy at which milk was both

The City Dairy: A Social and Family History

produced and sold; the term *Milk Shop* refers to a dairy from which milk was sold that was not produced on site.

The preferred situation of the early dairies was an end-terrace property. Such properties had the advantage of having access to the backyard, either down the side of the building or by going into the side street and knocking through a gateway from there. In the backyard there would be a stable for a horse and a space for garaging a milk cart, a midden for the muck and a loft for storing hay and straw; cowkeepers would also have a shippon (or 'cowhouse') for keeping an average herd of eight cows.

The milk business operated out of the ground floor of the property. The front room was the shop with a counter over which the milk was dispensed; this might have its own doorway at the front or side of the property, separate from that giving access to the residential part of the property. The back room was where the milk was held, ready for sale. If more space was required, for making butter or ice cream, or for making and storing cheese, then the building could be extended to the side or rear.

If the property had a cellar, then that was used for keeping everything cool. If not, there was usually a room deliberately kept cold for this purpose. This cold room was often referred to as 'the dairy'. I recall our cold room at Wellington Dairy. It was a stone-built outbuilding in a shaded corner to the rear of the milkhouse. For ventilation it had one window, set high in the wall, just below ceiling level, which did not receive any direct sunlight. The interior walls were whitewashed from floor

City Milkhouse – End-terrace properties were those most easily adapted to meet the needs of early dairymen. Bernard Gilpin, Cowkeeper. (Courtesy of Anne Poynter)

to ceiling and running along one side of the room was a worktop made from a single slab of thick slate. If you placed the flat of your hand on the slate, you could feel the heat being drawn out of you. Originally, this was where we put the milk from our own cows, ready for sale to the public; later, as we modernised, it became the home of a milk cooler, a table-top pasteuriser and a hand-operated bottling machine. My dad used to say that this was a dairy (room) within a dairy (building) within a dairy (business)!

The family lived upstairs. Cowkeeping families were often large as the business benefited from as many pairs of hands as possible. Consequently, it was common practice for the living quarters to be extended into the roof space or over the shippon. In his memoir of his Liverpool childhood, Jim Callaghan (2011) recalls a shippon of six cows being directly under his bedroom and 'looking down on them through the knothole in the floorboards we could feel the heat rising from their bodies.'

As cities expanded, the town planners recognised the need to accommodate dairying and cowkeeping businesses. New suburban developments included purpose-built milkhouses with all facilities provided: family living quarters, shop, dairy, shippon, milking parlour, stable, hayloft, midden, cart shed and a big yard. Many of these purpose-built milkhouses, being located in the suburbs, have survived city centre clearance programmes and still exist today, though their use has changed.

The Cowhouse or 'Shippon'

Although the terms *Milkhouse* and *Cowhouse* are often used interchangeably, in most cases they were separate buildings, designed with quite different functions in mind. Whereas a milkhouse was the building in which the family lived (upstairs) and from which the milk was sold (downstairs), the cowhouse – or, shippon – was the building in which the cows were kept.

Cowhouses, known as 'field barns', were common features on many rural dairy farms prior to the move to the cities. Indeed, the design of the city shippon is very much based on these original rural cowhouses. In the countryside, they were used to keep cows indoors during the winter, when the animals were unable to graze. Many still exist and remain fully functional. As part of its Heritage Lottery-funded project, *Every Barn Tells a Story*, the Yorkshire Dales National Park Authority researched the traditional cowhouses of Upper Swaledale that still stand today, and the families who worked them (**everybarn.yorkshiredales.org.uk**).

Some cowhouses were attached to the farmhouse, whilst others (as in Swaledale) were stand-alone buildings, located out in the fields; in either situation, space was not usually a limiting factor. That was not the case in the city, where space was at a premium, and shippons had to be shoehorned into tight backyards, walled-in by adjacent buildings.

These utilitarian buildings had many basic design features in common. The shippon was divided into stalls ('booses' or 'buses') in which the cow would stand,

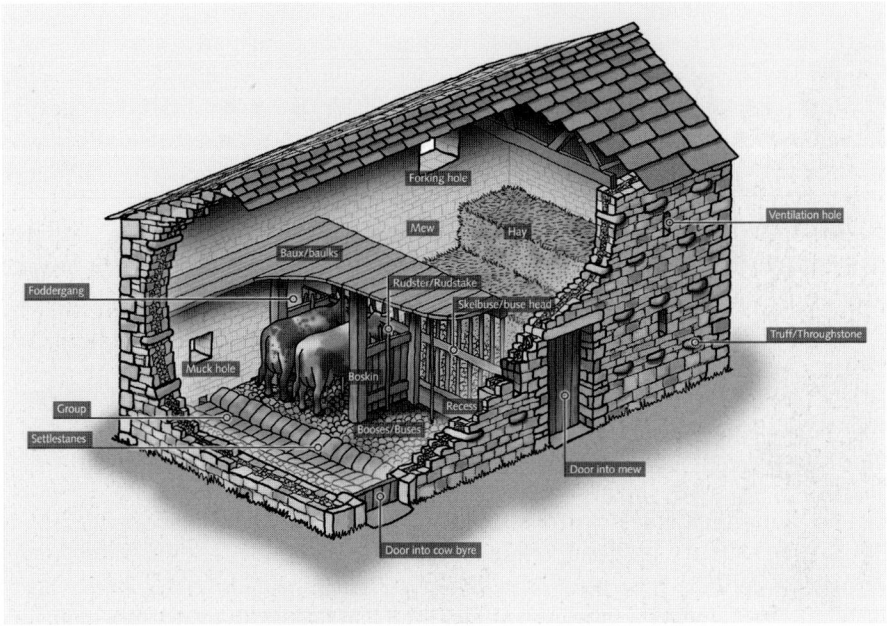

Traditional Cowhouse, Yorkshire – The design of city cowhouses was based on that of traditional 'field barns' in the countryside. (© Yorkshire Dales National Park Authority, 2019)

facing the wall. The cow might have been tethered to a pole ('rudstake') at the head of the stall and was separated from its neighbours by wooden or stone panels ('boskins'). At the rear of the stalls was a kerb of large stones ('settlestones'), which helped to form a gutter ('groop'). This stone-lined gutter ran behind the stalls and was where the muck collected. The muck would be swept to the end of the gutter where there was a hole ('muckhole') in the shippon wall. Muck was shovelled through the hole to the outside, where it was stored in a midden. A 'single' shippon had one row of cows down one side of the building; a 'double' shippon had two rows of cows, one down either side of the building.

Traditionally, hay and straw were stored in a separate part of the shippon, called a 'mew'. Because the hay could be stacked up to the rafters, the hole ('forkinghole') through which the hay would be forked into the mew was located high up in the shippon outer wall. Though the cows and the hay were kept apart by a wooden or stone divider ('skelbus'), a passageway ('foddergang') connected the mew and the stalls. Due to the lack of space in the city, as an alternative to the mew, hay might have been stored above the stalls in a loft ('baux' or 'baulks').

Though totally fit for purpose in the countryside, in the city this basic shippon design had to be adapted in the interest of public health and hygiene. The 1878 Contagious Diseases (Animals) Act began what would become a series of Dairies, Cowsheds & Milkshops Orders (see Appendix A). These Orders provided a structure for local authorities to register dairymen, cowkeepers and milk purveyors,

City Cowhouse, Liverpool – A typical cowkeeper's shippon and yard in the city centre. Selig Dover, Cowkeeper. (Courtesy of Liverpool Records Office)

and also provided new guidelines for the lighting, ventilation, cleansing, drainage and water supply of shippons. It was left to the discretion of each local authority to formulate new standards of design and practice, and the issuing of a licence to continue trading was dependent on the cowkeeper meeting these standards. Shippons had to change.

In an essay written in 1883, for the Royal Manchester, Liverpool and North Lancashire Agricultural Society, dairyman Frederick Stoner described how his local city shippons had adapted to the new standards:

- All internal walls must be whitewashed annually, in March.
- All floors are either brick or stone.
- A single shippon ought to be, at least, 14 feet wide: 8 feet for standing, 2 feet for gutter, and 4 feet for passage behind the cows.
- Stalls should be not less than 7 feet wide and dividers should extend no more than 4 feet from the wall (to enable the cow to lie down).
- Feed should be provided in tubs – not in fixed troughs.
- Single shippons should be no less than 8 feet high and double shippons no less than 9 feet high.
- All shippons must be ventilated separate from the loft, to enable the hot air to escape and create a flow of air through the building.

Rising Standards – As standards improved, city shippons were designed to accommodate herds of thirty cattle or more. (Author)

- Windows for ventilation should be 2 feet long, 1 foot 3 inches deep and hung with central hinges – one of these for every two cows, located immediately below the floor of the loft.
- Where possible, manure pits should be located at ground level and fitted with wooden covers.

The original small, cramped cowsheds were replaced by more spacious, purpose-built shippons that could accommodate thirty or more cows. In terms of their design and appearance, the practicalities of keeping cows, combined with the standards enforced by the local authorities, set shippons apart from the many other types of building in the cities.

Bringing Cows to the City

For the early cowkeepers, the preferred breed was the shorthorn as it had a relatively high milk yield but would fatten up well for the local beef market once its milking days were over; it was the ideal dual-purpose cow for the city cowkeeper (Mackenzie, 1910). Cows were brought into the city when they were newly calved and in full lactation and would spend approximately twelve months there, depending on the productivity of the cow. Once yield fell below about 3 gallons per day, the cow would be quickly fattened and sold locally for beef. Occasionally, if a cow turned out to be an exceptionally good milker, she would be returned to the home farm to be put to the bull once more.

Herds maintained through this practice of high-turnover replacement, rather than through breeding, were referred to as 'flying herds'. This was the most practical way of enabling a city herd to maintain its high milk output. In a collection of reminiscences published by Herefordshire Lore (2012), John Matthews describes the turnover of cows at his family's Bartonsham Dairy:

> Dad kept a 'flying herd', buying his cattle from Hereford Market when they were freshly calved and full of milk. Every Friday he would go to town and buy a few cows. Every Thursday he'd sell a few fat cows. When the cattle finished their milking life they were sold back at Hereford Market for meat.

Those cowkeepers who did not have access to a local cattle market were quick to take advantage of the opportunities afforded by the railways to transport cattle in and out of the city. Indeed, many city milkhouses were operated as satellite outlets for the home farm, with lots of to-ing and fro-ing between town and countryside.

The first cattle wagons were low-sided, wooden-floored open wagons with four wheels; in fact, they were much the same as the carriages used by third-class passengers, although without the wooden benches. But as train speeds increased, up to 20 or 30mph, the cattle began to suffer from this exposure. So, new wagons were introduced that were roofed and walled, with a big gap between roof and wall to ensure adequate ventilation. They were also equipped with moveable partitions, to separate the beasts during transit (Ginn and Goodman, 2016).

In the early 1890s, two sons of the Blackwell family, who were farming at Higher Clough, Dale Head, Westmorland, opened Canterbury Dairy in Window Lane, Garston. Cows were bred at Higher Clough and if they produced a particularly good milker, she would be sent to Garston where 'they never bulled them and a good cow would milk three to four years, if it was geld' (Leigh, 2004).

In the 1920s, Bernard Gilpin, who was farming at Green Bank, Crook, Westmorland, would herd his cattle along the country roads to the nearby town of Kendal, where they were loaded on to a train bound for Liverpool. Bernard had a brother, a son and two nephews who were city cowkeepers, all of whom looked to the family farm in Westmorland to supply their businesses with good milking cows (Anne Poynter, personal correspondence, 12 March 2017).

For those who could not access a supply of cattle from the home farm, there soon developed a plentiful supply from professional cattle dealers. These dealers would bring their cows into the city via the railways, twenty or so at a time. They would unload the cows and proceed to herd them through the city streets, going from one milkhouse to the next and doing business with the cowkeepers as they went, until the whole herd was absorbed into the city shippons. Dealers would also buy the cowkeepers' fattened cows and take them away to the abattoir.

In cities that were also ports, cows could be shipped-in and unloaded at the docks; for example, cattle from Ireland were regularly unloaded at the Pier Head in Liverpool.

The City Dairy: A Social and Family History

A Good Deal – Norman Shinkfield swapped cowkeeping for cattle dealing and became very successful. (Courtesy of Susanne Barton)

In his memoir, Frank Unwin (1984) recalls how cows were driven along the city's famous 'cattle trail' from the Pier Head to the market and abattoir: through Leeds Street, Alexander Pope Street, Richmond Row, Soho Street, Stafford Street and St Andrew Street. As well as causing chaos to local traffic, any householder who forgot to close a front door was likely to find a cow in their kitchen. The state of the streets after the passage of so much bovine traffic was such that they had to be hosed down at night.

To enhance their reputation as being suppliers of quality beasts, cattle dealers would enter their cows in local shows, many of which had special classes exclusively for dealers; also, a prizewinning cow would fetch a better price when sold on. Cattle dealers and cowkeepers worked hand in hand and it was not uncommon for a keeper to become a dealer, or to have keepers and dealers in the same family. In 1901, John and Norman Shinkfield were both living and working at the family dairy in Liverpool, assisting their father, Robert Shinkfield. When Robert retired, John continued as a cowkeeper, but Norman became a very successful cattle dealer. At different times, he was either a judge or a prizewinning competitor at the annual city cattle show.

The Milk Round

The working day would begin at around 5.00 a.m. with first milking, the milk then being ready to be taken out on the round by 7.30 a.m. First milking and first delivery were usually rushed, in order to have the milk on the doorstep in time for breakfast, and to make sure customers weren't tempted by another dairyman or milk hawker. If necessary, the cowkeeper would wait to have his own breakfast until after the first round was completed. Second milking took place at around 2.00 p.m. and second delivery commenced at 4.30 p.m. The afternoon routine was carried out at a slightly more sedate pace than that of the morning, as there was less of a mealtime deadline to meet.

For some, the answer to the problem of working countrymen's hours whilst following townsmen's social habits, was to take time out for a 'doss' between the end of first delivery and the beginning of second milking (Mellor, 2012). However, other dairymen (more than likely, those who didn't keep cows) preferred to spend that time providing a midday round; this was called the 'Pudding Round' as it arrived in time for pudding to be hastily made for the midday meal (Collacott, 2016).

Though a variety of barrows, perambulators and pushbikes were still employed for shorter rounds nearer the dairy, as the size of rounds grew, the horse-drawn, two-wheeled milk float became the preferred means of delivering milk. This vehicle was designed to meet the requirements of milk transportation, specifically, to accommodate the tendency of milk to curdle – to change into butter – when subject to excessive motion. Milk needed to be given as gentle a ride as possible, and three design features combined to make this so: wheels, axle and suspension.

Wheels – the two wheels were large for the size of the vehicle's body box or 'tub'. Large wheels give a smoother ride than smaller wheels as they turn more slowly and can more easily roll over unevenness in the road surface. However, a drawback to large wheel size is that the larger the wheels, the higher the axle is above the ground. This raises the centre of gravity of the whole vehicle, and the higher the centre of gravity of an object, the less stable it is.

Axle – the solution to the centre of gravity problem was to design an axle that was cranked. A cranked axle is bent twice at right angles near its ends, so that it is slung lower than the height of the wheel hubs. As well as lowering the centre of gravity and increasing stability, this design feature had the added advantage of lowering the tub, making it easier to load the vehicle with heavy items such as fully laden milk cans.

Suspension – to further protect the milk from the movement of the vehicle, the tub did not rest directly on the axle, but rather was borne above it on two leaf springs, one on either side. These were large bow-shaped affairs, running almost the full length of the tub. While the centre of the bow connected to the axle, the two ends were connected to the sides of the tub. The flexing of the bow absorbed the energy of bumps in the road.

The combined action of large wheels, cranked axle and sprung suspension enabled the tub to 'float' above the chassis. According to my father, who spent the first forty-five years of his life driving one of these vehicles, that is how the term 'milk float' came to be coined.

The City Dairy: A Social and Family History

The Milk Float – A vehicle designed for milk transportation. Thomas Ranson, Dairyman. (Courtesy of Tom Pollock)

Having designed and built a vehicle that could potentially 'float', what was then required was the right breed of horse to make this happen – ideally, a light draught horse that combined strength with speed; strength to pull the laden vehicle, and speed to get the milk delivered as quickly as possible. The dairymen's preference was not so much a breed of horse, but rather a type, variously referred to as a 'cob' or 'vanner'. These horses were originally bred to pull gypsy caravans; as such, their pedigree went unrecorded and consequently they were not at that time considered to be a breed. Characteristically, they were strong and mobile and could maintain a steady, economical gait for hours at a time; they were intelligent and took instruction very easily with quick response; they could live on limited grazing and had a calm temperament. This combination of characteristics made them ideally suited to dairy work in the busy city. In appearance they were either tobiano (piebald or skewbald) or uniform in colour with the occasional white face marking, and had a good feather on each leg. My father referred to the Joy's three milk horses as 'Irish Vanners': Danny was a bay, Rupert a chestnut and Peggy a black, and all three had white face blazes (Joy, 2014).

Prior to the invention of glass milk bottles, delivery took place in the street from the back of the milk float, the loose milk being dispensed into the customers' own jugs from the 'kit' (7–14 gallon can), using a measured ladle. Also, it would be delivered to the back door of the wealthiest households in a quart (2-pint) handcan:

City Dairies – Operations

When I was older, I would go out on the milk round with my eldest brother, Joe, in the horse and trap. Joe would drop me off, together with the milk churns, by the police station in Higher Lane, returning later to collect them. I would deliver the milk on foot with a churn and ladle – using the ladle to fill customers' jugs, or if customers were out, leaving a small can which then had to be collected later in the day. I remember on one occasion going back to Higher Lane but all the churns had disappeared. The policeman had played a joke on me and taken them into the police station.

(Unpublished interview with 84-year-old Janey Capstick, 1991)

Like farming, cowkeeping was a 7-day-a-week occupation, involving all members of the family. In between milking cows and selling milk on the rounds, there were many other daily tasks to be performed through the day: cattle and horses had to be mucked out, cleaned, fed, watered and exercised; the shippon and yard would be swilled down and brushed clean; stored fodder would be prepared for feeding to the cattle. Generally, the division of labour was as it had always been on the farm: women worked indoors and the men worked outdoors, though this arrangement was modified in the 1840s when many farmers adopted the almost revolutionary expedient of employing men as milkers (Mingay, 1989). Thus, the place where the sexes would most often work alongside each other was the shippon, at milking time.

Many Hands – Three or more generations of a family could be living and working at the city dairy. The Harper family, Chesnut Grove Dairy, Wavertree. (Courtesy of David Wilson)

Throughout the nineteenth century, the vital role played by women in the dairy business – be it on the farm or in the milkhouse – was as understated as their role in society in general. This situation seems not to have improved much by the turn of the century, as suggested by an article in the *British Dairy Farmers' Association Journal*, in 1917. Margaret Shanks, of Wensleydale, stated that dairying as a whole was carried out by men and women working together in closest partnership; she then qualified this statement by adding: 'although to read through a whole journal one would think that there was not a woman ever looked at a cow or handled a pail of milk!' (Yorkshire Dales NPA, 2020).

Inside the milkhouse, as tighter regulations were introduced, all surfaces had to be kept scrubbed clean and all utensils used in the production processes had to be scalded after each use. In the back room there might be butter and cheese to be made or cream to be separated, whilst in the front room there was a busy shop to run, with customers queuing in time for each milking. City dairies were open for business from dawn 'til dusk and often beyond, though some dairies closed for a few hours on a Sunday while the family attended church/chapel. There was so much work to be done that it was common to find three or more generations of a family working at the city dairy.

Fodder – A Moveable Feast

Most cowkeepers preferred to graze their stock whenever possible. But the closer they were to the centre of the city, the fewer opportunities there were for grazing. Indeed, as a city expanded into the surrounding countryside, even these few opportunities were lost, as former fields disappeared under bricks and mortar.

The loss of grazing due to urban and industrial expansion was a problem faced by the cowkeeping Joy family on numerous occasions across the generations. When, in 1873, my great-great-grandfather, Daniel Joy, first moved from Yorkshire to the industrial town and port of Garston, on the banks of the River Mersey, he was able to graze his cows on land that was formerly part of Dale Farm. However, this land was lost to an expanding dockland and its associated railway infrastructure. Daniel's son, Anthony, continued the family's cowkeeping tradition and grazed his cows on land that was formerly part of Island Farm. However, in 1900, that land was required for the creation of a new park and recreation ground. Anthony's sons, Percy and George, succeeded their father and grazed their cows on land at Dutch Farm, on the edge of town. But that farm disappeared in 1937, when a council-owned housing estate was built on the land. The one small field that survived the housing development finally succumbed to the need for a new school in the baby-boomer 1950s (Joy, 2016[1]).

The question of whether to locate their business closer to grazing land or closer to their potential customers was an ongoing dilemma for the cowkeeper. If suitable pasture was within walking distance of the dairy, it necessitated a twice-daily trip, there and back. Terry Clipson describes the daily movement of cows in Barton-upon-Humber in the 1940s. At about 9.00 a.m. the local cowkeepers would take their cows to the fields on the outskirts of town and then return them to the dairy at 4.30 p.m.:

> [The cows] would walk down the street ... two or three abreast in a longish line, taking up most of the width of the road. The cowkeeper would be at the back of them, geeing-up the ones that tended to dawdle. The front cows knew exactly where to go and which streets of the town centre to walk through. You knew if the cows had been taken out or brought back ... as there were cowpats on the road wherever they had been.
> **(bartonuponhumber.org.uk/stories/barton40s.htm)**

In the absence of grazing, cowkeepers had to make up the cows' fodder from what was available locally. Where possible they would obtain grass cuttings from the city's parks, gardens, playing fields and cemeteries, raking them up, then carting them back to the shippon. In the latter part of the nineteenth century, the Hogg family established a milkhouse at 3 Back Parkfield Road in the Aigburth district of Liverpool. The business was located only 500 yards from the magnificent 200-acre Sefton Park and the family had a special arrangement with the municipal parks department:

> Sefton Park was our 'farm' for over fifty years. The men of Parks and Gardens would mow the grass 5½ days a week and we would

Grass Cuttings – It was common practice for city cowkeepers to 'harvest' grass cuttings from municipal parks. The Hogg family at Sefton Park, Liverpool. (Courtesy of Angela Hallows)

rake it up and cart it away for the cows. We soon found out that one of the secrets of feeding grass to milk cattle is to feed it as soon after mowing as possible. We always found the cows gave less milk on Monday morning, when we were feeding them grass that had been cut on Friday or Saturday. Father had an arrangement with the park men to mow the thickest grass on Friday afternoon or Saturday morning to do us over the weekend.

(Unpublished Memoir of Thomas Hogg – Angela Hallows (née Hogg))

Another important part of the diet of the municipal cow was the spent grain obtained from local breweries and distilleries. Indeed, some town dairies were built attached to breweries, to facilitate the disposal of what, to the brewing business, was a by-product (Walling, 2018). Conversely, breweries in London cashed in on their by-product by setting up model herds of their own, notably that of Whitbread in Battersea. This symbiotic relationship between industry and agriculture evolved because the brewing/distilling season – from October to May (the warmer, summer months being unsuitable for malting and fermentation) – coincided with the cowkeepers' demand for feedstuffs during winter (Mathias, 1952).

The cows were fed a bushel (approximately 35lb) of grain per day, spaced out over the twenty-four hours. A typical daily regime might have looked like this: half a bushel of grains before first milking; then, a bushel of turnips and about 5lb of soft meadow hay before being turned out into the yard until noon; after being stalled again, a further half bushel of grains before second milking; after milking, another bushel of turnips; finally, in late afternoon, they'd be fed another 5lb of hay before being settled in the shippon for the night (Stout, 1978).

The cows' fodder would also include molasses from the city's sugar refineries; seed cake (such as linseed) from the vegetable oil refineries; greenstuffs from fruit and vegetable markets (e.g. in London, at Covent Garden and at Spitalfields); and hay from farms on the edge of the city. Additionally, local farmers would supply cowkeepers with surplus root crops in return for a cartload of cow muck.

Muck and Brass

Cows produce muck in significant quantities – that's just the way a ruminant's digestive system works. Back on the home farm it would have been spread on the land as a natural fertiliser, either by the cows themselves as they grazed the pastures, or manually by farm labourers. In the small city shippons, producing muck in such quantities could have been a liability, but the cowkeepers turned it to their advantage.

They contained the muck, temporarily, in a 'midden'; often formed by two brick walls (approximately 5ft high) built in the corner of the yard or, alternatively, in the form of a covered pit in the floor of the yard. Once the midden was full it would be emptied by hand using a muck rake and transferred into a cart. It was then taken away and sold to farmers, horticulturists and market gardeners on the edge of the city. The Hogg family had a long-running arrangement with the local council to dispose of their cow muck:

> Father had a contract with the Liverpool Corporation to supply the parks in and around Liverpool and they just about took all the manure the cattle made – except for a few loads for the gentry's house gardens, and several local allotments had their assured load too.
> (Unpublished Memoir of Thomas Hogg – Angela Hallows (née Hogg))

Of course, cattle weren't the only beasts contributing to the vast quantity of animal manure being produced in cities where, throughout the nineteenth century, the horse reigned as the principal form of transportation. In the mid-1800s, London's 17,000 cows were producing some 224,000 tons of manure per year, compared to the 620,000 tons being produced by the city's 54,000 horses (Atkins, 2012[1]). The movement of this waste on to adjacent farmland created a 'Charmed Circle' of well-manured land, surrounding each city. Some of this land was used to cultivate fodder crops, which were then transported back into the cities to feed the animals – creating a different kind of circle.

In late 1800s Liverpool, a cowkeeper could expect to make a good profit, selling his cow muck for 5 shillings per ton (Stoner, 1883). This trade in manure was lucrative enough to attract its own specialists and 'Muck Merchants' came into being, acting as a middle man between cowkeeper and farmer. Muck Merchants were still operating as late as the 1940s. Self-proclaimed Muck Man, John Mercer, recalls how he would take a cart to city milkhouses to empty the middens. By then, a midden serving a herd of thirty cows would need emptying once a week and a typical collection would generate a 6-ton load of muck to be carted away for sale to

Muck and Brass – Cow muck was stored, temporarily, in a midden until it could be sold to farmers as a natural fertiliser. A. Joy & Sons, Farmers and Cowkeepers, Wellington Dairy, Garston. (Author)

local farmers. The muck was bought from the cowkeepers for £1 per ton and then sold to the farmers for a profit of 10 shillings per ton. (Scott, 2016)

Alternatively, a cowkeeper wanting to dispose of his muck could miss out the middle man and do business direct with the farmer:

> The midden or manure pit was not too oppressive a sight. It was emptied possibly twice a week by farmers from the outskirts of Liverpool – potato and crop farmers, who would make an eight- to ten-mile journey each way to collect the manure. They used their own wagons for this purpose. One man, the driver, and our cowman would help load his wagon. Loads of three to five tons of manure each journey.
> (Unpublished Memoir of Edward Eubank Mason, 1980 – Robert Mason)

This business deal with the local farmers would sometimes take the form of an exchange, to the mutual benefit of both cowkeeper and farmer. Isabel Beck recalls her childhood in the 1920s, living at the family dairy at 189 Park Road in the Dingle district of Liverpool:

> I remember the smell of the dairy yard, seeing the hay brought in and fresh grass from farms in Ormskirk. Then they took away the manure on the empty wagon.
> (Unpublished Memoir of Isabel Beck, 1994 – Brian Phythian)

Clearly, whether it be in the 1800s or in the 1900s, cow muck played an important part in the business plan of a city dairy. So, that old adage, 'Where There's Muck, There's Brass', held particularly true for the city cowkeeper.

Regulation and Inspection

Keeping muck and milk separate was just one of many practices the cowkeepers had to demonstrate in order to acquire the necessary licences to carry out their trade. Though it varied from one local authority to another, the cowkeepers could find themselves preparing for three kinds of site inspection.

Firstly, there was the inspection of the milkhouse, including all the processes carried out there. This inspection was common to all dairymen, whether or not they kept cows. Passing such an inspection enabled the dairyman to display the words 'Registered for the Sale of Milk' in the dairy window.

Secondly, there was the inspection of the cowhouse, including all the practices carried out there. Passing this inspection required the cowkeeper to display the words 'Licensed to Keep x Cows' on or near the main entrance to the building; the x being the number of cows, and the cowkeeper was not permitted to exceed this number. Finally, the cowkeeper's herd was also subject to inspection. As well as the local authority examining the health of the cattle as part of its licensing regime,

City Dairies – Operations

Above left: **Licensed to Sell Milk** – Dairies were licensed by the local authority and were required to display that they were 'Registered for the Sale of Milk'. Edward Hall, Cowkeeper. (Courtesy of Bill Frith)

Above right: **Licensed to Keep Cows** – Shippons were licensed by the local authority and were required to display the number of cows for which they were licensed. A. Joy & Sons, Wellington Dairy. (Author)

the district cowkeepers' association would also make it a condition of membership that a cowkeeper's cattle pass a health inspection carried out by the association's own appointed veterinary officer.

Another type of inspection – not tied to the premises – was the 'spot check' implemented by the local authority's health inspectors, often in conjunction with the local police force. These unannounced inspections were targeted at the milk being sold, samples of which were taken away for immediate examination in a laboratory. The two principal checks carried out were for bacterial content (disease) and for fat content.

A milk-borne disease of great concern was tuberculosis; in particular there was the controversial question of whether tuberculous milk might be a contributor to tuberculosis in humans. When Liverpool Council engaged four of the country's most eminent bacteriologists to test the milk being sold in the city, 5 per cent of the milk from cows within the city was found to be infected, whereas this figure rose to 13.4 per cent when milk from rural farms supplying the city was tested. This resulted in the Liverpool Act of 1900, which enabled the council to extend its powers of inspection to include country cowsheds, with a view to preventing the importation of diseased milk (Hope, 1931).

The proportion of fat to water in milk was an issue of great contention for all dairymen, particularly so for those who were producing milk from their own cows. It was a complex problem made worse by the fact that the science for identifying adulteration or contamination was subject to extensive debate. One difficulty was trying to standardise a product that by its very nature varied from place to place and from cow to cow, and even from the *same* cow according to conditions at the time (such as diet, or whether it was the first or second milking of the day, or where the cow was in her milking cycle).

In 1900, the Wenlock Committee was established to consider the butterfat content of milk and cream. Its recommendations were embodied in the subsequent Milk and Dairies Order (1901). This laid down a standard of a minimum 3 per cent butterfat and 8.5 per cent solids-not-fat. Milk with content below these levels could be considered to have had water added and therefore deemed unfit for human consumption. Meeting this standard proved to be a tough challenge for milk producers. But the challenge was compounded by the fact that the legislation effectively shifted the burden of proof from the prosecutor to the milk producer; you were no longer innocent until proven guilty but were now guilty until proven innocent. When you take into consideration that the penalty for breaching this standard was at best a fine, and at worst the loss of the licence to trade – the end of your livelihood – then it is not surprising that this became the most disputed aspect of food quality legislation in Britain and remained so for many decades (Joy, 2021).

Many an innocent dairyman found himself in the dock being accused of adulteration based on the results of spot checks that subsequently showed his milk fell below the standard for fat content. As the burden of proof now lay on the accused, it was difficult to mount a defence. The length of the supply chain compounded the problem for the non-cowkeeping dairyman, making it difficult to identify where in the chain the adulteration had taken place; they could easily find themselves paying fines for the offences of others. Those who kept cows could 'appeal to the cow' and arrange for the inspector to take a fresh sample straight from the cow and to test that; if that sample also failed the test, then the cowkeeper was able to demonstrate that no adulteration had taken place. However, this was a risky ploy, as the fat content of the fresh milk may have changed since the original sample was taken. Undoubtedly, many deliberate adulterators were caught and rightly prosecuted, but some well-earned reputations were ruined through this somewhat heavy-handed approach to food safety.

On the flip side, cowkeepers were quick to take advantage of any scientific developments that would help increase their sales of milk. One popular theory was that infants and some invalids had more sensitive digestive systems that were unable to break down the protein (casein) in cows' milk. This property of milk is known as 'curd tension'; curds with high tension were described as being 'tough' or 'hard' and more difficult to digest. Though curd toughness seemed to be a characteristic of the individual cow, it was found that there was a greater chance of cows giving soft-curd milk in some breeds rather than others. Thus, an attractive proposition for the cowkeeper was to add to his herd a Holstein or an Ayrshire, in order to increase the chances of producing soft-curd milk. (Carpenter, 1934):

We were often asked for milk from a specific cow, referred to as 'babies' milk' as it was given to new-born babies unable to digest mixed milk from all the other cows.

(Unpublished Memoir of Mary Gaddas, 1984 – Rosemary McCaffrey)

To target this new market, cowkeepers advertised their product as being 'Special Milk for Infants' or 'Recommended by Medical Men for Invalids and Infants'. But the science was still not exact, and whilst some cowkeepers claimed to have a 'special' cow that gave milk suitable for sensitive digestive systems, others boasted that they had their own secret recipe of cattle feed that produced milk particularly suited to the needs of infants and invalids. There was some scepticism over such boasts, with suspicion that this may have been merely a marketing ploy on the part of the wily cowkeeper!

A further example of the cowkeeper targeting a niche market was the supply of milk to Jewish families, who had their own kosher dietary rules. The cows were milked in the presence of a Rabbi who ensured that the milk passed from the cow straight into the family's own jug without coming into contact with any of the man-made utensils normally used in the milking process (Hayes, 2018). Towards the end of the nineteenth century, the dairies in the East End of London benefited from the influx of a large Jewish population, which had fled persecution by a decaying Russian Empire.

As a result of this keenness by all parties to ensure a healthy supply of milk, dairymen could find themselves being inspected four or more times per year. Their livelihoods depended on them passing these inspections. When licences were issued in paper form, they would often be framed and displayed in a prominent

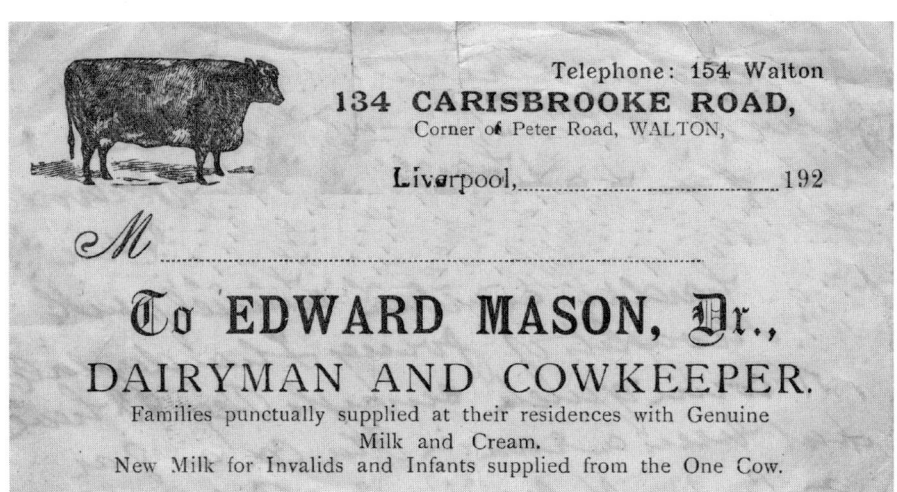

Invalids and Infants – Many cowkeepers kept a 'special' cow, giving soft-curd milk, suitable for sensitive digestive systems. Edward Mason, Dairyman and Cowkeeper. (Courtesy of Robert Mason)

position in the shop. As a means of demonstrating that they had nothing to hide from these inspections, many dairymen decided to throw open their doors to the general public so that their customers could see for themselves the high standards of cleanliness and hygiene that were practised. The phrases 'Inspection Welcome' or 'Inspection Invited' became common mantras and appeared on signs, hoardings and business stationery.

Trading Partners

The occupation and practice of keeping cows became integrated into the city economy. As well as the thousands of urban customers who received their milk fresh from the cow, other trades associated with cowkeeping included Cattle Dealer, Drover, Feed Merchant, Brewer, Miller, Farmer, Carter, Auctioneer, Cartwright, Wheelwright, Saddler, Blacksmith, Farrier, Muck Merchant, Slaughterer, Butcher, Veterinary and many, many more.

It was quite common for cowkeepers or their offspring to move into one of these related trades. My great uncle, William Cecil Joy, grew up living and working at the family's Wellington Dairy, but he spent the rest of his working life as a butcher with his own shop in Garston village (where the sign in the shop window read: 'Have you ever had the Joy of enjoying Joy's sausages?').

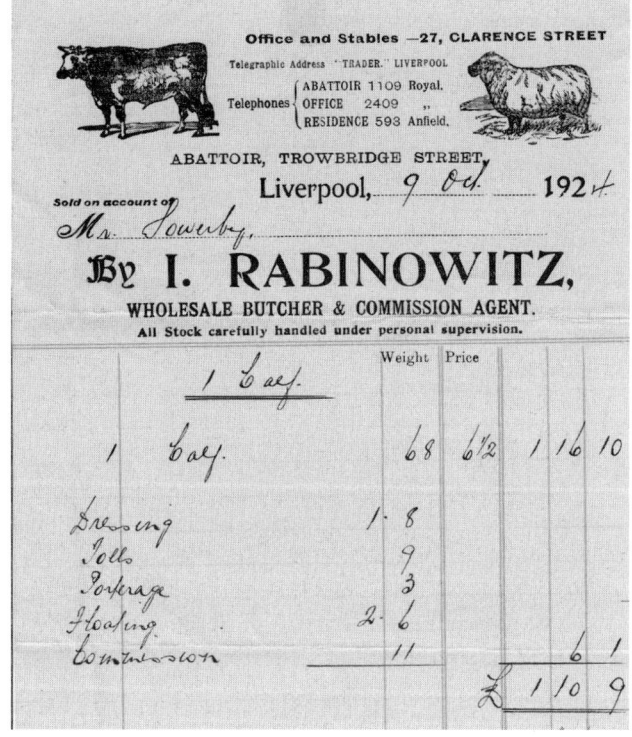

Jack of all-trades – Mr I. Rabinowitz was a livestock agent and a wholesale butcher who also ran a city abattoir. (Courtesy of Geoff Cannon)

It was also common to find some of these trades combined; for example, a blacksmith might also be a farrier, or a cartwright might also be a wheelwright. Mr I. Rabinowitz of Liverpool combined multiple trades; he was a wholesale butcher, who also bought and sold cattle on commission, and who also ran a city abattoir – he also had a lucrative sideline, supplying the Cheshire Hunt with horses imported from Ireland!

Showtime!

An important appurtenance of the cowkeeping way of life was participation in local agricultural or cattle shows. Those organised by the county agricultural societies were on a grand scale and would be held over two or three days. Smaller, one-day shows were organised by district cowkeeper and dairymen's associations. In both cases, there were many cash prizes and much prestigious silverware up for grabs.

A Prizewinning Dairy – Success at agricultural shows was an excellent way for dairymen to promote their business. Fawcett Harper, Farmer and Cowkeeper. (Courtesy of Kath Robinson)

Clearly, at county shows, city cowkeepers were at a disadvantage when competing against dairy farmers who were breeding their own cattle. So, when the county show came to Liverpool, in 1899, the Liverpool and District Cowkeepers' Association sponsored specific classes that were only open to its members. These classes reflected the different elements of the cowkeeping way of life. As well as classes for cattle and for best turnout (horse and milk float), there was also a competition to find the Best Kept Shippon, Milk-house, and Shop or Dairy. This involved an inspection of premises within a 7-mile radius of the town hall, carried out during the weeks before the show by a team of judges. The judging took into account general appearance, arrangements for convenience, economy of labour, cleanliness and hygiene, and air space, light and ventilation in the shippon. The results were announced on the day of the show.

These shows were red-letter days in the cowkeeper's calendar. All members of the family were called upon to prepare for the event whilst maintaining the daily routine of the dairy. The milk float received a fresh coat of paint, ornamental horse brasses and coach lamps were brought out of storage and, along with the harness, were cleaned and polished until you could see your face in them. On the day of the show, cows were cleaned and groomed to look their best, as was the horse, with plaited mane and tail. The annual show was an excuse for relatives from the countryside to spend a day in the city, lending a hand and enjoying the festivities. In this way, these events were also social occasions, presenting an opportunity for a day out, meeting up with family, friends and fellow professionals.

In a society that valued social rank, there was plenty of motivation to show that you were the best at what you did. But in addition to pride, there were also sound business reasons for participating. Picking up a prize at your local show presented an opportunity to publicise your business, to get one up on the local competition. As well as having your name and/or a photograph in the local newspaper, you could now promote yourself as a prizewinning dairy; certificates would be framed and hung up on display in the dairy shop; trophies and rosettes would be proudly displayed in the dairy window; titles and lists of prizes would appear on business stationery; and photographs of prizewinning cows or the prizewinning dairy would be used in leaflets designed to attract new customers. The cash prizes were also very welcome!

Chapter 3

Migration

Migration from rural areas to towns and cities was not a new phenomenon but industrialisation pushed the scale of such migration to a new high. Those in the dairy business participated in both Domestic and International migration. The reasons for such migrations are categorised as being either 'push' or 'pull' in nature. For most dairy-farming migrants it was the push of rural poverty combined with the pull of either business opportunities in the city, or of the prospect of a new and better life in the New World.

Those Who Left the Dales (Marriott, 2010) is a study undertaken by The Upper Dales Family History Group to celebrate its tenth anniversary. The study resulted in the publication of a fascinating collection of over 100 stories from the descendants of families who emigrated from this part of rural north Yorkshire, some to the towns and cities of England, others to the far side of the world. The 'sending' area for these emigrants included Swaledale, Arkengarthdale, Wensleydale, Bishopdale, Wharfedale and Langstrothdale. As pastoral farming was prevalent in these valleys, many emigrants were well equipped with the necessary dairying skills and knowledge to make a decent living further afield.

The decision whether to leave the home farm and try your luck somewhere else was not always an easy one to make. The grass may have seemed greener elsewhere but plenty of news filtered back to the rural villages that emigrants were experiencing mixed fortunes. It was the younger members of a family who were most tempted to migrate, but even they had reservations about the risks involved. This dilemma generated a degree of procrastination in some and fickleness in others. In her article in the *Dalesman* magazine, Patsy Mellor (1978) describes the vacillations of three Handley brothers from Garsdale:

> From time to time, Robert had various cowkeeping premises in the city, moving backwards and forwards between Liverpool and the Dales, unable to make up his mind where to settle. George and William both tried emigrating, as several of their uncles had done. George twice went to Australia, and when William gave up cowkeeping in 1911 he went for one year to relatives in Canada. Neither of them were able to settle down.

Domestic Migration – City Businesses with Rural Roots

For dairy folk, domestic migration to the city was not a one-off event. It was what social geographers refer to as a *Chain Migration*, meaning that one family from the same village would later follow in the footsteps of another family to the same city. Indeed, for many the link with the home farm was never broken, with a lot of to-ing and fro-ing between the two locations. The dairyman's children would spend holidays with their grandparents back on the home farm. Relatives from the countryside would come to help out at the milkhouse and to experience city life, some staying on to set up their own milkhouse, as the expanding city created new opportunities (Joy, 2016[2]).

The nature of this kind of migration led to some rural communities developing a strong connection with a specific city. For example, in the north of England, farmers from the Pennine Dales had a significant presence as cowkeepers in Liverpool. Joan Grundy's (1982) analysis of the 1871 census suggests that 36.5 per cent of Liverpool's cowkeepers had come from the Dales (defined as being parts of Westmorland, west Yorkshire and north Lancashire). In the south, farmers from south Wales had made their presence felt in London. Peter Atkins's (1977) analysis of Post Office directories identifies the number of London cowkeepers with Welsh surnames: they comprised 24 per cent of the capital's cowkeeping businesses in 1881, rising to 49 per cent by 1900.

This 'chain' was also reflected in the employment of staff, many of whom were recruited from the home farm parish and were friends or relatives of the cowkeeping

To-ing and Fro-ing – Relatives from the countryside would come to help out at the dairy and experience city life. William Metcalfe, Cowkeeper. (Courtesy of Kath Robinson)

family. Such staff would often live-in, especially young women, visiting the city for the first time. The business would also recruit from the local workforce:

> We had three men living on site, and also hired maids. Whereas the men mostly lived and ate on the premises, the maids were generally local girls who did not live-in. Occasionally, a maid from North Yorkshire would be hired on a six-month basis and then of course, she lived-in. Her wages in 1908–1911 would be about 5s per week, plus board.
> (Unpublished Memoir of Mary Gaddas, 1984 – Rosemary McCaffrey)

Another characteristic of chain migration is its reinforcement of the migrants' geographical and cultural identity. For dairymen, this was achieved through more than just keeping regular contact with the home farm. Although many miles from their community of origin, they created and maintained their own communities within the city. There were two principal mechanisms by which they achieved this: one based on religion and the other on profession.

Throughout the nineteenth century, religion was a dominant force in the lives of many people and the church or chapel formed the hub of their social life. Religious practices of village life were continued following the move to the cities. Megan Hayes (2015) describes the influence the chapel had on London Welsh life when the milk trade was at its height; services at such places of worship were often conducted in Welsh:

> Membership of a chapel or church was essential. Every denomination was represented in the capital just as in any village or town in Wales and as far as possible, the immigrants remained loyal to the sect they frequented in Wales. An application for membership would be forwarded to the appropriate place of worship as soon as the exile left Wales.

Religious practices, including 'chapel-going', were also strong amongst Dales dairymen who migrated to Liverpool (Scobie, 2008). The strength of this affiliation led to many city-born children of Dales parents being brought back to the village church or chapel to be baptised. The parish register of Burnsall, in Wharfedale, bears witness to this trend, recording the baptisms of a number of children from cowkeeping families whose place of birth is recorded as being a district of the city of Liverpool (Mellor, 2012).

The importance placed on attending church or chapel was illustrated by the fact that even the eight-till-late, seven-days-per-week operation of the dairy would be adjusted to accommodate this practice. It was not unusual to see the window display of the dairy's opening hours announce:

CLOSED ON SUNDAY FROM 11 TO 4

The City Dairy: A Social and Family History

The motivation behind establishing a local dairymen or cowkeepers' association may have been that of addressing collective and pragmatic business needs (e.g. creating an insurance scheme, or agreeing a pricing mechanism for milk), but such organisations also played an important role in engendering cultural identity. It was a place where the ups-and-downs and the ins-and-outs of the dairying way of life could be discussed with fellow countrymen in their native dialect – considered to be a foreign language by city dwellers. Aside from promoting the business interests of its members, these associations also had very active social programmes, including grand dinners, tea dances, Christmas parties, and day trips to the seaside, to the countryside or to agricultural shows etc.

The Liverpool Cowkeepers' Association held an annual 'picnic' for its members and their families. This involved an excursion by train, either north to Cumbria, east to Yorkshire, or south to Cheshire or North Wales. In 1897, the *Liverpool Mercury* (4 June) reported on one such event, which that year took the cowkeepers to Ripon, in Yorkshire. The party of 148 boarded a train at Lime Street station at 7.50 a.m. and had returned by 10.50 p.m. that evening, after enjoying the sights of Studley Royal and Fountains Abbey.

The favourite destinations for the Croydon Dairymen and Cowkeepers' Association were the south-east coastal resorts, such as Eastbourne or Hastings. In 1905, their trip to Brighton was covered extensively in the *Croydon Chronicle and East Surrey Advertiser* (29 July). The London and Brighton Railway Company had placed several saloon carriages at the disposal of the party, which left East Croydon station at 9.25 a.m., reaching Brighton by 11.00 a.m. Activities on offer included admiring the splendid properties on the King's Road, browsing the High Street shops, enjoying the sea front and pier, or a coach trip to Worthing; culminating in an evening meal at Mutton's Hotel, after which many fine speeches and celebratory toasts were made. The reporter, who accompanied the party, captured the spirit of the day in rhyme:

> If you're waking, call me early;
> Call me early, do you hear?
> For tomorrow's hurly-burly
> Is the pleasantest of the year.
> If I miss this demonstration
> There will be deuce to pay,
> For tomorrow I'm in Brighton,
> For it is the Dairyman Day!

An important function of such occasions was that they provided the perfect opportunity for friendships to blossom and for young people to meet their potential spouses. So, even though they might be hundreds of miles from their place of origin, it was common for city dairy folk to marry within that same dairying community, generating a myriad of genealogical links between dairy families and perpetuating their cultural distinctiveness.

Further evidence that migrants retained their sense of cultural identity, despite spending many years (sometimes, decades) living in the city, was that upon

A Grand Day Out – Cowkeepers' and dairymen's associations organised extensive programmes of social events for members and their families. (Courtesy of Edith Margaret Royle)

retirement, the original dairymen might return to the home farm, which was still held in the family; if they had made enough money, they might even buy it outright. Jon Stobart and Alastair Owens (2000) describe this farm-milkhouse bipolarity as 'an inter-generational family lifestyle pattern' in which the cowkeeping income eased pressure on the rural small-farming family and allowed some accumulation of savings for a return to farming. When this happened, the city milkhouse might be sold or otherwise passed on to the family's grown-up children. In this way, both rural farms and city milkhouses would serve the same family through several successive generations.

International Migration – The New World

From 1850 up until the beginning of the Second World War, mass migrations were occurring worldwide as people went in search of employment and a new, better life. Particularly popular with British citizens were the existing and former British colonies, such as the USA., Australia, New Zealand, South Africa and parts of Canada. And of particular interest to British dairymen were those countries where the right combination of climate and soil supported a healthy dairy industry. Accordingly, many dairymen moved overseas and, utilising their existing dairy skill set, became 'ranchers'. One such example exists in my own family history.

Hilda Mary Joy (known as Mary) was born in Ilkley in 1882, the only child of Augustus Bowdin Joy and his wife Elizabeth (née Brumfitt). Under her stage name of 'Rose Garden', she became a professional 'Actress Vocalist' and toured with Mr Robert Courtneidge's company in the *Mousme*. However, in 1912 Mary left her stage career when she married Yorkshireman Norman Stones and the couple emigrated to Van Anda, Vancouver, in British Columbia, where they acquired and ran a dairy farm – they became ranchers. The passenger lists show that Mary made a number of journeys back and forth across the Atlantic Ocean, as she visited her ailing mother back home in Yorkshire. Following the outbreak of war in 1914, the couple decided to sell their ranch and return to England. On 1 May 1915, in New York, they boarded a ship bound for Liverpool. The ship they boarded was the largest passenger ship in the world at that time: the Cunard-owned RMS *Lusitania*. On 7 May 1915, 11 miles off the southern coast of Ireland, the ship was torpedoed and sunk by a German U-boat. Norman Stones survived the sinking, but the body of his wife was never recovered. (**davejoy-author.com/hilda-mary-joy-1882-1915---rms-lusitania.html**)

Despite the possibility of hardship or even of tragedy, emigration was generally looked upon as a good thing: an opportunity for a surplus workforce to move to a country that was in need of workers. The British government, poor law unions, charities and independent philanthropists worked together to fund assisted emigration schemes, which included benefits such as cut-price passage, agricultural training and financial aid to purchase farmland. Many who participated in these schemes were successful in making a new life for themselves; members of the extended family were then sent for to try their own luck in the new world. However, this was not always the case and many others, who did not fare as well, either perished or returned to their homeland after a few years.

In the early 1900s, the Australian economy was crying out for workers and the Commonwealth relaunched its initiative to encourage British citizens to migrate 'down under'. Passage assistance was resumed in 1906. The uniform maximum assistance was £6 for an adult, equating to half the minimum fare. A publicity campaign was rolled out through cinemas, newspapers, lectures and posters. A new film unit prepared the material. As a result of this initiative migration boomed: 146,602 British migrants arrived in 1912, and many more in the two subsequent years before the outbreak of war. The Joy family history also provides an example of this antipodean emigration.

George Eric Wright was born in Liverpool in 1890, the son of George Wright and Hannah (née Joy). Hannah was born in Bolton Bridge, Yorkshire, and had come to Liverpool as a child when her father, Daniel, became a cowkeeper at 10 Railway Street, Garston. The Wright family took over the business when Hannah's father died, in 1896, and young George began his apprenticeship in keeping cows and running a dairy. In 1913, George left the family home to try his luck down under – giving his occupation as *Farmer* (UK Outward Passenger Lists) – he emigrated to Australia, where he put his dairy skills to good use working on the sprawling 300-acre *Maryland* estate, lying a few miles outside of Sydney. When war broke out in 1914, he did his patriotic duty and enlisted with the 3rd Battalion, Australian Imperial Forces – Private 1853. He saw action at Gallipoli and in Egypt before being shipped to a different theatre of war: the Somme Valley in northern France.

Migration

A Dairyman Abroad – George Eric Wright was a Garston dairyman who emigrated to Australia in 1913. (Author)

On 24 July 1916, during the Battle of Pozieres, Corporal George Eric Wright was killed in action (KIA); he was just 26 years of age. After his death, his mother, as next of kin, completed and submitted a standard form containing the 'Particulars Required for the Roll of Honour of Australia in the Memorial War Museum' (**awm.gov.au/ collection/ C1380265**). These particulars included his 'Calling' as a 'Dairy Farmer' and his connection with the Maryland address in New South Wales prior to his enlistment. It was from this information that I was able to piece together George's life as a dairyman while he was living and working in Australia (Joy, 2018).

Although there was a tendency for families to migrate in chains, there are examples of members of the same family migrating not only to different cities but also to different continents. In her self-published book, *A Bit Akin – The Story of a North Craven Farming Family*, Faith Finegan (1994) describes various migrations of the Wolfenden family. An initial domestic migration to keep cows in the city of Liverpool, led to the next generation of Wolfendens being brought up within sight of the River Mersey and its docks – the stepping off point to the New World:

> Three of James's sons and a grandson left Waterloo for Canada, as did Bert's adopted son, Tom. It wasn't just the menfolk who emigrated. Cousin Robert's eldest daughter [Lena] … went out to British Columbia in 1911. She used to come home on holiday every few years and one of our visits to Liverpool was to see her off.

By way of contrast, another young Wolfenden who decided to emigrate was Captain Tom Wolfenden. Perhaps migration was in his blood as his father, Thomas Wolfenden, a farmer from Tosside, had spent some time in America before returning to England to become a cowkeeper in Liverpool. Captain Tom married Annie Marguerite Rothwell, in 1906. But, rather than follow his relatives to America or to Canada, he decided to emigrate to New Zealand, the couple setting sail for Auckland after their marriage. Between 1907 and 1915 they had five children, all born in Auckland, and they had their own dairy. Captain Tom was a retailer of milk, but when the men he employed were called up, he was unable to manage the dairy business on his own and so took a farm. This branch of the Wolfenden family made a successful life for themselves, dairying down under. Captain Tom Wolfenden died in Auckland, in 1931.

Inward Migration – Welcome to Britain

One other type of migration that may have played a part in shaping the lives of your dairy ancestors is that of inward migration, whereby people from overseas relocated to this country and subsequently became dairymen. Ironically, in their native countries these people would have experienced similar forces of 'pull' and 'push' to those experienced by British citizens who were seeking a better life abroad. One such 'push' factor, prevalent in mainland Europe during the nineteenth century, was that of religious persecution.

In late 1800s Belorussia, the Russian government was actively repressing Belorussian culture and Jewish families in particular were being subject to ruthless persecution. This led to many fleeing the country and seeking a new life elsewhere. One such family was that of Joshua Dworetski. By 1901, Joshua had fled his homeland and relocated his family to England; he anglicised his surname, changing it to 'Dover'. He spent the rest of his life as a cowkeeper in Liverpool, first at 57 Prescott Street and later at 14 Shannon Street. Joshua's son, Selig, assisted in the running of the Shannon Street dairy and inherited the family business when Joshua passed away, in 1932. Selig, in turn, was then assisted in the running of the dairy by his wife and his two children. Selig's granddaughter, Janis Stout, recalls some of the family stories:

> My father and his younger sister both grew up at the dairy. He told tales of milking the cows before going to school and university and of putting out fires when an incendiary bomb landed on the cowshed in the blitz.
> **(davejoy-author.com/cowkeepers-from-russia.html)**

Although the Dover family's dairy at Shannon Street survived the bombings of 1941, it was unable to survive the redevelopment of this part of the city centre. The building was demolished in the mid-1960s to make way for the construction of Liverpool Metropolitan Cathedral.

Chapter 4

Rise and Fall of the City Dairy

The 'Hay-day' of the Cowkeeper

Once legislation was introduced requiring cowkeepers to be licensed, it became possible to record the number of cows being kept in towns and cities. Licence records were referred to in the annual reports published by the city's Medical Officer of Health. The figures from these reports suggest that the number of city cows reached a peak between the turn of the century and the beginning of the First World War:

The Number of City Cows 1911–1913
- Birmingham   575
- Bradford   4,400
- Burnley   726
- Halifax   2,500
- Leeds   2,000
- Liverpool   6,428
- London   3,096
- Manchester   1,943
- Newcastle   497
- Norwich   567
- Nottingham   860
- Preston   304
- Salford   195
- Sheffield   2,400
- Sunderland   171

(Adapted from Atkins, 1999)

This peak in city cowkeeping activity perhaps reflects the continued attrition of the rural hinterland by the relentless march of industrialisation and urban expansion. In their study of milk supply in the Midlands town of Darlaston Green during the early 1900s, Peter Carter and Dennis Parker (2019) describe the emergence of town cowkeepers, as traditional farming in the area became marginalised by the growing prominence of mining and metalworking. During this time, the town's milk was supplied by a number of cowkeeping urban dairies run by the Andrews, Foster, Holland, Small and Worrall families.

In August 1913, as a result of an agreement reached by the major dairy companies in London, newspapers around the country predicted the 'Doom' of the milk can as a vessel for milk delivery. The agreement in question entailed the adoption of a new set of rules and regulations, based on those already in existence in New York. Foremost among these were the requirements that: 'Milk shall be delivered to the consumer only in sealed bottles, which have been sealed at the dairy' and 'Milk shall be delivered to the consumer within thirty-six hours from the time at which it was drawn'. From this it was anticipated that 'milk will no longer be ladled out in dusty streets, catching the germs that hover around' (*Western Gazette*, 22 August 1913). This change of practice by the London dairy companies did indeed set a trend that would spread across the country, but the expediency with which the bottle replaced the can was tempered when Britain was drawn into the conflict in Europe.

The First World War

The First World War resulted in thousands of men joining the forces and being shipped across the English Channel to fight in Europe. This affected all industries and businesses in the country, including farming; it was a commonly held belief that 'agriculturists make good soldiers' (Roberts, 2007). The impact on cowkeeping was lessened by the fact that the cowkeeper's wife (sometimes referred to as a 'cow-wife') was more than capable of stepping into her husband's shoes and running the business in his absence. Also, having a large family and being able to call upon relatives from the countryside to come into the city and lend a hand, helped in this respect. This was how many cowkeeping and non-cowkeeping dairies continued after the man of the house became a casualty of war. Indeed, it was a common occurrence for the widows of dairymen to continue running the business, under their own name and with the assistance of their grown-up children.

The shortage of labour resulted in the dairymen of many towns and cities collectively announcing that they would be reducing the number of deliveries through the day. The usual practice of two deliveries per day – one in the morning and a second one in the afternoon, to coincide with milking times – was reduced to just one delivery per day, between the hours of 6.00 a.m. and 12 noon, Sundays and weekdays.

Another way in which the First World War affected the city dairyman was the British army's persistence in the use of horses for both combat and transportation. As popularised in Michael Morpurgo's 1982 novel *War Horse* (subsequently a successful play and film of the same name), the army purchased thousands of horses from farms across the country and transported them to the various theatres of war abroad. This had a direct impact on all dairymen who used horses in the delivery of milk. Edward Mason recalls, as a boy, the family's Carisbrooke Dairy in Liverpool being visited by officers from an artillery unit. They had come to inspect Edward's favourite horse, Muddle, and he was afraid they would take the horse away. Although Muddle was quite capable of pulling the milk float, to Edward's

Rise and Fall of the City Dairy

War Horse – During the First World War, thousands of working horses were acquired by the army and used to carry supplies to the front. Richard Harper, Cowkeeper. (Courtesy of Roy Thwaite)

great relief, the officers considered the horse not to be big enough to pull a gun carriage (unpublished Memoirs of Edward Eubank Mason, 1980 – Robert Mason).

But there was also another, indirect, impact on those dairymen who kept cows. Huge quantities of fodder were needed to feed these war horses, necessitating the Forage Department of the War Office in purchasing all the best hay in the country. As hay was essential in maintaining a herd of cows in the city, cowkeepers were forced to find alternative sources of sustenance for their beasts. The solution to this problem was for cowkeepers to arrange for their cows to be turned out on to any and every available piece of grazeable land in the city; school playing fields, sports pitches, golf courses, cemeteries, highway verges, commons, private grounds, public parks and gardens were all utilised in this way. For a brief period, the city cow emerged from its backyard shippon and once more impinged upon the consciousness of the urban populace.

Problems caused by the scarcity of labour, of provender and of dairy cows were compounded by an increase in the price of all these commodities. This inevitably meant an increase in the price of milk to the customer. But this was a time of great hardship for everyone, and the dairymen wrestled with the problem of how to provide affordable milk whilst making enough profit with which to make a living.

The matter was taken out of the dairyman's hands in 1916 when the Ministry of Food was created with powers to regulate the supply and consumption of food. This was implemented through local Food Committees whose remit was to ensure people adhered to rationing and, where food was available to be purchased, that it was at a reasonable price. But these measures failed to quell a growing dissatisfaction amongst consumers who suspected milk distributors of profiteering from what by then was considered to be a basic human need. Foremost amongst these consumers were women, the guardians of the family, who organised protests, boycotts and marches, demanding cleaner and cheaper milk (Valenze, 2011).

In 1917, the first grading scheme for milk was introduced. The National Clean Milk Society (NCMS) had been founded two years earlier, with the stated aims of raising the hygienic standard of milk and milk products, and of educating the general public as to the importance of a clean and wholesome milk supply. Of great concern was the elimination of milk-borne diseases, in particular that of tuberculosis. Robert Koch had isolated the tubercle bacillus responsible for the disease back in 1882, but it was not until 1895 that the First Royal Commission on Tuberculosis had expressed its considered opinion that the consumption of tuberculous milk was a contributory factor to human tuberculosis; subsequently, the 'Royal Commission Appointed to Inquire into the Relations of Human and Animal Tuberculosis', was set up in 1901.

Pressure from groups such as the NCMS, and from the general public, resulted in the 1917 Milk (Special Designations) Order, with its requirement that Grade A milk had to be produced under exceptionally clean and hygienic conditions from a herd certified by a vet to be free from tuberculosis. Although some cowkeepers were suspicious of the motives of what they saw as the 'wealthy and elite' clean milk campaigners, their defiance gradually lessened as it became obvious that the standard for graded milk was within the reach of those who practised the ordinary rules of cleanliness.

Between the Wars

After the war, the call for cleaner and cheaper milk continued and the inter-war period became a time of massive change in the dairy industry in Britain. The trade in milk was booming: in the 1920s, over sixty express milk trains were running daily into London on the Great Western Railway alone, with the entire network transporting 282 million gallons of milk every year. Tankers began to replace the traditional metal milk churn as the principal means of transporting milk by rail. Just seven of these 3,000-gallon tanks could replace 2,000 churns, without all the manpower and delay that the loading and unloading of milk churns required (Ginn and Goodman, 2016).

The adoption of pasteurisation was slow at first; only 1.5 per cent of our milk supply was being pasteurised in 1926. One reason for this was that the early pasteurisation machinery was unreliable. The so-called 'flash' process, in which milk was heated very quickly to a high temperature in batches and then cooled, was eventually banned by the Milk (Special Designations) Order (1923) and replaced for the next couple of decades by low temperature (63–71°C for 30 minutes) machines. Eventually, in the 1940s, the HTST (High Temperature Short Time) method was adopted, whereby milk was heated for 12–20 seconds at 75–76°C (Atkins, 2000).

Rise and Fall of the City Dairy

The milk bottle came into its own and proved to be a big hit with the public; it soon replaced the traditional kit and ladle used to dispense loose milk on the doorstep. In addition to introducing standardisation in terms of quantity (purchasing by the pint, or fraction thereof), it also brought with it advantages in terms of quality. Firstly, it enabled the customer to see the product – its colour and, most importantly for many a housewife, to see the 'cream line'. Secondly, the need for the bottle to be secured, so that its contents did not spill, necessitated the introduction of a top that could be sealed.

Bottles of sterilised milk were originally sealed with glass plugs, but these were replaced by metal 'crown' seals that required a separate opener to lever them off. Pasteurised milk was sold in wide-necked bottles that were sealed with waxed, paperboard 'pogs'; these were inserted into the wide mouth of the bottle and sat on a narrow ledge that ran around the inner surface, just below the lip. A disadvantage of the paperboard seal was that it left the pouring lip uncovered, exposing it to possible contamination.

A constant bugbear for the city dairies and the dairy companies were those unscrupulous milk vendors who dishonestly saved themselves some expense by using other people's milk bottles. Although such activity was illegal under the 1887 Merchandise Marks Act, and was punishable by a fine or imprisonment, still it became widespread. In response, the Milk Vessels Recovery Inc. was formed in 1920 by milk traders throughout the country for the express purpose of preventing misuse by unauthorised persons of the property of its members. This non-profit organisation was financed by its members through the sale of shares and annual subscriptions. It not only took steps to recover its members' property but also worked with the authorities to prosecute those responsible. By 1943, it had caused well over 2,000 prosecutions to be instituted in the High Court, and also in the police courts throughout the country (Enock, 1943).

In 1920, the National Milk Publicity Council of England and Wales (NMPC) was formed from representatives of producers, wholesalers, retailers, distributers, consumer groups and the public health sector. Its aim was to launch a national publicity campaign to raise awareness of the health value of pure milk. At the same time, voluntary milk clubs had begun to appear in schools, whereby willing teachers organised a supply and collected money from the children. This movement took off in 1927 when the NMPC lent its support by promoting contacts between schools and their local suppliers. The milk was served in one-third pint bottles at the price of one penny. By 1933, over 1 million children in England and Wales were involved in milk clubs, a new market of about 9 million gallons per annum (Jenkins, 1970).

In the 1930s, an increasing awareness and concern about public health and hygiene led to the introduction of the foil milk bottle top, which not only provided an airtight seal but also fully covered the pouring lip. Early foil tops were manufactured using a thick-gauge foil with an underlining of greaseproof paper, and had a pull-tag to make it easier for the customer to remove them when opening the bottle. They were pre-formed, stamped and cut by a specialist foil cap manufacturer and supplied to the dairy ready for application to the bottle. The dairy used a special cup with a rubber fitting which would press the caps into place on the bottles (Hudson, 2010). The combination of glass bottle and securable seal not only proved very popular with customers for its convenience but also greatly limited the opportunity for adulteration or the risk of contamination once the milk had been bottled.

One prominent high street dairy company was unaffected by the clean milk movement and was immune to the trend for bottled milk. The reason being that although its shops carried the title 'Dairy', the Maypole Dairy Company did not sell milk. Established in the Midlands by George Watson in 1887, Maypole specialised in the manufacture and sale of margarine. Indeed, by 1918, through a chain of over 800 shops (with splendidly tiled fronts), the company held a 50 per cent share of the UK margarine market. They also sold butter, cheese, eggs and tins of condensed milk, but margarine accounted for 85 per cent of the company's sales. As such, the Maypole Dairy was not in direct competition with those city dairies dealing in milk (**letslookagain.com/2015/05/milking-profits-a-history-of-the-maypole-dairy-co/**).

To cope with demand for bottled milk, large processing plants were developed and these were supplied by the railways, which by then were replacing the traditional metal milk churn with glass-lined milk tanks, and also by road haulage, using glass-lined tankers. New distribution depots were created in the cities to cope with this tidal wave of bottled milk. The Medical Officer for Health of the Borough of Hammersmith, J.B. Howell, described the system of operation being implemented at that time by one of the (unnamed) larger dairies under his purview:

> All milk to this dairy is delivered direct from the farms to a private railway siding on the premises. From the time of its arrival until it leaves the premises in bottles, the milk is subjected to the minimum of exposure and handling. After pre-heating, the milk is passed through a series of pipes to a number of centrifugal clarifiers. From these it is conveyed by a further series of pipes to a pasteurising plant of the Holding type, from whence, after cooling, it is passed to numerous automatic bottle-filling machines. In use at these premises are some of the largest bottle washing machines in the world. An average of 40,000 gallons of milk per day is dealt with at this dairy.
>
> (Howell, 1927)

Milk bottles were popular with the non-cowkeeping dairyman as they were easy to handle and they did away with the need to measure out each customer's order. Even so, health and hygiene requirements meant that milk bottles did generate their own workload. In 1933, Sloper's Dairy in Laindon, Essex, began to use milk bottles (**laindonhistory.org.uk/content/people/family_memories/slopers_dairy**). Their rounds included a number of local schools to which they supplied large churns for the kitchens and third-of-a-pint bottles for each and every child. Mrs Sloper handwashed every bottle, five days a week – a formidable task.

Rise and Fall of the City Dairy

The introduction of milk bottles was not as popular with the cowkeepers, as bottling introduced what they considered to be an expensive and unnecessary process into their simple supply chain. Long after milk bottles became the norm, some cowkeepers continued to serve loose milk, either using the kit and ladle, or delivering handcans to the doorstep. In his memoir about the working horses of Liverpool, Harry Wooding (1991) recalls, as a boy in the 1930s, being woken each morning by the sound of his local cowkeeper, Ernie Hudson of Lovat Street:

> [He] was always up and around early, delivering milk in 1 pint and half-pint milk cans, which made an almighty noise in the early hours, plus the fact that he always wore clogs with irons on the soles and heels ...

Mr Hudson, described as being as strong as an ox, added to the clatter of milk cans and clogs by yodelling as he delivered the milk!

The inter-war period also saw the rise of a new type of dairyman – the Milkman. For the most part, dairymen, whether they kept cows or not, had been self-employed, as these were family businesses. However, many of the large wholesale dairies that were processing and supplying milk in bulk also developed a retail/delivery arm to their corporate operation. This entailed managing a fleet of vehicles (in corporate livery) and a workforce (in corporate uniform) to deliver bottled milk to the doorstep.

Unlike traditional dairymen, milkmen were not self-employed but were employees of the corporate dairies. They were not farmers and they were not keepers of cows and they did not turn milk into butter or cheese; their job did not require any of these dairy skills. They were not involved in sourcing the milk in any way; their job was purely delivery. They did not live on the premises, they worked contracted hours and at the end of the working day, collected their pay and went home. Consequently, many of these milkmen were transient and few viewed delivering milk as a job-for-life.

Despite the differences between the traditional dairyman and the corporate milkman, the latter still worked long and arduous hours involving up to three deliveries: a 4.00 a.m. start was followed by the first round of the day; after returning to the depot for something to eat, a midday round was carried out; the final delivery took place later in the day, after which all carts, churns and utensils had to be cleaned and sterilised, finally finishing work at 7.00 p.m.

In 1924, in an attempt to improve conditions for milkmen, the Transport and General Workers' Union presented its Dairy Workers' Charter to the London dairy trade. The charter demanded the following: a minimum wage of £4 a week; abolition of the commission system; a six-day, 48-hour week; a roster for relief work; time-and-a-half for overtime; double time for Sundays and public holidays; fourteen days of annual holiday; the proper stamping and gauging of all utensils; and the abolition of all service agreements. Although these demands may have been prophetic of future working conditions, at the time they were being tabled there were the beginnings of an economic depression and although some minor concessions were made, the charter was rejected.

The City Dairy: A Social and Family History

Milk delivery to the doorstep reverted to its pre-war frequency of at least twice per day; in some areas the 'Pudding Round' was reinstated. In her poem, *The Milk Ponies*, Jan Struther (1932) humorously described the midday delivery to her home in Wellington Square, Chelsea. Whereas at six in the morning the milk ponies took great care to come very quietly into the square, at twelve o'clock they noisily champed:

> Here's cream for your puddings,
> Here's butter from Devon,
> Grade A for the baby, At Number Eleven;
> And all the price, We want you to pay
> Is best loaf sugar – Three lumps a day.

The 1930s saw the emergence on the high street of a new type of dairy outlet, imported from America: the Milk Bar. Unlike the traditional city dairy, milk bars were places where people – mainly young people – congregated to consume milk products (milk shakes, ice cream etc.), rather than purchase them for consumption at home; they were cafes rather than shops. Black and White Milk Bars Ltd and Strand Milk Bars Ltd opened up chains in the capital, whereas National Milk Bars Ltd spread their brand throughout the provinces of England and Wales ('Milk Bars March', article in *News Review*, 4 February 1937).

A further major development in the country's dairy industry was the creation of the producer-owned Milk Marketing Board (MMB), in 1933, at a time when tens of thousands of dairy farmers were struggling financially. The aim of the MMB was to find buyers for every drop of milk produced in the UK. With a workforce of some 7,000, it set about creating a stable market for the country's milk producers by guaranteeing a minimum price for all milk produced and by creating local networks of producers, processors and distributors. As a co-operative, it was the largest agricultural model of its kind in British history.

Although creating a level playing field for all milk producers appeared to be a quite laudable and fair exercise, and was welcomed by the wholesale producers, it was not at all welcomed by producer-retailers. Due to their shorter supply chain, producer-retailers had previously enjoyed a distinct business advantage over wholesalers, but this advantage was gradually eroded as the MMB imposed a levy on the producer-retailers. Cowkeepers began to feel the pinch.

The demise of Carisbrooke Dairy began when the Liverpool Co-operative Society opened a store directly across the road from the dairy and began selling cheap milk. The Mason family watched helplessly as more and more of their customers began buying milk from their 'hated rivals'. Edward Eubank Mason, when forced to close the dairy's accounts, following the death of his father in April 1934, vehemently conveyed the frustration of the struggling cowkeeper:

> As a concluding statement, at the price of 6d per quart of milk we definitely were losing money and this business was <u>not</u> paying for itself. Milk as from 1 May 1934 was reduced to 5½d per quart. The

last sentence is added 'without comment'. The Milk Marketing Board are working for the large firms, for example, Co-operatives and in a few years I do not have any hesitation in stating that the number of firms will be greatly reduced. Our firm – Edward Mason, Cowkeeper and Dairyman – would have been wiped out in a few months!

(Unpublished Memoirs of Edward Eubank Mason, 1980 – Robert Mason)

In the face of so many rapid changes affecting the whole of the dairy industry, those dairymen responsible for the distribution of milk formed their own trade organisation. The National Dairymen's Association came into being in 1937 with the following stated objectives: to promote, watch over and protect the interests of all persons concerned in the retailing of milk; to originate and promote improvements in the law or regulations which affect the industry, and to oppose measures not in the interests of the trade; and to assist individual members on all matters relating to their business. The association was financed by subscription and at the end of 1942 approximately 7,000 members were enrolled, all of whom received their monthly copy of *The Milk Industry*. It represented its members at tribunals, advised them on all matters pertaining to National Service, helped settle disputes with the MMB, and successfully opposed proposals in the House of Commons, which it claimed would have promoted the interests of co-operative societies to the detriment of the producer-retailers (Enock, 1943).

Despite all these pressures threatening not only the survival of their business but also the survival of their way of life, some cowkeepers dug in and equipped themselves to compete in this new market. They invested in small-scale pasteurising machines and in hand-operated bottling machines; they even procured their own milk bottles, stamped or moulded with the name of the dairy. Others, who were either unable or unwilling to make such an investment, opted to dispense with their cows and bought in bottled milk for retail; they became non-cowkeeping dairymen. Both continued to trade as family-owned businesses.

The National Dairymen's Association – This national association was formed in 1937 to protect the interests of all persons concerned in the retailing of milk. (Author)

The Second World War

During the Second World War, many city people were evacuated to the countryside to escape the bombings. Demand for milk dropped accordingly, but the milk industry went to extraordinary lengths to maintain a level of service in our blitzed cities. When milkmen were recruited to the forces, their jobs were filled by older men, women and boys, often from the same families as those who had gone away to fight. In his book, *The British Milkman*, Tom Phelps (2011) describes how United Dairies had 198 men killed in action and also lost thirty-five members of staff in the bombings.

In Liverpool, the larger dairies entered into a mutual arrangement whereby if one company's property suffered bomb damage the other companies would take on the processing of that milk to enable the affected business to continue. Hanson's, having one of the most modern plants in the country, were able to help out other dairies in this way. This wartime co-operation between the city's rival dairies also extended to rationalising transport and milk delivery. Hanson's had over 100 rounds to maintain in the absence of men who had enlisted and James Hanson later heaped praise upon the many stout-hearted women who took on this role, 'delivering milk in fair weather or foul, seven days per week' (Hanson, 1939). This voluntary rationalisation by the big dairies in Liverpool pre-empted the coming of a national scheme for milk delivery.

The nationwide rationalisation of milk rounds was part of a plan to enable transport resources (petrol, tyres, drivers, vehicles etc.) to be redirected to support the war effort. On 3 June 1942, Major Lloyd George, Parliamentary Secretary to the Ministry of Food, announced proposed changes in the marketing of milk designed to maximise economies in its distribution. All contracts between individual producers and purchasers would be terminated; the MMB would then purchase all milk from producers and simultaneously sell that milk to the Ministry of Food for resale to distributors and manufacturers. A new pricing structure to meet the cost of distribution was being prepared. In the meantime, all dairymen serving urban localities with a population of over 10,000 – some 516 towns – would be constituted into wartime associations to prepare schemes of rationalisation suited to local requirements. Where distributors failed to produce a scheme the Ministry of Food would introduce its own scheme after considering local circumstances.

'*One Street – One Milkman*' was the principle underlying the new zoning arrangements; although the local co-operative societies were allowed to continue serving their existing customers wherever they lived. All milk retailers were required to become members of their local wartime association and to complete a questionnaire listing the name and address of all their existing customers. This information was then used to redraw the milk rounds in the city or town in question. As the retailers had an active part in the process there was a considerable degree of self-policing to ensure the zoning was as fair as possible and that everyone had the same number of customers as before; though there was some concern on the part of the family businesses, that the co-operative societies were receiving preferential treatment.

The scale of this operation varied between locales according to the size of population, the size of the area being covered and, correspondingly, the number of existing milk retailers. In London, it was reported that of the 6.338 million registered customers, 4.5 million had to be transferred to a new retailer (*The Scotsman*, 21 April 1943). Accordingly, the precise details of the rollout of the new arrangements also varied from place to place. Nevertheless, to make the transition as smooth as possible, all areas set about providing customers with plentiful information and advice in preparation for their local launch date.

Publicity included the production of Street Lists, showing which dairy was delivering in which street, posted in local newspapers and displayed in public places, and also of postcards, delivered to each household by the postman, stating who the new supplier would be. In Coventry, Street Lists were deposited for inspection at public libraries, British Restaurants, sub-post offices, the Municipal Lodgings Bureau, the Citizens Advice Bureau, day nurseries, municipal clinics and relief stations as well as at the Food Office and the Council House (*Coventry Evening Telegraph*, 27 April 1943). In Trowbridge, 1,857 households received postcards, notifying them of the changes (*Trowbridge Advertiser*, 27 February 1943).

The Aberdeen Dairyman's Wartime Association urged householders who were about to have a new milkman to keep a lookout so that deliveries would not be unduly delayed (*Aberdeen Press and Journal*, 23 April 1943). In Cardiff, the public were asked to give 'great help' by providing jugs or other utensils for each of the final three days' supply by their present dairyman in order that all bottles could be in the possession of their owners before the rationalisation commenced (*Western Mail*, 6 May 1943). In the interests of promoting good health, customers in Leicester who had previously purchased pasteurised or other designated milk were advised that they had a right to insist on their usual grade of milk from their new dairyman (*Leicester Evening Mail*, 27 April 1943).

The Milk Rationalisation Scheme. Street Lists for Ramsgate

As reported in the *East Kent Times and Mail*, 17 November 1943

Sharp's Dairies	Cambrian	Claremont	Coronation Road
Alexandra Road	Cottages	Gardens	Denmark Road
Ann's Road	Cannon Road	Clarendon	Downs Road
Alma Road	Cavendish Street	Gardens	Dumpton Park
Alpha Road	Chapel Place	Cliffs End Farm	Road
Ashburnham	Chapel Place	Coast Guard	Duncan Road
Road	Lane	Cotts.	Dundonald Road
Ayton Road	Chapel Road	Cliff Cottages	Ellington Place
Belmont Road	Charles Road	Clifton Road	Ellington Road
Beresford Road	Chatham Place	Crescent Road	Eagle Hill
Boundary Road	Chatham Street	Cumberland Road	Eagle Yard
Bursill Crescent	Cheriton Avenue	Cliftonville	Effingham Street
Bush Avenue	Carlton Avenue	Avenue	Elms Avenue
Buxton Road	Chilton Lane	Codrington Road	Elmstone Road

The City Dairy: A Social and Family History

Ethelbert Road
Fairlight Avenue
Finsbury Road
Forge Lane
Farm Road
Gilbert Road
George Street
Goodwin Road
Grange Road
Granville Avenue
Grosvenor Road
Grove Road
Guildford Lawn
Hatfield Road
Haine Road
Highfield Road
High Street
High St. St. Laurence
Holbrook Drive
Hollicondane Road
Harbour Street
King Edward Road
King's Avenue
London Road from St. Laurence Ave to Nethercourt Circus
Lorina Road
Manston Road
Marden Avenue
Marlborough Road
Mayforth Gardens
Meeting Street
Memel Place
Minster Road
Mill Cottages
Morden Cottages
Nethercourt Gardens

Nethercourt Hill
Newington Road
Norman Road
North Avenue
Paradise
Park Road
Pegwell Road
Pegwell Avenue
Percy Road
Picton Road
Poplar Road
Prices Avenue
Princes Avenue
Queens Avenue
Richmond Road
St. Lukes Avenue
St. James Avenue
Saxon Road
Southwood Road (7–174 and 61–149)
Seafield Road
South Eastern Road
Stanley Place
Telham Avenue
Thanet Rd. Northwood
Upper Dumpton Park Rd
Vale Road
Whitehall Road
Winstanley Crescent
Willson's Road
Woodville Avenue
York Terrace
York Street

Page's Dairies
Abbotts Hill
Albert Road
Albion Hill
Albion Road

Alliance Road
Arklow Square
Artillery Road
Augusta Road
Avebury Avenue
Avenue Road and Syndale Place
Albion Place
Alfred Cottages and New Alfred Cottages
Alma Place
Balmoral Place
Bethesda Street
Belle Vue Road
Brights Place
Broad Street
Brockenhurst Road
Brunswick Street
Belmont Street
Belle Vue Cottages
Camden Square
Church Hill
Camden Rd and Cotts.
Cecilia Road
Cottage Road
College Road
Church Road
Dane Crescent
Dane Park Road
Dane Road
Dumpton Park Drive
Ellen Avenue
Erdley Square
Flora Road
Garden Row
Granville Marina
Hardres Street
Hereson Road

Hollicondane Terrace
Honeysuckle Road
Hardres Road
The Harbour
Hibernia Street
Irchester Street
King Street
Kent Terrace
La Belle Alliance Sq.
Leonards Avenue
Leopold Road
Lillian Road
Lyndhurst Road
Montague Road
Monefiore Avenue
Muir Road
Montefiore Cottages
Mews Cottages
Newcastle Hill
Penshurst Road
Prestedge Avenue
Plains of Waterloo
Packers Lane
Queens Road
Rosebery Avenue
St. Andrews Road
St. Davids Road
St Georges Road
St Patricks Road
Salisbury Avenue
St. Pauls Cottages
St. Lukes Road
School Lane
Shaftesbury Street
Staffordshire Street
Sydney Road
Thanet Road

Rise and Fall of the City Dairy

Trinity Place	Liverpool Lawn	St. Laurence Avenue	Newlands Road
Turner Street	Leopold Street		Northwood Road
Truro Road	Military Road	Lorne Road	Pysons Road
Unity Place	Nelson Crescent	Mays Road	Violet Avenue
Union Road	Paragon Street	Napleton Road	Woodford Avenue
Union Street	Paragon	Queen Bertha Road	
Vincent Place	Priory Road		
Victoria Road	Prospect Terrace	Rawden Road	**Abbott's Dairies**
Victoria Terrace	Queen Street	Royal Esplanade	Allenby Road
Victoria Parade	Rodney Street	St Laurence Avenue	Bradley Road
Winterstoke Crescent	Rose Hill	St. Mildreds Avenue	Bolton Street
	Royal Crescent		Central Road
Wallwood Road	Royal Road	St. Mildreds Road	Coleman Crescent
Warten Road	Sion Hill	Southwood Road	
Waterloo Place	St. Augustines Road	Stancombe Avenue	Fitzroy Avenue
Wellington Crescent	Spencer Square	Watchester Avenue	Gwyn Road
	Spencer Street		Hillbrow Road
West Dumpton Lane	Townley Street	Warre Avenue	Margate Road (2–230 and 1-129)
	Vale Square		
Stonelees Dairies	Vereth Road	**Hawes' Dairies**	Nixon Avenue
Addington Street	West Cliff Road	Clements Road	Princes Road
Adelaide Gardens		Cox's Lane	Queensgate Road
Albert Street	**Sevenscore Est.**	Homeleigh Road	Roman Road
Church Avenue	Bloomsbury Road	Hopes Lane	Stanley Road
Chartham Terrace		Margate Road (232 on to Boundary)	Station Approach Road
Cannonbury Road	Clarence Road		
Cross Street	Durlock Avenue		Wheatley Road
Cliff Street	Edith Road	(131 on to Boundary)	Wilfred Road
Harrison Terrace	London Road		Winifred Avenue
Hertford Street	From Grange Road to	Marrose Avenue	
James Street			

Inevitably, there was a degree of disgruntlement on the part of some customers who had established a good relationship with their regular milk supplier over many years. Also, amongst their many other challenges, dairymen now had to adapt to new rounds and to the requirements of new customers. Despite this, on the whole the new arrangements worked out well for both dairyman and customer.

The Food Control Committee at Tynemouth hailed their scheme a success. The chairman of the local dairyman's association, Mr H.F. Davies, said that the greatest trouble was on the first day when he had to knock everybody out of bed to ask how much milk they wanted, but by the end of the week everyone was satisfied. (Though he also reported two instances where neighbours informed him that people on his new list had been dead and buried for years!) Tynemouth's Food Executive Officer, Mr F.G. Egner, praised the 100 volunteers, mostly women, who had undertaken all the clerical work to bring the scheme to fruition. He went on to say it was a wonder the scheme had not been introduced sooner as it had saved a lot of time and energy (*Shields Daily News*, 20 January 1943).

Indeed, the new arrangements seem to have achieved the overall aim of conserving resources, and economies were reported both locally and nationally. For example, the town of Arnold, in Nottinghamshire, witnessed a reduction in round size: '39 streets to eight streets, 51 to 13, 34 to five, 113 to 39, and 139 to 33'. (*Nottingham Journal*, 22 February 1943) When the matter was debated in the House of Commons, on 8 March 1944, Colonel J. Llewellin informed the House that over the country as a whole, which had 676 rationalisation areas, it was estimated there had been a saving of 6,700 men, 2,150 women, and of 39,000 gallons of petrol per week.

When petrol was rationed, deliveries of milk continued, using the horse and cart; the trusty steed once more making its worth felt. Milkmen would stay up all night with their horses to calm them during the bombings, as would cowkeepers with their cows. When a property had been demolished, the milk was left at the bombsite in the knowledge that neighbours would know if the family had survived and where they were staying and would pass it on to them. As people moved, dairies traded customers to keep rounds compact. If a dairy property was bombed, neighbouring dairies would adapt their own rounds to make sure the level of service was maintained. Through this extraordinary contribution to the war effort the milkman – and his endearing horse – found a special place in the hearts and minds of the British people.

Though our dairy ancestors managed to survive the war-torn first half of the twentieth century, the rapid technological and economic changes that marked the second half proved to be their undoing. First the cowkeeper succumbed, followed soon after by the family dairyman, leaving only the suburban milkman as a remnant of the city dairying tradition.

The Last Cowkeeper

The Blitz brought previously unimaginable death and destruction to our major towns and cities. Though many of the traditional city cowkeepers had had their businesses bombed out of existence, some, mainly located in the suburbs, survived the bombings. But even these had to take a long, hard look at the viability of continuing to keep cows in the city. With the development of refrigeration and pasteurisation the shelf life of milk had been greatly extended – the need for milk that was fresh from the cow became a thing of the past and the notion of 'from cow to customer' was replaced by that of 'from field to fridge'. Also, public perception and, therefore, the local authority policy, had changed; cowkeeping was now considered to be a 'dirty' trade (or, at the very least, a smelly trade) that was no longer seen as being appropriate in a residential area. The close bond that had once existed between cow and customer in the city was no more and the era of the town cow was coming to an end:

From Cow to Customer? – By the end of the Second World War, the bond that had existed between city cow and customer was no more. (Courtesy of Sue Smith)

> **CARS MORE ACCEPTABLE THAN COWS** A garage was more acceptable than a cowkeeping business, a woman resident said at an inquiry at the Municipal Annexes, Liverpool, today. The inquiry … was into the refusal of Liverpool City Council to grant permission for a garage at 8 Tawd Street. Opening the case for the appellants, Mr Steel said the premises were 80 to 100 years old and had been occupied by Mr Thomas Illingworth, father of the appellants, since 1940 in his business as cowkeeper. In June 1954, the Corporation served a dangerous structure notice on him and he decided that it was not an economic proposition to carry out the repairs. He gave up the business of cowkeeping …
>
> (*Liverpool Echo*, 10 May 1955)

In London, David Carson's dairy in Swedenborg Square, near the Tower of London, was the last in the East End. During the war, when so many of the remaining London cowkeepers went out of business, he had survived by reducing his herd to just six cows. Sadly, the post-war shortage of labour, the increasing cost of feed and the high cost of tuberculin-tested cows finally forced Mr Carson to give up cowkeeping, and the last cow left the East End in 1954. Not too far away, in Lugard Road, Peckham, fourth-generation cowkeeper, John Jorden, was surviving with a herd of between thirty and forty beasts. But, despite a deal to cease delivering and just sell his milk direct to United Dairies, he still could not cover his costs. It appears that when Mr Jorden ceased trading, in 1967, this marked the end of cowkeeping in London (Stout, 1978).

The City Dairy: A Social and Family History

The longevity of Liverpool's cowkeepers earned the city the title of being the 'Last Stronghold of Town Cowkeepers' (Hill, 1956). They did their best to compete with the corporate dairies. They formed their own limited company, Dairy Farmers Creamery (Liverpool) Ltd (known as D.F.C.), and built a pasteurisation and distribution centre in a factory in Kirkby at a cost of £70,000. The creamery opened in 1951 and at its peak was supplying 11,000 gallons of milk per day.

> We get Fragrance from the Roses,
> And Honey from the Bee,
> But Milk as Fresh as a Daisy
> Comes to you From D.F.C.
> DELICIOUS FRESH CREAMY

However, in 1966 the Kirkby operation was bought out by J. Hanson & Sons (by then, part of Unigate), and two years later it was announced in *The London Gazette* (18 April 1968) that the company had been voluntarily wound up following an Extraordinary General Meeting held on 25 March 1968.

The Liverpool and District Dairy Farmers' Association (formerly, the Liverpool & District Cowkeepers' Association) continued up until 25 April 1975, when it was finally wound up by the then secretary, Mr Thomas Hogg. It was just three months later that Mr Joe Capstick, of 4 Marlborough Road, Liverpool, ably assisted by his teenage son, Maurice, moved his cows into the Lancashire countryside and the last true city cowkeeper was gone. A way of life that had spanned nearly two centuries had finally come to an end.

End of an Era – The Liverpool and District Dairy Farmers' Association closed its books on 25 April 1975. (Courtesy of Andrew Williamson)

Open All Hours

The end of cowkeeping did not mean the end of the city dairy. As the supply of milk from cowkeepers diminished, it was replaced by milk supplied by one of the large dairy companies. But, although sales from the dairy and the milk round could continue, being a retailer of milk was not as profitable as being a producer-retailer; if it was going to remain viable, the dairy – as a shop – needed to diversify. In addition to milk, dairies had traditionally sold eggs, cheese, butter, ice cream, and even poultry, sausages and cuts of meat. (Indeed, the Maypole Dairy had previously demonstrated the principle of a city dairy not dependent upon the sale of milk.) So, it was not a huge leap for them to morph into more general stores, combining dairy with grocery, or even becoming a newsagent and tobacconist. The bottling of milk had inadvertently facilitated this diversification by ensuring milk could be sold alongside other goods without risk of contamination.

In London, the large dairy companies, such as Express Dairies, United Dairies and the Co-operative Dairies, were viewed by the small, family-run businesses as being 'the opposition'. Despite this, more and more dairymen and their families were forced to sell up to the large conglomerates. Some just sold off their milk rounds to the big dairies and continued running the shop. The Daniel family had set up a dairy in Morton Terrace in 1931, but they sold their milk round and continued

The Corner Shop – City dairies survived by evolving into corner shops and convenience stores. (Author)

doing business until 1995 by selling milk over the counter, along with bread, cereal and general groceries (Hayes, 2018).

Reminiscences of early dairies refer to there being one at the end of every street (Mellor, 1978). This rather romanticised view is undoubtedly an exaggeration. But implicit in this description are the qualities of 'corner' (they needed access to the backyard), and of 'convenience' (they needed to be close to their customers). Maybe it is not so surprising then, that many of these dairies seamlessly joined the ranks of those other most British of institutions: Corner Shops and Convenience Stores.

The Joy family history provides an example of the transformation of a city dairy. In 1901, George Wright was a cowkeeper, living at Dale House, Garston, with his wife, Hannah (née Joy) and their two children. By 1911, they had relocated, and opened a dairy at 260–262 Garston Old Road. The family were living above the shop and they were no longer keeping cows, as indicated in the census of that year: George was a 'Milk Dealer', and his son an 'Assistant Milk Dealer', but Hannah's occupation was given as 'Confectioner' – diversification had begun. By the time of the 1939 register, George had retired, but Hannah was now running the show; her occupation was given as 'Sub-Postmaster, Sweets and Tobacco Dealer', and that of their daughter, Hettie, was given as 'Post Office Counter Clerk'. Eventually, Hettie succeeded her parents and ran the shop as a newsagent's, until her death in 1964. Today, the shops on that block at the end of Garston Old Road have all been converted into residential properties (Joy, 2018).

Hettie Wright, my first-cousin-twice-removed, was perhaps typical of her generation of dairymen and women: born in the early 1900s, she spent all her working life in the family business, and inherited it when her parents retired. In contrast, my generation of baby-boomers had different aspirations. Neither the prospect of working in a shop, from dawn 'til-dusk, seven days a week, nor that of being out on a milk round in all weathers, were attractive propositions for the generation that allegedly 'never had it so good'. Despite this natural wastage caused by children leaving to pursue alternative careers, many of these family businesses made the necessary changes and persevered.

Although milk was still stocked by these remodelled dairies, its importance was greatly diminished. In her book, *The Corner Shop*, Babita Sharma (2019) describes the reaction of her shopkeeper parents when a neighbouring competitor reduced the price of his milk:

> Mum and Dad would not be drawn into battle on this particular item. There was no point in fighting over spilt milk because the mark-up for us was minimal. It could be anything from 0.5 to 1 per cent and we preferred to keep our price the same rather than be accused by the customers of profiteering on an essential item whose price was set by government tariff. In any case there were plenty more items in our shop besides milk that would bring in the bacon.

Things became even more difficult for corner shop businesses with the arrival of that other American invention: the supermarket. Ironically, companies with their roots in the dairy industry were key players in driving the supermarket movement in the UK. Premier Supermarkets, a subsidiary of Express Dairies, are often credited with opening the UK's first true supermarket in Streatham, South London, in the early 1950s. Around the same time, the Asquith family merged with Associated Dairies, and Asda was born. Initiatives such as these heralded the beginning of a retail revolution that would spread to every corner of the nation over the next two decades. As well as competing with those corporate dairies still involved with doorstep delivery, supermarkets also dealt a further blow to the smaller, family businesses. Joan Fenney recalls the impact of the supermarket upon the family's dairy in Liverpool:

> As soon as they built the supermarkets people said 'No, we won't leave you', but they did. You dreaded getting a note in the bottle saying 'No milk 'til further notice'. You knew very well that they wouldn't start again.
>
> **(bbc.co.uk/news/uk-england-merseyside-14855763)**

Milk bars also succumbed to the supermarket's impact. These high street cafes had flourished in the decades following the war, proving to be an important facet in the development of youth culture in Britain; they were widespread and were places young kids could go and hang out by the jukebox or play on slot machines (Horn, 2009). Although they were the venue of choice for the younger generation throughout the Swinging Sixties, few survived beyond the 1990s. In 2010, John Frost, managing director of National Milk Bars Ltd., reflected on how the company had struggled against coffee shop and supermarket cafe competition:

> It's become out of date with the next generation, so if we were looking to continue we'd probably have to upgrade and become a more coffee-like operation. But that market is pretty flooded at the moment. There's a lot of competition. Tesco has moved in … and it tends to suck up trade in the high street.
>
> **(bbc.co.uk/news/uk-wales-mid-wales-12038590)**

As the city dairy metamorphosed, a few of the family-run businesses doggedly maintained their milk rounds. They kept their independence but at the same time, under the umbrella of the MMB, became part of the distribution network of the corporate dairies who supplied them with their milk. As with the dairy, the milk round also had to modernise. The dairymen who had traded in their horse and cart for a petrol-driven van, now traded that in for an electric milk float. Essentially, they were no longer dairymen. Apart from the family name adorning their vehicle, to the man in the street they were indistinguishable from the employees of the dairy companies. They had joined the ranks of what had become a symbol of the British way of life: the Milkman.

No Milk Today

When the post-war baby boom contributed to an increase in demand for doorstep milk, 'Milkman' seemed to be a relatively secure occupation. Indeed, during the late sixties and early seventies between 40,000 and 45,000 milkmen were delivering to over 18 million UK homes (99 per cent of households). However, by 2014 that figure had fallen to just 4,000 milkmen delivering to 2.5 million homes (11 per cent of households). Customers were expressing a preference for the convenience, price, freshness and longevity of milk bought from the supermarket, rather than having it delivered to their doorstep (Ward, 2016).

As doorstep delivery diminished, the small-scale family business found it more and more difficult to make ends meet. Most of the milkmen that remained were either employed directly by a dairy company or were operating a franchise. Under a franchise arrangement, the milkman was self-employed, but the dairy company owned the round; the milkman bought his milk from the parent company, which provided him with a float on a rental basis.

More recently, a sterling effort to buck this trend is being made by those dairy farmers who, finding themselves in a twenty-first century version of the 'Goldilocks zone' on the edge of town, have reinvented the producer-retailer. As well as providing an on-site farm shop for their produce, these dairy farmers are producing, processing and bottling their own milk and then delivering it door-to-door locally. It seems the old From-Cow-to-Customer approach, combined with the reintroduction of reusable, glass milk bottles, fit well with the modern demand for sustainability. Pembertons Farm Shop & Dairy is located on the edge of the township of Lytham St Annes, in Lancashire. It is a family business, established over 130 years ago, that began delivering milk to the local community in the 1950s, and then opened a farm shop in 2017, selling dairy, meat and groceries, and incorporating a vending machine selling raw milk. Not surprisingly, the company emphasises the economic, environmental and health benefits of 'buying locally'. As well as milk, their (up-to-four-times-a-week) doorstep delivery service also includes cream, butter, eggs, yogurts, milkshakes and potatoes (Pemberton, 2022).

Nevertheless, Dairy UK's (2021) estimate is that only around 3 per cent of the UK's fresh milk is now being delivered directly to the doorstep by milkmen and women (**dairyuk.org/the-uk-dairy-industry/#doorstepdelivery**). In his book, *No Milk Today: The Vanishing World of the Milkman*, Andrew Ward (2016) attributes this gradual disappearance of the milkman to a combination of factors: price deregulation; European rulings; improved refrigeration, including the popularity of refrigerators in the home; increased shelf life; supermarket initiatives, such as selling milk in larger-volume, plastic containers, and as a loss leader product; competition from soft-drink companies; the dissolution of the MMB; changing diets; traffic/delivery restrictions; and, in the face of all this, the relative powerlessness of all those involved in the dairy industry – including the milkman.

As well as tracking the decline of this icon of Britishness, Andrew's book is also crammed with humorous anecdotes and funny folklore collected from generations of milkmen, many of whom were continuing a family tradition.

A Legacy of Laughter

There are at least two famous British comedians who had dairying connections and who are worthy of special mention: Tommy Handley and Benny Hill.

Although Tommy Handley (1892–1949) had a long theatrical career, he became a household name mainly due to his role in the BBC radio show *It's That Man Again*, which boosted national morale during the war years. When interviewed about his early life he replied that he came from a family of dairy farmers in the middle of Liverpool; the interviewer was uncertain whether Tommy was being serious or if this response was just another example of the comedian's typical Scouse sense of humour. Of course, Tommy was being quite sincere as he was born in 1892 in a milkhouse at 13 Threlfall Street, Toxteth. His father's family had been farmers in Garsdale, Yorkshire, before moving to Liverpool to become cowkeeping dairymen.

Whereas Tommy Handley's primary medium for his comedy was radio, Benny Hill (1924–1992) brought his brand of comedy to the nation via television. *The Benny Hill Show*, with its slapstick sketches full of double entendre, was one of the most-watched programmes in the UK. But Benny's other claim to fame was his 1971 chart-topping Christmas comedy hit *Ernie (The Fastest Milkman in the West)*. The lyrics and storyline of the song were inspired by his early experience of working as a milkman in Eastleigh, Hampshire. In December 1940, at the age of 16, Alfred Hawthorne Hill (as he was christened) joined James Hann & Sons, then trading as Dorset Dairies. At that time, 25 per cent of the dairy's staff were serving in HM Forces and another 25 per cent were on standby. For a period of eight months, assisted by his horse, Daisy, young Alfred Hill carried out a round that encompassed Eastleigh and the village of Fair Oak. He left the dairy in August 1941 to pursue his showbiz career (Phelps, 2015).

Just as popular as the song, was the accompanying video (**youtube.com/watch?v= 8e1xvyTdBZI**), which includes footage of Ernie driving a traditional two-wheeled, horse-drawn milk float. Like all such milk floats, Ernie's carries the name and address of the proprietor, in this case: E. Price, Marlow-on-Thames, Bucks - Phone 2481. However, the real-life owner was not named Ernie, but rather, Edward. Eddie Price, of Berwick Farm, lent his vehicle and his favourite horse, 'Regency Cream Boy', to Benny Hill for use in the video. Interestingly, the livery also advertises the sale of 'Super Cream Line'. This is a reference to milk that has been pasteurised but not homogenised; the cream has not been mixed in with the milk and so still forms a 'cream line' in the bottle. Following his No. 1 hit, Benny Hill was one of a number of celebrities to appear, throughout the 1970s, in Unigate's series of TV milk advertisements featuring characters called the *Humphreys*.

The storyline of Benny Hill's song plays upon some of the popular folklore surrounding the job of milkman. This was nothing new, as the milkman, 'serving' all the housewives on his round, had been the subject of bawdy jokes since the days of the music hall. But, as reported in the *Daily Express* on 1 January 1969, it seems that at least one dairy took this implied misbehaviour seriously and provided a special course for trainee milkmen to teach them about 'the dangers of the amorous housewife', and about the 'importance of keeping the relationship on a friendly basis without going too far,' (Jenkins, 1970).

The Yorkshire-based publisher, Bamforth & Co., started producing saucy, seaside postcards as early as 1910. After the Second World War, Bamforth's artists began to satirise classic comic archetypes and the milkman's blushes were not spared. Today, a search of the Internet (or a summer stroll along Blackpool's Golden Mile) provides copious examples of such randy milkman postcard images, many of which have become collector's items (Hearn, 2013).

Dairyman Eric Joy's favourite piece of lascivious milkman mythology was the story of *The Gold-Top Babies*. The story goes that in a single neighbourhood a dozen ginger-haired babies were all born in the same year to non-ginger parents. The only thing the households had in common was that they were all served by the same milkman, known to his mates as 'Ginger Tom'! (As a foil to Eric's humour, his wife, Alice, would regularly announce in public that all her kids were the milkman's!)

But seriously, setting aside these tongue-in-cheek slurs on the character of our beloved milkman, whether your ancestor was a Cowkeeper, Dairyman, Milkman or even the more politically correct, 'Rounds Person', you may take some considerable pride in the knowledge that they were part of what we can rightly claim to be the greatest doorstep, food-delivery service in the world.

A Legacy of Laughter – Bamforth & Co. produced saucy seaside postcards satirising classic comic archetypes, including the milkman. (Author)

PART TWO
Research Guide

Chapter 5

Researching Your Dairy Ancestors

As you would expect, information about your dairy ancestors can be found in most of the major classes of archival and printed sources. But there are also less well-known sources that are peculiar to this way of life. Both are included in the descriptions that follow. They are presented in alphabetical order, though some are grouped for convenience and there may be some overlap. The wealth of information contained in the census records make them worthy of more detailed investigation and these are described separately in Chapter 6.

Births, Marriages and Deaths

It was common practice for certificates of birth, marriage and death to include a detail about Occupation or Profession, as it also was for registers of baptisms and burials. As the family in question supplied this information, the term 'Cowkeeper' would have been used without ambiguity, whereas that of 'Dairyman' might require further corroborative information from other sources to identify exactly what kind of dairyman they were. In the case of births, the occupation of the father would be given and for deaths, the occupation of the deceased. For marriages it might be given for any or all of the following: the groom, the bride, the groom's father, the bride's father.

Records of birth and baptism can also provide evidence of the migratory nature of the dairying way of life. First, there is the difference in the place of birth between child and parent, typically with the parent being born in a rural area and the child being born hundreds of miles away in a city. Second, there is the difference between a child's place of birth and their place of baptism. This might reflect the common practice of city-born children being brought back to their home village for baptism. The Daggett family were originally farmers in Wharfedale. On 7 June 1882, Alice Daggett, the daughter of John William and Ann Daggett, was baptised at St Wilfrid's Parish Church, Burnsall; her abode is given as 'Garston, Liverpool' and her father's occupation as 'Cowkeeper'.

In addition to recording the occupation of the deceased, death certificates also recorded the cause of death. Because cows produce a lot of heat (through digesting their food and turning it into milk), the atmosphere in shippons was characteristically very humid, often in stark contrast to the weather outside, as James Hanson (1939) recalled:

The cowsheds were kept warm, registering about 65 degrees. Coat and vest were discarded at 5 a.m. My time for years was 4.30 a.m., and one would sweat heavily, although it might be snowing outside. No time was allowed for breakfast – just a drink of hot milk or porridge – before we went away for two to three hours delivering the milk.

Moving from a warm shippon to a cold yard or dairy resulted in many cowkeepers suffering from respiratory problems. Thus, common causes of death amongst the cowkeeping population were conditions such as bronchitis or bronchial pneumonia. In this respect, some cowkeepers were their own worst enemy: in mid-nineteenth century London it was a common misbelief amongst dairymen that milk yield could be maximised in warm shippons (Atkins, 2012[2]). As a result, their buildings were often poorly ventilated with inadequate lighting, cleansing and drainage. Apart from creating an unhealthy working environment, these conditions also created the perfect environment for the spread of airborne cattle diseases.

Another common cause of death amongst dairymen and their families was tuberculosis, sometimes recorded on the death certificate as 'Phthisis' or 'Consumption'; the latter term was coined as a result of sufferers seeming to waste away as they were slowly 'consumed' by the disease. It was also known as 'the white plague' due to the extreme anaemic pallor it induced in patients. Although tuberculosis in humans could be contracted from cattle infected with the bovine variety of the disease, passed on either by airborne means or by consuming contaminated meat/milk, for many decades this fact was disputed. In 1901, eminent scientist Robert Koch famously challenged the received wisdom of the day: that tuberculosis could spread from animals to humans. The storm of debate that followed, and the scientific uncertainty so caused, only served to forestall or dilute any positive action to tackle the problem (e.g. by making pasteurisation compulsory), leaving both dairymen and their customers at risk.

Neither were dairymen immune to the everyday stresses, strains and risks of running their own business. In 1893, 64-year-old cowkeeper David Hughes, of 55 Thirlmere Road, died after he was punched in the face during an altercation over an outstanding debt (*Liverpool Echo*, 7 June 1893). In 1897, 24-year-old cowkeeper Frank Stott was found dead, hanging by the neck, in a loft adjoining his shippon; his suicide was 'supposed to be due to business troubles' (*Liverpool Mercury*, 29 January 1897). In 1925, 37-year-old cowkeeper Samuel Allen, of Laburnum Road, was found hanging by a rope fastened to a ceiling beam in the loft of his shippon; at the inquest it was reported that he 'had worried over monies that were owing to him' (*Liverpool Echo*, 31 July 1925).

Where a death is thought to be due to anything other than natural causes, an inquest is held to provide the details needed for the death to be registered. When, in 1872, my great-great-grandmother, Mary Joy, took her own life, there was an inquest. Subsequently, her death certificate recorded her cause of death as: 'Drowned herself in a mill pond whilst in a state of temporary insanity' (Joy, 2017[2]).

Business Accounts

Although accounts are essential documents for a going concern, they are perceived as being of little value once a business ceases to trade and all statutory requirements have been met. Historically, once such documents had served their purpose they were more likely to be deposited in a bin than in the local archive. Indeed, it was the lack of such records for farming businesses that led the Museum of English Rural Life to undertake a project during the 1960s, from which it established a modest collection of farm accounts. These documents now provide much more than a statement of the financial position of the business. The detail contained therein provides fascinating insights about a whole way of life.

The historical business accounts of city dairymen, being scarcer than those of farmers, are even less likely to have found their way into archive collections. They are more likely to be discovered at the bottom of a box of family papers, left in a loft, in a cellar, or in some other obscure place. The business accounts of Messrs T. Sowerby & Sons were rescued from a house clearance, by family historian, Geoff Cannon.

The Sowerby family were long established cowkeepers in and around Liverpool. By the 1950s, the family business was located in the district of Knotty Ash. The profit and loss account for year ended 31 March 1952 contains the following information about how the business was being run:

MESSRS. T. SOWERBY & SONS.
256, East Prescot Road, Knotty Ash, Liverpool.
PROFIT AND LOSS ACCOUNT FOR THE YEAR ENDED 31ST MARCH, 1952.

			1951		
Stocks:- Provender	165. 0. 0.		10,771	Sales	
Dairy Produce	20. 0. 0.				
Bottles	50. 0. 0.		20	Home Consumption	
Discs	18.15. 0.				
Manure	2. 0. 0.	235. 15. 0.	349	Manure Sales	
Stock of Cows (31)		1,085. 0. 0.	1,245	Cows Sold (37)	
Cows Purchased (38)		2,153. 10. 0.	1,085	Stock of Cows (32)	
Dairy Produce		5,797. 16. 1.		General Stocks - Provender	165, 120. 0. 0.
M.M.B. Levy		111. 9. 4.		Dairy Produce	20, 24. 13. 9.
Provender		3,439. 13. 5½		Bottles	30, 25. 0. 0.
Wages, Keep and National Insurance		738. 1. 8.	236	Discs	19, 5. 0. 0.
Rent 2/3rds Dairy Assessment		26. 13. 4.		Manure	2, 3. 0. 0.
Rates - General 1/3rds thereof	6.13. 0.		748	Milk Marketing Board Subsidy	
Water	16. 9. 8.	23. 2. 8.			
Gas 2/3rds thereof		7. 7. 1.			
Electricity - Power	43.19. 8.				
Lighting 1/3rd thereof	1.16. 4.	45. 16. 0.			
Coal ½ thereof		24. 1. 1.			
Insurances		10. 3. 2.			
Telephone		7. 11. 10.			
Motor Expenses ⅞ thereof		259. 18. 1.			
Stable Expenses		78. 5. 1.			
Carriage		11. 5. 0.			
Repairs and Renewals		212. 18. 10.			
Stationery, Postages and Discs		74. 17. 2.			
Sundry Expenses		102. 7. 1.			
Hire Purchase Interest		30. 0. 8.			

Business Accounts – Messrs T. Sowerby & Sons. Profit and loss account, 1952. (Courtesy of Geoff Cannon)

- Value of stock held, in the form of: Provender [cattle feed], Dairy Produce [milk/cheese/butter], Bottles [bespoke milk bottles], Discs [bespoke, waxed cardboard bottle tops] and Manure [cow muck, to be sold as fertiliser].
- Number of cows bought and sold [an illustration of the 'flying herd' approach].
- Annual expenditure on cows [38 in number], cattle feed [provender] and business overheads [building running costs are proportioned between business and domestic use].
- Payment of a producer-retailer levy to the Milk Marketing Board and receipt of a subsidy from the same source.
- Annual income from sales of dairy produce and of manure.
- Depreciation on equipment used in the business, including: Refrigerator, Milking Machine, Bottle Washer, Dairy Utensils, Stable/Farm Utensils and Delivery Vehicles [Cycle, Motor Van and Motor Car].
- Previous sale of Horse, Float and Harness [as the business modernises and moves from horse-drawn to motorised delivery].

The family business was a partnership of two brothers and the annual profit of £767 was split equally between them.

Census Records *(See Chapter 6)*

County Agricultural Societies

The structure and organisation of agriculture in the UK began to gather pace in the mid-eighteenth century: The Board of Agriculture was formed in 1793; the English Agricultural Society held its first show in 1839; and 1876 marked the founding of

The County Show – City cowkeepers were prominent at local agricultural shows, providing a day out for the whole family. J. Hogg & Sons, Cowkeeper. (Courtesy of Janet Dalton)

The British Dairy Farmers' Association. This movement also saw the formation of agricultural societies based on county boundaries, established to represent the interests of their members within that county – farmers of all description, including city dairymen.

These county agricultural societies were properly constituted and administered. Their meetings were all minuted and their accounts audited. The highlight of their year was the organisation of their annual county agricultural show; a substantial public event, lasting for up to three days.

The activity and business of the county agricultural society was captured in the form of an annual report or 'Journal'. These documents not only included the annual accounts of the society but also details of their membership. It was common for these journals to include in their back pages a full list of the society's members' names and addresses. In addition to this, the journal gave a detailed description of the annual show, including a list of all the prizewinners and photographs of owners showing off their prizewinning beasts.

Many county agricultural societies still exist today and have their own archives. Alternatively, a collection of their journals may be found at the county branch of the National Archives.

Diaries, Memoirs and Reminiscences

Diaries are records written at the time, rather than retrospectively. Not everyone kept a diary and the further back in time you go the scarcer they become, due to the low level of literacy of the population. These records were usually standardised, printed and bound booklets bought from stationers. Some had dated pages for daily entries whilst others merely consisted of faintly lined blank pages – the latter were also referred to as Memorandum Books. The amount of detail recorded in these diaries varied according to the need, inclination or whim of the owner.

In 1857, 32-year-old Daniel Joy of Hebden, Yorkshire, acquired a pocket-size Improved Metallic Memorandum Book, manufactured by W. Sinclair of Otley, Yorkshire (Joy, 2017[1]). The 'improved metallic' refers to the binding of the book being constructed of two very thin sheets of metal, covered in a tightly woven fabric. If this design was to protect and extend the longevity of the book, then in Daniel Joy's case it seems to have worked as the book in question was handed down through the next five generations of Joys.

Sadly, although the metallic cover has survived intact, only a few tattered pages remain of the content. But upon these Daniel had listed the names and dates of birth of his siblings and the dates of birth and godparents of his own children – invaluable information in piecing together the Joy family history. On another page, Daniel had kept an account of the number of 'loads of manure' he had sold to a Mr Atherton during 1878–79. This is of interest because by then Daniel had left Hebden and had relocated to Garston (which, in those days, was a township in its own right, located to the south of Liverpool), where he was keeping cows, making this a written record of the practice of cowkeepers selling cow muck to farmers on the edge of the city.

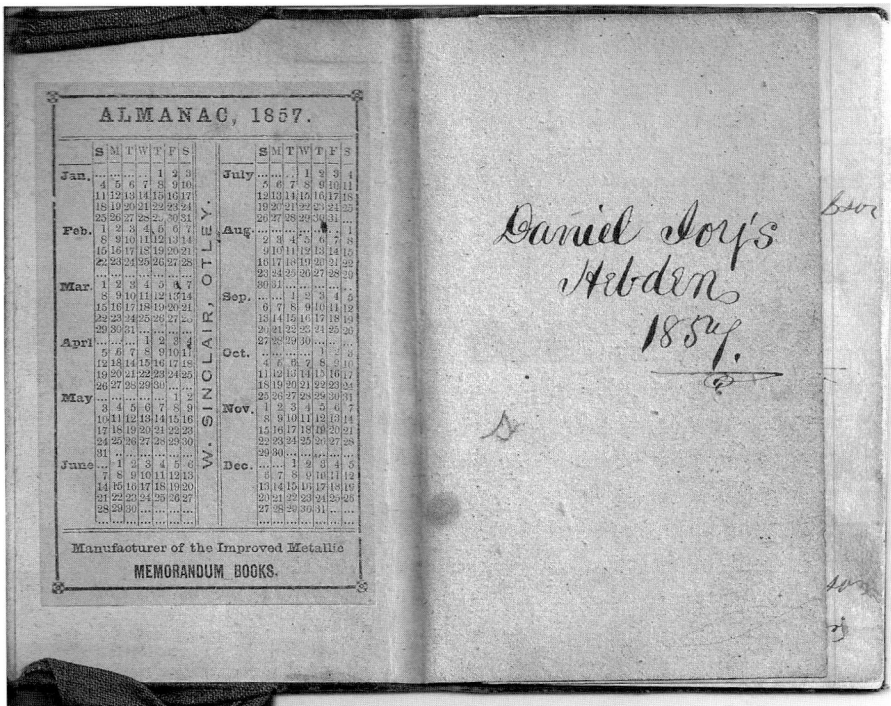

Daniel Joy's Diary – Personal diaries can be a rich source of information for the family historian. (Author)

Diaries were personal accounts of both the extraordinary and the mundane in individual lives, often containing personal thoughts and opinions. Although at the time they were written the author might have considered the content to be private in nature, as with most historical records containing personal information, the privacy factor diminishes with the passage of time, as there is no one left to be affected by the contents. In recognition of the huge family and social history value of diaries, the Great Diary Project was launched in 2007. The project receives, rescues, archives and makes publicly available a growing collection of thousands of previously unpublished diaries. The collection is available to the general public at London's Bishopsgate Institute, but a list and description of each diary can be viewed online (**thegreatdiaryproject.co.uk**).

Unlike diaries, both memoirs and reminiscences have been written retrospectively. The boundary between the two is becoming somewhat blurred as more and more information is posted for general consumption online. For convenience, let's define a memoir as being an autobiographical book intended for general publication whereas a reminiscence is a written recollection of a previous experience, usually short and not intended for publication. An example of the former would be my own memoir, *My Family and Other Scousers: A Liverpool Boy's Summer of Adventure in '69*. Examples of the latter would have been difficult to come by in the past, as they were neither intended nor suitable for publication. However, the coming of the Internet has meant these snippets of information, previously intended for family consumption only, are now being presented to a wider audience.

In addition to the blogs and websites of the many local and family history groups (see Chapter 8) there are also the chat or forum sites where people can post and share their recollections of either working in a city dairy or being served by one. At the time of writing there were ongoing discussions about cowkeeping dairymen on sites run by Rootschat, Family Tree Forum, British Genealogy, Genes Reunited and Ancestry:

> That cowhouse in Bryanston Road I remember well. As kids we used to look up through a vent grill in the wall and you could see a cow's nose looking back at you. A school-friend of mine who sat next but one to me used to work there before he came to school, and didn't we know it, phooaaarr.
>
> Stan Cotter, 12 May 2014

> In the 1950s and 1960s, Carol's Dairy on Walton Breck Road provided our milk. They delivered in a horse and cart. As school kids we would ride on the dray and help with deliveries. The owner was killed when he fell off the cart and was kicked to death by the horse. Yet they still delivered for years after that, the same horse I think.
>
> Alan Brooks, 8 August 2014

> I remember my poppy telling me he used to deliver milk on his horse and cart in the Liverpool 8 area, in the early 1900s, using a milk churn and people would come out with their milk jugs to be filled. We also had the dairy shop that sold all kinds of fresh food: eggs, bacon, cheese, etc. In the 50s and 60s we modernised and had an electric handcart and two milk floats, a Bedford open flat back and a small Morris Minor flat back.
>
> Stephen Caldwell, 11 August 2014

> I have such clear, vivid memories of it. Playing in the warm brewer's grain brought by Wilson's, going out on the horse-drawn dray doing deliveries, Uncle Henry taking the horse off to the local schools to mow the grass with a gang mower and bringing it back for the cows.
>
> Victoria Lyon, 24 July 2016

District Cowkeepers' and Dairymen's Associations

In addition to being part of a county-level organisation dealing with agriculture in its broadest sense, many city dairymen were also involved with district associations, dealing specifically with the city dairy profession. They were based

The Professionals – Many city dairymen were members of local associations. Dairyman William Ingham and fellow professionals. (Courtesy of Philip Ingham)

around the main towns and cities, but their official titles varied slightly in form, e.g. Edinburgh & Leith Cowkeepers' Association, Grantham & District Dairymen and Cowkeepers' Association, Bradford & District Dairy Farmers' and Cowkeepers' Association. A list of what were some of the more active associations is included at Appendix B.

Perhaps it is because these local associations did not produce their records in bound journal form, that such records tend to be scarcer and more difficult to locate than those of the county agricultural societies (though the county archive is always worth a try). The records of the Hull Cowkeepers' and Farmers' Association have been preserved as they were kept by a local firm of solicitors, who also acted as secretary to the association. The records, which cover the years 1881–1972, are now available at Hull History Centre. A description of all papers included in the collection can be viewed online (**catalogue.hullhistorycentre.org.uk/files/l-dscf.pdf**).

Despite the scarcity of formal records, these local associations were very busy, and their annual activities, such as outings, Christmas parties, annual general meetings and cattle shows, and their lobbying of local and central government, all provided good fodder for local newspapers, where they were reported on regularly, often in great detail.

Electoral Registers

Generally, electoral registers are a list of names and addresses, without reference to occupation/profession. However, many do include a one- or two-word description of the type of property being occupied. The ubiquitous description 'house' is sometimes supplemented with 'and shop', or 'and stable', both of which allude to a type of occupation. However, when the additional description is given as 'and shippon', that is a more specific indication that the resident was keeping livestock – typically, cows – on the premises. As an example of thoroughness, the 1904–05 Electoral Register of Liverpool, describes the Joy brothers' property at 21 Calton Avenue as: 'house, shop, yard and shippon'.

Family Lore, Myths and Legends

A word of caution here, about information that is not first-hand, for the accuracy of what has been passed down the generations by word of mouth cannot always be trusted. If unrecorded, such information is subject to the foibles of memory and interpretation of more than one person in succession, making it susceptible to distortion. The lesson I learnt when researching the history of the Joy family was to seek corroboration from other, documented, sources – of course, with the power of the Internet at my disposal, that is now so much easier for me to do than it ever was for anyone of my father's generation or older. To spare any third-party blushes, I'll use my own family research to illustrate this point.

In 1978, when my great-aunt Kathleen responded to Patsy Mellor's request for information in her *Dalesman* magazine article, 'Cowkeepers From the Pennine Dales', she submitted a version of the family's history that had been passed down to her by word of mouth. In her defence, her letter is quite explicit in declaring that some of the information is 'hearsay from my father'. With regard to the move from Yorkshire to Liverpool, the anecdotal family history sent to Patsy reads as follows:

> **1863** – Two brothers, Richard and Orlando Joy, settled in Garston, then returned to Hebden.
>
> **1873** – Brother Daniel Joy came to Garston and farmed in Railway Street, and George Joy came to Ash Grove, Wavertree.

First up, Richard and Orlando were not brothers, they were cousins and I have been unable to find any evidence that Richard ever left Hebden, where he was a successful farmer. Orlando, on the other hand, is listed in the 1861 census along with his brother, George, and his sister, Hannah, keeping cows in Lovat Street, Liverpool. As he was something of an entrepreneur (archived newspapers), it is quite possible that Orlando established a dairy in Garston in 1863; however, to date, I have no documented evidence to corroborate this claim. Following his marriage, in 1876, Orlando did return to Yorkshire, but not to Hebden. Instead, he became an innkeeper in Ilkley (West Yorkshire Alehouse Licenses 1771–1962).

It seems likely that Daniel Joy's move to Garston from Yorkshire did indeed take place in 1873, following the tragic death of his wife the year before; subsequent records (censuses and trade directories) confirm that he spent the rest of his days at the dairy in Railway Street and he is buried in the church graveyard across the road from where he lived (gravestone inscription). However, his brother, George, had already moved from Lovat Street to Wavertree by 1866 (Marriage Certificate) and specifically to Ash Grove in Wavertree by 1868 (Electoral Register).

The same verbal account of the family history was told to me by my father. It had originated from my great-great-grandfather, Daniel Joy, and by the time it reached me, it had been passed down by word of mouth through five generations. This brief example shows how details of people, places, dates and relationships can become distorted through the 'Chinese Whispers' effect of word-of-mouth passage through successive generations. So, *caveat emptor*.

Funeral Cards and Eulogies

Funeral cards (or memorial cards) were sent out to family, friends and the local community to provide notice of a forthcoming funeral. Recipients were expected to attend the funeral or risk offending the family; some cards were used as tickets to gain admission to a funeral. Funeral cards were often 'collected' and mounted in albums as a permanent reminder of, or tribute to, the deceased.

As well as providing information about the date and place of the funeral, the cards frequently contained information about the date and place of death. The relevance of this information to the dairying way of life is that it discloses the common practice of the bodies of city dairymen and their families being returned to their rural place of origin for burial in the traditional family grave. Whether it was the dairymen of London being returned to the churchyards of Cardiganshire, or

> IN AFFECTIONATE REMEMBRANCE OF
>
> **ANN,**
>
> The beloved wife of William Metcalfe,
>
> Of 2, Vicar Road, Liverpool,
>
> Who died November 1st, 1929,
>
> **Aged 50 Years.**
>
> And was interred at the Cemetery, Sedbergh,
>
> November 5th.

Funeral Card for Ann Metcalfe – It was common practice for the bodies of city dairymen and their families to be returned 'home' for burial. (Courtesy of Kath Robinson) those of Liverpool being returned to the dales, for many there was a strong desire for their rural home to be their final resting place – a desire respected by their surviving family.

Ann Nelson (1879–1929) was born into a farming family near Sedbergh, Yorkshire. She was one of six siblings who relocated to Liverpool to become dairymen and in April 1904 she married cowkeeper William Metcalfe. Ann and William had five children and the family ran a dairy at 2 Vicar Road. When Ann died in 1929, at the age of 50, she had spent half her life living and working in the city and it was the home of her children. However, as her funeral card bears testament, though she died in Liverpool on 1 November, she was interred four days later at the cemetery, Sedbergh, in accordance with her wishes.

Eulogies were tributes to the deceased, usually delivered as a speech at the funeral by a family member or friend. The original notes, or a transcript of these appearing in the local parish/church magazine, were often kept by the family – along with the funeral card and order of service – as a lasting memoriam to the deceased. A handwritten eulogy to my great-grandfather, Anthony Joy, read at his funeral on 25 February 1927, makes reference to Anthony's life as a Liverpool dairyman who had his origins in Yorkshire (Joy, 2017[2]):

> When a young man, he joined his father in business and some here may remember the old dairy in Railway Street and the farm and the fields where now are the railway sidings. Anthony Joy was a member of the Liverpool & District Dairy Farmers and Cowkeepers Association for some 40 years and an official for many of those years. Although this was his home, he was a true son of Yorkshire and inherited many of the characteristics of that great county, where in Craven district he was almost as well known as in Garston.

Licence Registers

Legislation was introduced that granted local health authorities the power to licence properties for the keeping of cows or for the sale of milk (see Appendix A). As these locally designed licensing schemes were rolled out, they began to generate what would become formidable databases about the dairying way of life. Each licence issued would be recorded in a register, indicating the name of the licensee, the address of the licensed premises and, where relevant, the number of cows they were licensed to keep on those premises.

For example, the London Metropolitan Archives hold the relevant registers of the London County Council. These include the following:

- Register of Licensed Cowhouses
- Register of Cowkeepers, Dairymen and Purveyors of Milk
- Register of Premises approved as Dairies
- Street Index of Dairies, Cowsheds etc.

When genealogist Linda Newey was researching her husband's family history, she found his ancestor, John Newey, listed in a Register of Cowkeepers & Dairymen, kept at Worcester City Archives (**fouroaksgenealogy.co.uk/case-studies-fruitful**). The Dairyman Register 1879 to 1886 consisted of two volumes, one of which was an alphabetical index of cowkeepers and dairymen. John Newey was included as entry number 683, registered on 29 April 1879 at Severn Side, Claines, Worcester, as a 'Cowkeeper and Purveyor of Milk', trading from a cowshed 'on the premises' from which milk was sold 'wholesale'.

In addition to registers, there were also annual reports produced by a city's Medical Officer of Health, which were presented to the local Health Committee. These included statistics related to the number of licences issued and also, when appropriate, a commentary on any issues that had arisen during the year, such as occurrences of disease, or successful prosecutions for adulteration. As these reports were presented to the local Health Committee, today they form part of the archived records of the relevant local authority.

Maps and Satellite Images

In researching your dairy ancestors there are two loci in which you might be interested: that of the home farm and that of the city dairy. Though neither of these may still exist today as physical buildings, if you are armed with basic address information it is still possible to identify their respective locations using old maps of the area in question. Since 1981, Alan Godfrey has been reprinting old Ordnance Survey maps and his catalogue now holds more than 3,000 titles covering the majority of towns and cities in the UK (**alangodfreymaps.co.uk**). Most of these maps are based on the Ordnance Survey 25-inch (or 1:2500) and show virtually every building on every street, including the yard, if one was present. Each map includes information on the history of the area and extracts from the relevant street directory (in which your ancestor might be listed). They come ready-folded and pocket-sized, so they are easy to carry as you explore.

Though Godfrey's maps might not cover the more rural areas of the country, there are now online tools that do, such as the *Side-by-Side Geographical Reference Map Viewer* provided by the National Library of Scotland on its free and easy-to-use website (**maps.nls.uk/geo/explore/side-by-side**). This site enables you to select from a collection of old maps and to view these alongside modern satellite images of the same location. Using your cursor and the zoom facility, you can pinpoint the exact location of your ancestral home. Of particular use to the family historian are the 6-inch (1888–1913) and 25-inch (1892–1914) maps, as these, again, show individual buildings and farmsteads.

TheGenealogist has on its website a map facility specifically geared to the needs of the family historian. Its *Map Explorer* feature uses layers of georeferenced maps to help you trace your ancestor's property over time. There are three layers, which can be viewed on top of one another – like sheets of paper – and you can change the transparency of one layer to view the layer below. The *Base Layer* can be used to select a modern Ordnance Survey (OS) map, Open Street Map or a Bing Satellite Image. The *Historic Layer* can be used to select a range of OS maps from the 1890s to the 1960s. Finally, the *Record Set Layer* provides access to record sets such as the Lloyd George Domesday survey or to Tithe Maps. This layer has the ability to show *Pins*, map markers that link directly to the records so you can see who was living in a particular property. The intention is to add further maps and data sets as the feature is developed. At the time of writing, *Map Explorer* is available to all Diamond subscribers to TheGenealogist (**thegenealogist.co.uk/maps**).

Military Records

Your ancestor's military records can provide information about occupation and situation prior to enlistment and may also contain clues about how they may have utilised their occupational skills whilst in military service.

My grandfather, Anthony Percival Joy, was a third generation cowkeeper and farmer. He spent his entire life living and working at the family's Wellington Dairy in Garston, south Liverpool, producing and retailing milk. As a 'producer' of milk, he grew up breeding livestock, tending and milking cows, making cheese and butter, and treating and bottling milk. As a 'retailer' of milk, using a horse and cart for delivery, he had a second skill set related to stable work and horsemanship. The only time he ever left the dairy was when he went away to fight for his country. Although it seems that his First World War military records were amongst the so-called 'burnt records' destroyed during the Second World War, his surviving medal records show that after enlisting with the King's Liverpool Regiment, he was subsequently transferred when the Labour Corps came into being. The significance of this transfer is that the Labour Corps was formed primarily to facilitate the transportation of supplies to the front. Those supplies included foodstuffs and their principal mode of transport would have been by packhorse. As such, Granddad's occupational skill set would have been put to good use in the Labour Corps.

By the time of the Second World War, it was the turn of my father, Anthony Eric Joy, to be called up. Unlike those of the First World War, the military records pertaining to the Second World War are much more complete. It is possible for descendants of military personnel to obtain copies of these records from the Ministry of Defence's Historical Disclosure Division, at the Army Personnel Centre in Glasgow, though you have to provide proof of your relationship by sending a copy of your ancestor's death certificate. Further information and guidance is available on the GOV.UK website (**gov.uk/guidance/request-records-of-deceased-service-personnel**).

My father had an occupational skill set similar to that of my grandfather. Upon enlistment his then occupation is variously recorded as either 'Farmer' or, more unusually, as 'Farm Horseman'. Initially, he joined the Manchester Regiment, but like his father he was subsequently transferred – this time to the Royal Army Veterinary Corps. He was assigned to the No.1 Reserve Veterinary Hospital, Depot and Training Establishment situated on the racecourse at Doncaster. This assignment enabled Dad to put to much better use his skills, experience and knowledge gained as a dairyman, especially those pertaining to horsemanship. (In later life he would regale us with his army stories: training or 'breaking-in' remounts for army work; maintaining stable-room for some 600 animals; spending time assigned to local farms; and about the friendships he forged with soldiers of a similar background to him – farmers, cowkeepers, dairymen, horsemen etc.) Interestingly, his army record includes periods of 'Agricultural Leave'. Traditionally, this was special, unpaid leave granted to farm workers during harvest time, though the dates on which it was granted to Dad suggest it was also used at other times of the year – perhaps in recognition of the contribution to the war effort being made by family dairies, maximising domestic food production. The final record of the link between occupation and military service is given on Dad's Release Papers. Apart from his Trade on Enlistment being given as 'Farmer', his testimonial reads as follows: 'A very hardworking and conscientious man. Has a good knowledge of horses and stable work.' In all, he spent six years and 115 days as a soldier, before returning home to recommence working at Wellington Dairy. (He would also wish me to mention that his Military Conduct was described as 'Exemplary'!)

Newspapers

The local newspapers of the day are a rich source of information about your city dairy ancestors:

Public Events: the county agricultural shows and the district dairy/cattle shows were events of great pageantry and celebration with fierce competition for the top prizes; this made excellent fodder for the local newspapers. As well as eloquent descriptions of the extravagant goings-on, attended by VIPs, the reports also

Hold the Front Page! – City cattle shows provided plenty of prizes, pomp and pageantry for the local press. Tom Hogg, Dairyman. (Courtesy of Angela Hallows)

included a list of prizewinners, often with the street address of their family-owned dairy business. Your dairy ancestor might also get a specific mention if they were either a show judge or a member of the show committee.

Obituaries: when some of the more prominent dairymen passed away, the newspapers printed quite extensive obituaries with descriptions of their businesses and listing those in attendance at the funeral. When cowkeeper Matthew Whitfield died in 1888, his obituary included a list of all the members of the Liverpool & District Cowkeepers' Association who attended his funeral.

Situations vacant: dairymen placed employment notices in the local papers. 'Wanted: Experienced Milk Maid' or 'Experienced Cowman wanted' and 'Must be a good milker' were common descriptions. The notices included the name and address of the business and a contact telephone number.

Adverts: newspapers were used extensively for advertising the family's dairy business, but also used were parish magazines, as they targeted a more local customer base. Apart from giving the full address of the premises, these adverts might also be illustrated, incorporating the business's logo or an appropriate image of a cow.

Court Proceedings: unfortunately, some dairymen fell foul of the law, either through deliberate transgression or through no fault of their own. As natural cow's milk consists of 85–95 per cent water, it was tempting for some to add more water to their milk, to increase the quantity and, therefore, their profit. This is what Charles Dickens (1851) was alluding to when he referred to the water pump as 'The Cow with the Iron Tail'. Of course, such adulteration of milk was illegal and offenders could find themselves facing a fine and/or having their licence withdrawn:

> No sympathy can be felt for those milk dealers who still reckon 'the cow with the iron tail' as among the most profitable of their cattle. Two such were dealt with at the Liverpool Police Court yesterday. In one the delinquent was Edward Capstick, of 38, Coleridge-street, of whom it was proved that with regard to one sample purchased at his shop nearly 20 parts of water had been added to every 100 parts of the milk, which was also deficient in cream; and the analysis of a second sample showed it had been mixed with a small quantity of water but that two-thirds of its cream had been abstracted. It seems a pity that the seller should escape with so light a penalty as 20s and costs, especially as his lie had nearly got another milk seller into trouble who purchased from him.
>
> (*Liverpool Mercury*, 3 January 1884)

A further sanction on cowkeepers found guilty of adulteration was expulsion from the local cowkeepers' association. Clearly, the Liverpool Cowkeepers' Association was of the opinion that its members were above such practices, as demonstrated by the following emphatic letter to the editor of the *Liverpool Mercury*, written by John Verity, the chairman of the association:

> WATERED MILK – TO THE EDITORS OF THE LIVERPOOL MERCURY.
> Gentlemen, – Adverting to your report under this heading of the case in which a milk dealer at Wavertree was fined by Mr Raffles for 'selling adulterated milk to the Royal Infirmary', and in which it was alleged, in defence, that the milk was watered 'for the purpose of throwing up the cream', and that there was not a single milk-dealer in Liverpool who did not 'water his milk,' I should be obliged if you would allow me to point out: 1. That in the trade, 'Cowkeepers' and 'Milk dealers' are quite separate and distinct. 2. That whether the statements in defence be true or not, so far as regards the class of people known as milk dealers, i.e. those persons who merely retail country milk, and are not producers by their own cattle as the cowkeepers are, such statements are certainly untrue in regard to Liverpool cowkeepers, who do not require to water their milk for any purpose whatever. 3. The association on behalf of which I write feels it necessary to give an emphatic contradiction to the statements of the Wavertree milk dealer, which are calculated to bring into disrepute a very useful, hard-working, and honourable body of tradesmen.
> (*Liverpool Mercury*, Thursday, 27 February 1890)

Adulteration of milk was classed as a misdemeanour rather than a felony, so cases tended to be dealt with either by magistrates' courts or by police courts. These were local proceedings and were reported – often in great detail – by local newspapers, a vast collection of which can be searched and viewed online at The British Newspaper Archive (**britishnewspaperarchive.co.uk**).

The Cow with The Iron Tail – Adding water to milk became a criminal offence. (Courtesy of the artist, Heather Joy)

Oral History and Living Memories

Reminiscences can be somewhat random and fragmented in nature, but another, more complete, form is oral history – the video and/or audio recording of people providing their living memories. At first glance, the idea of cows being kept in cities might seem to be something from a long bygone age. Of course, it is not as bygone as all that; as the era of city animal husbandry continued up until the mid-twentieth century, it is still within living memory. Not only are there those living today, in their seventh decade or more, who were part of a dairying family, but also there are many others who were either employees or customers of those families. All have their own first-hand experiences of witnessing the life and/or work of the city dairyman who delivered milk in the local neighbourhood. If you are fortunate to have access to someone with living memories, then sit them down, listen and make a record of what they have to say, as advocated by The Oral History Society (**ohs.org.uk**).

In 2002, the Joy family sat 83-year-old Anthony Eric Joy in front of a cassette recorder, pressed PLAY/REC and captured ninety minutes of Eric describing his childhood at Wellington Dairy, Garston. When Eric passed away in 2007, the recording was kept as a priceless family treasure. In 2017, the recording was transcribed and posted on the Internet:

> My earliest recollection is from about 1922 (age 3). I was sitting in the milk float with my father going under Allerton Station Bridge, with a train above. The horse, Daisy, was terrified of steam trains. All I could see of her (she was a bay horse with black points) was her rump above the front of the trap, as I was so small. My dad was holding me with one hand and driving her with the other.
> **(davejoy-author.com/anthony-eric-joy-1919-2007.html)**

Postcards

The Post Office first issued postcards, without images, in 1870. These were printed with a stamp to cover the cost of postage, which was included in the purchase price. Then, in 1894, publishers were granted permission by Royal Mail to publish picture postcards, which could be sent through the post. These early cards carried pictures of landmarks and scenes from the place of posting. Photographic studios were quick to capitalise on this developing market by turning family photographs into postcards, to be sent to loved ones at home and abroad.

For a semi-literate working class, living away from home, the postcard was a convenient alternative to having to write many pages and deal with the palaver of using writing paper and envelopes. Sentiments could be expressed in the few short sentences that would fit on to the limited space afforded by a postcard, fulfilling the obligation or necessity of keeping in touch with home. Though the narrative of postcards may have been limited, they provide the family historian with evidence of what the writer

Researching Your Dairy Ancestors

A Postcard from Home –
Photographic studios turned family photographs into picture postcards.
(Courtesy of William Franks)

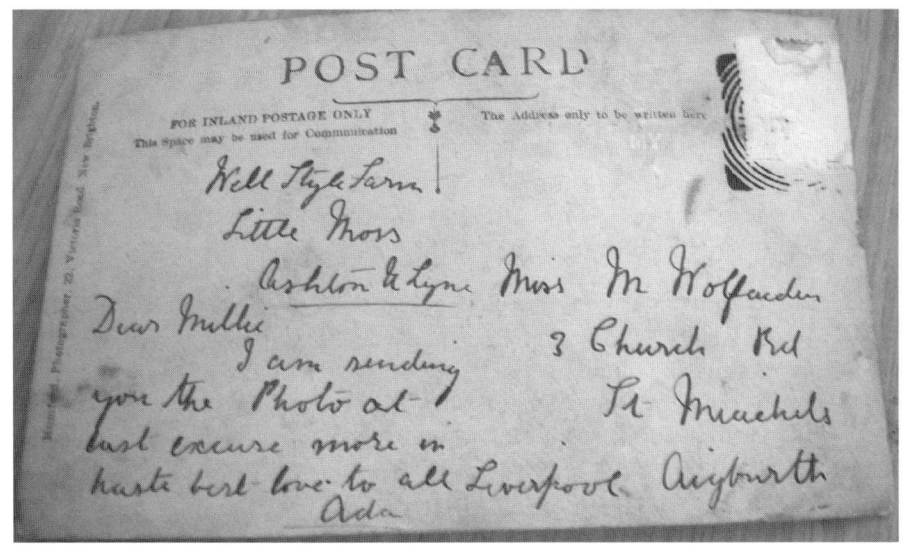

was doing (content) and where (picture) and when (date stamp) they were doing it.

Mary Irving, of Sedgwick, Cumbria, was researching her family history when she came across a collection of picture postcards from the early 1900s. They had been sent by her mother, Isabel Stewardson (known as Bell), who was born in 1893 in Witherslack, Cumbria, and who had spent her teenage years working away from home as a servant girl. From these postcards, Mary was able to trace her mother's journey, working on a series of farms in south Cumbria. Then, between 1909 and 1911, Bell's address for correspondence was given as c/o Mrs Taylor, 3 Church Road, St Michaels, Aigburth, Liverpool. A check of the census records and trade directories indicated that this was a milkhouse being run by Richard Taylor, Cowkeeper and Dairyman, originally from Cartmel Fell, Cumbria. Mary discovered that her mother had been employed as a milkmaid and was able to correlate this information with an old photograph of Bell taken outside the address: 'Bell is the taller of the two girls. Bell's move at this time reflected a trend when many people moved from the north to run or work in dairies, which sold fresh milk to townspeople.'

Bell Stewardson (right), a City Milkmaid from Witherslack – City dairies recruited workers from rural areas. (Courtesy of Vera Haydock)

Trade Directories

Trade directories were first published at the end of the eighteenth century. There were many different publishers but perhaps the best known are Pigot, Gore and also Kelly. The latter initially produced official Post Office directories but continued to dominate the market even when the Post Office appellation was dropped. The usual format was for each directory to cover a county area; as well as trade listings, they also provided a description of the geography and economy of the county in question. Trades were listed in a number of different ways within in a single directory volume – alphabetically, according to Street, Surname or Profession. From the 1930s onwards, trade directories were gradually replaced by telephone directories. Kelly's finally ceased publication in the 1960s.

Though most branches of the National Archives will hold a sizeable collection of trade directories for their respective counties, a number are now being made available online. The Historical Directories project was carried out by Leicestershire University with the aid of a Big Lottery grant. It involved the digitisation of selected trade directories in England and Wales covering the period from the 1760s through to the 1910s on a county-by-county basis. The project is now complete, but the collection of selected directories, from a variety of publishers, is available online (**specialcollections.le.ac.uk/digital/collection/p16445coll4**) and provides free access to scanned images and full-text. It can also be accessed via Ancestry by subscription.

The publishers of directories wrestled with the same problem of defining the trade of the city dairyman, as did the census enumerators. In alphabetical trade directories you might find your dairy ancestor listed under 'C', 'D', 'F' or even 'M'.

'C' is for 'Cowkeepers'. It's a pretty safe bet that all listed here actually kept cows and sold milk.

'D' is for 'Dairymen'. As stated previously, this is a bit more ambiguous as it could refer to anyone who sold milk. To make matters worse, some tradesmen were listed under both categories – under 'Cowkeepers' and also under 'Dairymen' – in the same directory. Apparently, trying to separate out these two professions presented too great a dilemma for certain directory publishers, so they lumped them all together under the title of 'Cowkeepers & Dairymen'.

'F' is for 'Farmers'. Cowkeepers located in the outer city had access to fields, used for both grazing and for growing fodder crops. Though, like their inner-city compatriots, they had shippons located on street corners or tucked away behind other buildings, they preferred to call themselves 'farmers'. Even so, some would still be double-listed under one of the other two categories mentioned above.

'M' is for 'Milk Dealers'. This more generic term could be applied to anyone who participated in the milk supply chain. Though initially it was used to describe non-cowkeeping dairymen, latterly it leaned toward those involved in the bulk supply or wholesale sectors of the industry. As well as the corporate dairies, this group also includes the larger family businesses, many of which started out as Cowkeepers or Dairymen. These listings often provide more than one address, usually a head office and a number of depots.

As the distinction between these different trades was so blurred, when using trade directories to trace your ancestors it is worth checking their entries in all of the alphabetical listings – street, surname and trade – as each may contain different information. For example, a residential address might differ from a trade address for the same family; or a name classed as 'Dairyman' in the trade list might be tagged with the profession of 'Cowkeeper' in the residential list.

One other characteristic of the dairy businesses listed in trade directories was the addition to the name of the business of the term '& Son' or '& Sons'. This underlined the family nature of this way of life, with the milkhouse being handed down through the generations. Having spoken with many daughters of dairymen, they are quite adamant that they did as much work as their brothers, but the convention of the day prevented their contribution being recognised in the naming of the business. However, following the death of a spouse, widows who continued to run the business under their own name were still described as 'Dairyman' or 'Cowkeeper' and were listed in directories accordingly.

Transport Tickets

Prior to the 1968 Transport Act, tickets for buses and trams were produced by local councils or corporations in their role as the area's passenger transport authority. To maximise income, the reverse of the ticket was sold to local businesses as advertising space. Although the routes of buses and trams would have taken them beyond the catchment areas of local dairies, many such family businesses took advantage of this relatively cheap form of advertising. The amount of space available on the reverse of a ticket was limited, but it was enough to carry essential information such as the name and address of the business. The *Milk Bottle News* website features a collection of tram tickets from across the country and ranging in dates from the 1920s to the 1960s, on the reverse of which are a variety of adverts for both family and corporate dairies (**milkbottlenews.org.uk/features/tram-tickets/index.html**).

Wills and Probate

A will is a document in which a person records their wishes about what happens to their estate when they die and often who they wish to be responsible for carrying out those wishes. The content of wills varies greatly, from a simple listing and apportionment of the testator's estate, to personal messages to their successors. Obviously, as far as the family historian is concerned, the more information the better.

Probate is a legal document issued by a Probate Registry that confirms the validity of a will and is issued to an executor. Probate records are usually much more to the point than the actual wills but may still contain pertinent genealogical information such as the deceased's full name, address, occupation, date and place of death. The record will also list the value of the deceased's estate and the names and occupations of the main executors.

Probate records may provide descriptions of occupation, for the deceased and for their executors. If the deceased was retired, this might be indicated as a prefix, e.g. Retired Dairyman or Retired Cowkeeper. If the executors are also the children of the deceased, their occupation will indicate whether or not they have continued in the family tradition of dairying.

Copies of wills and probate records can now be obtained online. GOV.UK provides a *Find A Will* search facility for any documents produced since 1858. Copies can be downloaded for a small fee (**probatesearch.service.gov.uk/#wills**).

Chapter 6

Census Records

The first modern UK census took place on Sunday, 6 June 1841 and it has taken place every ten years since then (except in 1941). In accordance with the legislation under which each census was carried out, these records cannot be released to the public until 100 years have passed. Those census records published to date took place as follows:

- Sunday, 30 March 1851
- Sunday, 7 April 1861
- Sunday, 2 April 1871
- Sunday, 3 April 1881
- Sunday, 5 April 1891
- Sunday, 31 March 1901
- Sunday, 2 April 1911
- Sunday, 19 June 1921

The family historian should bear in mind that spring was a busy time on the home farm, with lots of calving and muck spreading to be done. This might account for some members of the dairyman's family being absent from the city at the time of the census. If they had returned to the home farm to lend a hand during this busy period, they would appear on the census for the relevant rural parish.

Census Information

Each householder was required to complete a census schedule providing the address of the property and the name, age, sex, occupation and place of birth of every person residing there. From 1851, this list was extended to include details of each resident's relationship to the householder, their marital status and the nature of any disabilities. The enumerators then collected these schedules and copied them into census enumerators' books (CEBs). As the original schedules prior to 1911 have long since been destroyed, the majority of census records now available to us are the CEBs.

Once completed by the enumerators, the CEBs were then sent to the Local Registrar Office, where they were examined and revised by a registrar before being approved and signed off by a superintendent registrar. From there the books were sent to the central census office where an army of clerks subjected them to a further process of revision, generating a fresh array of alterations and annotations. Finally, the CEBs were passed to a second army of clerks whose job it was to process the data, extract information and produce various tables.

In such a lengthy paper trail, each step makes it possible for information to be lost, changed or reinterpreted. Although written guidance was provided for those involved at each stage of the information-gathering process, it was not always adhered to and even when it was, there still remained room for interpretation and ambiguity. This was particularly so when it came to describing 'Occupation'.

Occupation

With regard to how the census records describe the occupation of your dairy ancestors, the critical distinction is, as always, whether or not they were keeping cows. Although a simple head-of-household declaration of 'Cowkeeper' would have started off the information trail on the right foot, such a description was not always forthcoming. It is evident from trade listings, from adverts and from shop signage captured on old photographs, that those keeping cows variously described themselves as 'Dairyman' or 'Dairyman & Cowkeeper' or even 'Dairyman & Farmer'. If these descriptions were reproduced in the census schedules, they would not have made the enumerator's task any easier.

When transferring descriptions of occupations from the census schedules into the CEBs, an enumerator had two other points of reference: their own local knowledge of who did what and the written instructions provided to enumerators by the census office. The latter would have encouraged the enumerators to use descriptions that would facilitate the classification of occupation later in the information-gathering process.

It was necessary to classify or categorise occupations in order to glean information about the economic structure of society. A number of different methodologies were adopted and adapted throughout the nineteenth century. Evidence of this approach is apparent in the census records where the enumerator/analyst has overwritten the original entry with the appropriate class/category description according to the methodology of the day. Depending on the classification being used, you may find the label 'MILK' or 'DAIRY' or 'DAIRYMAN' has been added to (or written over) the original occupation description of the city dairyman and his contingent of staff, post-census and in a different hand from the original entry. Alternatively, an existing key word in the job title – such as the word 'Milk' in 'Milk Dealer' or 'Dairy' in 'Dairyman' – may have been underlined in dark ink. In later censuses, classification used code numbers instead of words.

Consequently, when tracing your dairy ancestors through sequential census records, it can be difficult to ascertain whether a change in the description of occupation reflects a real change in how that person was making a living, or merely a change in the system of classification. William Cowper Calvert, a Liverpool dairyman of Yorkshire stock, was successively recorded as being 'Milk Dealer' (1891), 'Cowkeeper' (1901) and then 'Dairyman' (1911).

Even when presented with an unambiguous description of 'Cowkeeper', the poor enumerator still had a decision to make. For, despite its prevalence, as late as the census of 1921, official sources were still not recognising the practice of keeping cows in the city as an occupation in its own right. Perhaps this was due to it involving a unique combination and sequence of work tasks that were necessary in order to provide a service from cow to customer. Essentially, it involved three distinct activities: 1) the keeping of cows; 2) the production of milk; and 3) the sale/delivery of milk. Unfortunately, the guidance provided to the enumerators spread these tasks over a number of different classes of occupation:

- *Cattleman* – does all work required in rearing and tending of cattle; drives them to and from sheds and pasture; feeds in winter with roots and cattle cake; cleans sheds; attends cows at calving and feeds calves.
- *Dairyman* – works in dairy; turns separator or churn or controls engine or dynamo so doing; keeps dairy and utensils clean; cleans the skin of the cows daily; moves them to place of milking or feeding; milks cows twice daily; carries milk to dairy, cools it by tipping pails into cistern of water-cooling apparatus and runs it from taps into cans for transit or for further use in the dairy.
- *Milkman* (also milk carrier, milk deliverer and milk hawker) – sells or delivers milk in cans or bottles at customers' houses from hand barrow, float, or van; keeps book record of amounts delivered and makes returns to shop; collects accounts; usually also sells cream, butter and eggs; may clean barrow, float or van, tend horse in stable, etc.

To further complicate the dilemma, *A Dictionary of Occupational Terms Based on the Classification of Occupations used in the Census of Population, 1921* (published in 1927), includes 'Cowkeeper' as an Agricultural Occupation, and lumps it in with the likes of: beastman, byreman, byrewoman, cowman, herdsman, neatherd, ox feeder, ox man, stock keeper and stockman.

Thankfully, in many cases common sense prevailed and the occupation was correctly recorded as 'Cowkeeper'. But, even in those instances where the chosen terminology to describe the occupation of the head of the household is less precise (e.g. Dairyman, Milkhouse Keeper, Milk Dealer or Retailer of Milk), the census record might contain other evidence pertaining to the cowkeeping vocation.

In addition to the occupation credited to the Head of Family, there were also a number of secondary occupations held by other family members or by live-in employees; these might indicate that cattle were being kept on the premises. 'Cowman', 'Cow Boy' and 'Shippon Worker' were three of the most obvious – why employ one of these if you didn't keep cows? In completing his return for the 1911 census, my great-grandfather, Anthony Joy, left no room for doubt as to the occupation and situation of his two eldest sons, describing them both as 'Cowkeeper's son. Working at home.'

That these occupational descriptions were usually assigned to the men is indicative of the traditional division of labour within a dairy business, with the women working indoors and the men working outdoors. The place where these two roles overlapped was the shippon, as both men and women were involved in hand-milking the cows – indeed, it was thought by many that cows would 'let down their milk more readily for women than for men' (Armstrong, 2007). If a wife's contribution to the family business was acknowledged at all in the census records, it was generally understated, typically labelled with the ubiquitous 'Domestic Duties' or the slightly better 'Assisting in Business'. An exception to this rule was the less common practice of recording the cowkeeper's wife's occupation as that of 'Cowkeeperess'. This was the term used to describe the occupation of Bessie Sunter, wife of Liverpool cowkeeper Thomas Sunter, in the 1881 census (Ref: RG 13/3438, Folio 85, Page 27).

Of course, the understatement of the role of women, not just in the family but also in society as a whole, was not something peculiar to the census records or to the dairy trade. In the UK, the 1918 Representation of People Act granted the right to vote to women over 30 with property interests, but it was not until the Equal Franchise Act of 1928 that women were granted equal voting rights to men. It is worth the family historian bearing in mind that some women refused to participate in the 1911 census as a way of demonstrating their support for the Suffragette Movement and its fight for women's rights.

The take-away from this is to be wary when using occupational terms to assist you in researching your ancestors. Remember that the occupational terms given in the CEBs are at best only a good approximation of the occupations carried out by individuals (Woollard, 1998). So, look to other clues in the census record to help in building the picture of how your ancestor earned a living – what they did and how they did it.

Occupational Status

From 1901, a further column was added to the census sheet. Each working member of the household was categorised according to their occupational status as either 'Employer', 'Worker' or 'Own Account'; the latter referred to someone who was self-employed, or who was living off their savings/investments. As dairymen were usually running their own business, they were categorised as either living on their 'Own Account' or, if they were employing staff, as an 'Employer'. An employee, such as a Milkmaid or a Cowman, would be categorised as a 'Worker'.

Used in combination with other census data, occupational status can assist in piecing together a person's situation. For example, a dairy 'Worker' with a 'Relation to Head of Household' of 'Servant' suggests someone living on site at their place of work – the dairy. Alternatively, a dairy 'Worker' with a 'Relation to Head of Household' of 'Boarder' suggests someone not living on site at the dairy, but rather someone living off-site in a boarding house or other temporary accommodation.

Similarly, occupational status might also provide a clue as to whether the premises in which the person was living was a dairy. For example, even if a Head of Household was described as 'Dairyman' or 'Cowkeeper', if their occupational status was that of 'Worker' it suggests that they were employed at a dairy elsewhere (usually nearby, often in the same street).

Property

A further clue as to whether or not cows were being kept might lie in the description of the property. There was more than one term used to describe the business premises. 'Milk House' typically referred to a property with a shop downstairs, family living accommodation above and a shed out back where the cows were kept; whereas, the term 'Milk Shop' was usually reserved for those premises that did not keep cows but just sold milk. The term 'Dairy' began as a reference to the room in which milk was stored or turned into butter or cheese, but it became much more generic and was used as a way of describing the whole of the business, whether or not cows were kept. It was regularly adopted as the business name, e.g. 'Daisy Dairy' or 'Swift's Dairy'.

As the practice of keeping cows required space – usually a shippon and yard, in addition to the house – it was common to find these businesses located at the end of the street, where they had access to the side of the property or access to the rear via an alleyway. So, house numbers tended to be the highest or the lowest in the street.

An alternative solution to the need for space was for the business to straddle two adjacent properties and for this to be reflected in the street address, e.g. property number given as '31–33'. The property in which the cows were being kept might simply be recorded on the census sheet as being 'Unoccupied' as there were no persons actually residing there. But occasionally, an enumerator with a particular eye for detail would include a description of the combined property, labelling one as 'Milk House' and the other as 'Shippon'. Indeed, the very conscientious enumerator would even include comment on the content of the shippon, stating the number of cows being kept there at the time, e.g. 'shippon with 28 cows'.

Place of Birth

The records may also contain evidence of the chain migration that was common to both cowkeepers and non-cowkeeping dairymen. Although the head of the household and his wife may well have a place of birth hundreds of miles away from the city – in the rural areas of England, Ireland, Scotland or Wales – their children were born in the city and were growing up fully participating in the family business. The same clue of *Place of Birth* applied to the live-in employees, many of whom were relatives or friends of the family, from back at the home farm, who were offered employment in the city milkhouse. A word of caution: although this translocation was typical of the dairying way of life, these waters could be muddied if a pregnant mother insisted on returning to the home farm to give birth, away from the bad air of the city!

Analysing Census Records

Census records contain both objective facts (*Name, Age, Relation to Head* or *Marital Status*) and more subjective descriptions (*Property* and *Occupation*). In isolation, a single fact or description may add little to our understanding of how the people referred to in the records actually lived their lives. But, when taken together, the whole becomes bigger than the sum of the parts and a clearer picture emerges of the lives and times of our dairy ancestors.

The following examples, transcribed from census records, have been selected to illustrate the variety of terms used to record the city dairy and its occupants. Additionally, by examining a number of records, certain characteristics of the dairying way of life become apparent. The census references quoted are those used by The National Archives.

William Mason. 1881 Census (Ref: RG 11/263. Folio 59. Page 55.)

William Mason was born in 1806 in Llanfihangel Y Creuddyn, a parish in Cardiganshire. By 1861 he had married Anne Jones and the couple were farming locally. However, by 1871 they had followed the path of the ancient Welsh cattle drovers, from Cardiganshire to London, where they were keeping cows and running a city dairy. By 1881 William was a widower but was still running a dairy.

William Mason. 1881 Census (Transcript). London, Islington. RG 11/263. Folio 59. Page 55.

ROAD, STREET and No. or NAME of HOUSE	HOUSES		NAME and Surname of each Person	RELATION to Head of Family	CON-DITION as to Marriage	AGE last Birthday of		Rank, Profession or OCCUPATION	WHERE BORN
	In-habited	Unin-habited (U)				Male	Female		
36 + 38 Queensbury Street	2		William Mason	Head	Widower	75		Dairyman + Cowkeeper	Llanfihangel Y Creuddyn, Cardiganshire
			William Mason	Son	Unm.	43		Cowman	Cardiganshire
			James Mason	Son	Unm.	27		Milk Carrier	Cardiganshire
			Mary Mason	Dau.	Unm.		24	Housekeeper	Cardiganshire
			Morgan Mason	Son	Unm.	22		Dom. Servant	Cardiganshire
			Agnes Mason	Serv.	Unm.		15	Dom. Servant	London

The following features are of note in the 1881 census:

- *Street Name/House Number* – the family and their business are occupying two adjacent properties – *36 and 38 Queensbury Street* – providing a footprint large enough to accommodate a dairy business that was keeping cows. Both properties are shown as being occupied.
- *Relation to Head of Family* – as was typical of these family businesses, William, a *Widower*, is being assisted in the running of the dairy by those of his children who are not yet married.
- *Occupation* – William's occupation is described as *Dairyman & Cowkeeper*. His two eldest sons are given the occupation of *Cowman* and *Milk Carrier*, respectively. These titles illustrate the two sides of the dairy business: producing milk and selling milk. The term *Milk Carrier* usually referred to selling milk out on the round, rather than in the dairy shop.
- *Place of Birth* – William was one of many farmers from *Cardiganshire* who became cowkeepers in London.

Census Records

Henry Peel. 1881 Census (Ref: RG 11/3619. Folio 15. Page 24.)

Henry Peel (1845–1920) came from a farming family. He was born in the parish of Easington, Forest of Bowland (now in Lancashire, but in those days it was within the boundary of the West Riding of Yorkshire). By 1871 he had moved to Liverpool to become a cowkeeper. There he met and married Elizabeth Alice Kinrade. Their first child was born in the city in 1872. When Elizabeth died, in 1875, Henry married her sister, Mary Kinrade. By the time of the 1881 census, Henry and his family were keeping cows in Moon Street and continued to do so until Henry retired – he is recorded in the Isle of Man census of 1911 as a 'Retired Dairyman'.

Henry Peel. 1881 Census (Transcript), Liverpool. Ref: R G 11/3619. Folio 15. Page 24.

ROAD, STREET and No. or NAME of HOUSE	HOUSES Inhabited	HOUSES Uninhabited (U)	NAME and Surname of each Person	RELATION to Head of Family	CONDITION as to Marriage	AGE last Birthday of Male	AGE last Birthday of Female	Rank, Profession or OCCUPATION	WHERE BORN
39–41 Moon Street		1 U	(Stables & Cow House)						
43 Moon Street	1		Henry Peel	Head	Mar.	36		Cowkeer' *Dairyman*	Yorks. West Riding
			Mary Peel	Wife	Mar.		37		Isle of Man, Lezayre
			Robert Peel	Son		9		Scholar	Lancs. Liverpool
			Francis Peel	Son		7		Scholar	Lancs. Liverpool
			Isabella Harrison	Niece			13	Scholar	Isle of Man, St Jude's
			Bridget Murphy	Serv.	Unmar.		20	Servant	Lancs. Liverpool
			Robert Lightfoot	Serv.	Unmar.			Servan. *Dairyman*	Chester

The following features are of note in the 1881 census:

- **Street Name/House Number** – *43 Moon Street* is the property in which the family are living, but next door is the property numbered *39–41 Moon Street*, described as a *Stables and Cow House*. This adjacent property was where Henry kept his cows and his horse(s) and milk float. Also, the numbering of other properties in the street indicates that Henry's house was located at the end of the street, a typical location for a cowkeeping business.
- **Relation to Head of Family** – the family unit consists of a married couple and their two sons. Also living with them is a 13-year-old *Niece* and two *Servants*, both in their twenties. The two sons and the niece would have been expected to lend a hand in the business, before and after school. The female *Servant* would have worked indoors for most of the time, whereas the male *Servant* would have been working with the cows or out on the round, delivering milk.
- **Occupation** – Henry's occupation of *Cowkeeper*, and that of the male *Servant*, have subsequently been overwritten with the classification of *Dairyman*.
- **Place of Birth** – Henry and his wife were not native to Liverpool, but both of their sons were born in the city. The hired help was also local.

James Fothergill. 1881 Census (Ref: RG 11/3707. Folio 25. Page 44.)

James Fothergill (1849–1912) was from a farming family in Westmorland. In 1880 he married Esther Newton and the couple moved to Liverpool in time to be recorded in the 1881 census, living in Moorgate Street. Their stay in the city was relatively short-lived, as by the time of the next census James was once more farming in Westmorland.

The City Dairy: A Social and Family History

James Fothergill. 1881 Census (Transcript), Liverpool. Ref: R G 11/3707. Folio 25. Page 44.

ROAD, STREET and No. or NAME of HOUSE	HOUSES		NAME and Surname of each Person	RELATION to Head of Family	CON-DITION as to Marriage	AGE last Birthday of		Rank, Profession or OCCUPATION	WHERE BORN
	Inhabited	Uninhabited (U)				Male	Female		
1-3 Moorgate Street		2U	Yard & Shippon						
5 Moorgate Street	1		James Fothergill	Head	Mar.	32		Milk Dealer	Westmorland
			Esther Fothergill	Wife	Mar.		26		Westmorland
			Thos Fothergill	Son		2mo			Liverpool
			Joseph Dakin	Serv.	Unmar.	21		Cowman	Askrigg, Yorks.
			James Newton	Bro. in Law	Mar.	28		None	Longsleddale, Yorks.

The following features are of note in the 1881 census:

- **Street Name/House Number** – the low house numbers indicate that this was a property at the end of the street. *1–3 Moorgate Street* is recorded as being a *Yard and Shippon*, with the family living next door at *5 Moorgate Street*.
- **Relation to Head of Family** – in addition to their newborn son, to assist in the running of the business the couple have living with them a male *Servant* and also Esther's 28-year-old brother.
- **Occupation** – James's occupation is given as *Milk Dealer*. This could be interpreted as being someone who merely sold milk. However, the fact that his servant is given the occupation of *Cowman*, plus the fact that the business is located next door to a *Shippon*, are strong indications that James was keeping cows and producing milk, as well as selling it.
- **Place of Birth** – James and his wife were both from *Westmorland*, but their son was born in *Liverpool*. The places of birth of their *Servant* and of their relative (*Brother-in-law*) are indicative of chain migration.

Mary Prescott. 1881 Census (Ref: RG 11/3595. Folio 14. Page 21.)

Mary Prescott (née Whalley) was born in 1827, in Bickerstaffe, located in rural west Lancashire. In 1856 she married Edward Prescott, whose family had been farming in Lancashire. The couple were married in Liverpool and became city cowkeepers. They had dairies in Collingwood Street (1861) and then in Bostock Street (1871). When Edward passed away, in 1880, Mary continued to run the business with the help of her grown-up children.

Mary Prescott. 1881 Census (Transcript), Liverpool. Ref: R G 11/3595. Folio 14. Page 21.

ROAD, STREET and No. or NAME of HOUSE	HOUSES		NAME and Surname of each Person	RELATION to Head of Family	CON-DITION as to Marriage	AGE last Birthday of		Rank, Profession or OCCUPATION	WHERE BORN
	Inhabited	Uninhabited (U)				Male	Female		
67 Bostock Street		U							
69 Bostock Street	1		Mary Prescott	Head	Widow		54	Cowkeeper keeping 15 cows	Bickerstaffe, Lancs.
			James Prescott	Son	Unmar.	20		Cowkeeper	Liverpool, Lancs.
			Mary Prescott	Daur.	Unmar.		17	General Servant	Liverpool, Lancs.
			Edward Prescott	Son		15		Cowkeeper and Assistant	Liverpool, Lancs.
			William Prescott	Son		13		Scholar	Liverpool, Lancs.

Census Records

The following features are of note in the 1881 census:

- **Street Name/House Number** – the family are living at *69 Bostock Street*, next door to *67 Bostock Street*, which is recorded as being *Uninhabited*. Although no description is given for this adjacent property, it is likely that this is where Mary was keeping her cows.
- **Relation to Head of Family** – Mary is now a *Widow* and has succeeded her husband as *Head of Family*. It was not unusual for the widows of cowkeepers to continue the business under their own name. The other occupants are her four grown-up children. It was commonplace for the children to grow up in the family milk business and either to eventually take it on, or to set up a new business of their own.
- **Occupation** – Mary is recorded as a *Cowkeeper keeping 15 cows* and this description is dittoed for her eldest son. The keeping of that number of cows would necessitate the use of the adjacent property (67 Bostock Street). Though the 17-year-old daughter is described as a *General Servant*, the 15-year-old son is described as *Cowkeeper and Assistant*. This reflects the typical division of labour at a city dairy: the women worked indoors and the men worked outdoors.
- **Place of Birth** – Mary was born in rural *Lancashire*, but once she and her husband had become city cowkeepers, all of their children were born in *Liverpool*.

John Parker. 1881 Census (RG 11/680. Folio 36. Page 4.)

John Parker (1834–1918) was born in Camberwell, the son of a dairyman. When he married Hannah Lettes Mack, in 1867, his occupation was that of Cowkeeper. However, in 1891, although still living locally, in Peckham, John found himself in that 'Goldilocks zone', on the edge of town – far away enough to have access to fields for dairy farming, but near enough to operate a dairy, selling milk to the local town dwellers.

John Parker. 1881 Census London (Peckham). RG 11/680. Folio 36. Page 4.

ROAD, STREET and No. or NAME of HOUSE	HOUSES		NAME and Surname of each Person	RELATION to Head of Family	CON-DITION as to Marriage	AGE last Birthday of		Rank, Profession or OCCUPATION	WHERE BORN
	Inhabit-ed	Unin-habited (U)				Male	Female		
Hanover Street Hanover Dairy	1		John Parker	Head	Mar.	40		Cowkeeper + farmer of 54 acres. Employing 11 men.	Camberwell, Surrey
			Hannah L Parker	Wife	Mar.		34		Bermondsey
			John Parker	Son	Unm.	13		Scholar	Peckham
			Walter Parker	Son	Unm.	12		Scholar	Bermondsey
			Emma Parker	Dau.	Unm.		7	Scholar	Peckham
			Ada Parker	Dau.	Unm.		6	Scholar	Peckham
			Alice Parker	Dau.	Unm.		4		Peckham
			George Parker	Son	Unm.	2			Peckham
			Mary Parker	Dau.	Unm.		1		Peckham
			Charles Parker	Son	Unm.	5m			Peckham
			Florence Bates	Ser.	Unm.		18	Domestic Servant	Lincolnshire
			Mary Jane Halkey	Ser.	Unm.		16	Domestic Servant	Peckham

The following features are of note in the 1881 census:

- **Street Name/House Number** – rather than being given a house number, the property is recorded under its business title of *Hanover Dairy*. This title places the emphasis on the sale of milk (dairy) rather than the production of milk (farm).
- **Occupation** – John's occupation is described fully as: *Cowkeeper and farmer of 54 acres, employing 11 men*. Clearly, this is a larger operation than merely running a city milkhouse. The business is a combination of dairy farm and town dairy. It is unusual for other family members not to have an occupation related to the family business, but in this case the workforce (11 men) is living off-site.
- **Place of Birth** – Peckham's edge-of-town situation at that time meant that John did not need to migrate to access an urban market for his liquid milk. He was born locally, as were his children.

Agnes Capstick. 1911 Census (Ref: RG 14/22310. Schedule 224.)

Edward Capstick and his wife, Agnes (née Nelson), were married in Garsdale, in 1875. They had moved to Liverpool by the time their third child was born, in 1880. They had a succession of dairies in the city and by 1911 were keeping cows at 42 Handfield Road, Crosby.

Agnes Capstick. 1911 Census (Transcript) Liverpool. Schedule No. 224.

NAME and SURNAME	RELATION to Head of Family	AGE at last Birthday		PARTICULARS as to MARRIAGE	PROFESSION or OCCUPATION		BIRTHPLACE
		Male	Female				
Agnes Capstick	Head		58	Married	Cowkeeper & Dairy	916	Dent, Yorks.
Rose Capstick	Daughter		24	Single	Dairy Work	916	Gargrave, Yorks.
Edward Capstick	Son	20		Single	Working in Shippon	916	Wavertree, Liverpool
James Capstick	Son	19		Single	Working in Shippon	916	Lark Lane, Liverpool
Joshua Dugdale	Grandson	3					Waterloo, Liverpool

Postal Address 42 Handfield Road, Waterloo

The following features are of note in the 1911 census:

- **Relation to Head of Family** – as Edward was away, visiting their daughter's farm in Middleham, Agnes is assigned as *Head of Family*. As well as three of their grown-up children being present, the third generation of cowkeepers is represented by the presence of the *Grandson*. Family dairy businesses were often handed down for many generations.
- **Occupation** – in her husband's absence, Agnes's occupation is given as *Cowkeeper & Dairy*. If her husband had been present, perhaps Agnes's occupation might have been described merely as *Dairy Work*, as is the

case with her daughter. The occupation of both sons is given as *Working in Shippon*. These descriptions continue to reflect the traditional division of labour between men and women in the dairy business. Each description of occupation has been overwritten with the code 916 (*Milksellers, Dairymen*).
- **Place of Birth** – Agnes was born in *Yorkshire*. Her eldest daughter was also born in *Yorkshire* but her sons were both born in *Liverpool*, reflecting the point in the family history when the move to the city took place. The grandson represents the second generation of the family to be born in Liverpool.
- **Street Name/House Number** – 42 Handfield Road is an end-terrace property. The absence of an adjacent property identified as a *shippon*, suggests that the cows may have been kept at the rear of 42 Handfield Road, accessible by a side passage at the end of the terrace.

The corollary of this is, of course, that census entries for non-cowkeeping dairymen, who were simply retailers of milk, do not include these various indicators that milk was being produced on site.

The 1939 England and Wales Register

Though not part of the decennial national census regime, the 1939 Register has proven to be a key reference for genealogists. Carried out on 29 September, it documents the lives of 41 million people. Originally undertaken to facilitate the production of wartime National Identity Cards, it was subsequently used in the tracking of evacuees, the production of ration books and then, later, as the basis for creating the National Health Service Register. Its importance for the family historian is not just the detailed information recorded for each member of the household (including date of birth), but also because it fills a thirty-year gap in census data: the 1931 census records were destroyed in a fire during the war and the 1941 census did not take place due to the ongoing conflict. Its importance for those with dairy ancestors is that it provides a final snapshot of the city dairy immediately prior to its post-war decline.

Chapter 7

Literature Review

Although there are many publications on the history of the farming way of life and the dairy industry, there are fewer dealing with the specific occupation of city dairymen, and fewer still of practical use to the family historian. Some of the excellent books that do exist are listed below:

A Bit Akin: The Story of a North Craven Farming Family by Faith Finegan (F.W. Finegan, 1994). Faith Finegan's delightful self-published book tells the story of the Wolfenden family who farmed in the Craven district of Yorkshire, some of whom went on to keep cows in Liverpool and abroad.

A Brief History of Milk Production: From Farm to Market by Bert Collacott (Old Pond Publishing, 2016). This brief history of the Milk Marketing Board also includes a potted history of cowman Arthur Thomas Godbold (1893–1968) and references to various other dairying families.

Britain's Wartime Milkmen: From the Great War to the Second World War by Tom Phelps (Chaplin Books, 2015). This follow-up to *The British Milkman*, focusing on the war years, is similarly packed with images and stories of city dairies and the families that ran them.

The British Milkman by Tom Phelps (Shire Publications, 2011). Tom Phelps's detailed and lavishly illustrated history of the occupation 'Milkman' is crammed with photographs and vignettes of family dairies in the city.

Cows, Cobs and Corner Shops by Megan Hayes (Y Lolfa, 2018). This sequel to *The London Milk Trail* describes the establishment and subsequent history of the many family-owned Welsh dairies and corner shops that sold milk in London.

The Cowkeeper's Wish: A Genealogical Journey by Tracy Kasaboski and Kristen Den Hartog (Douglas and McIntyre, 2018). This family history begins in the 1840s with young Benjamin Jones and his wife-to-be, Margaret Davies, leaving their home in Aberaeron to begin a new life as cowkeepers in the London borough of Southwark. The authors then use a myriad of archived sources to piece together, in great detail, the lives and times of the couple's descendants over the next 100 years.

Literature Review

Fields of Discovery: On the trail of Liverpool's Cowhouses by Duncan Scott (DWS Publications, 2016). Duncan Scott's second book about dales families that came to Liverpool, includes more detailed histories of the Herd, Wilson, Capstick and Harper families.

Liverpool Cowkeepers by Dave Joy (Amberley Publishing, 2016). In this book I have used my own family history to tell the story of the Liverpool cowkeepers. The book also includes potted histories of other families who kept cows in the south of the city.

The Liverpool Cowkeepers by Patsy Mellor (P.J. Mellor, 2012). Patsy Mellor's self-published booklet is based on a combination of her research into her own family history, and an appeal in local newspapers for information about Yorkshire families who moved to Liverpool to keep cows. As well as a description of the cowkeeping way of life, the booklet also includes the responses to this appeal for information, listing the families alphabetically by surname.

The London Milk Trail: The Story of Welsh Dairies in the City by Megan Hayes (Gwasg Carreg Gwalch, 2015). A fascinating book that traces the history of the many families from Wales (in particular, from Cardiganshire) who began as cattle drovers, but who became dairymen in London.

Milk, Herefordshire by Bill Laws (Herefordshire Lore, 2012). Herefordshire Lore is the county's reminiscence group, which records and publishes people's memories. This edition of Little Herefordshire Histories is packed with memories and anecdotes from Herefordshire families involved in the production, sale and delivery of milk over the past 100 years.

The Milk Supply of East Yorkshire 1850–1950 by Alan Harris (East Yorkshire Local History Society, 1977). This concise but factual account of dairying in the East Riding of Yorkshire includes references to cowkeeping families in the cities of Hull and York.

No Milk Today: The Vanishing World of the Milkman by Andrew Ward (Robinson, 2016). As well as charting the demise of the British milkman, this book is crammed with anecdotes and folklore collected from generations of dairymen across the country, many of whom were continuing a family tradition.

The Old Dairy at Crouch Hill by John Hinshelwood (Hornsey Historical Society, 1999). This is the story of the Friern Manor Dairy building (now a restaurant) and the rare decorative sgraffito panels that adorn its exterior. It is also the story of a London dairying family, the Taylors, beginning in the 1840s.

Those Who Left the Dales by The Upper Dales Family History Group (2010). Described as a 'Migration Archive', this is a collection of over 100 family stories based on letters sent home from those who left the dales between 1700 and the end of the nineteenth century. It includes a comprehensive index of surnames and place names.

Urban Cowboys: Lost Worlds of Doorstep Milk by Duncan Scott (DWS Publications, 2010). Duncan Scott describes his book as 'an illustrated biographical essay'. It traces the history of the Capstick family (and its various branches) from their Cumbrian roots, farming near Howgill, through their years of keeping cows in Liverpool, to becoming milkmen in Lymm, Cheshire.

Chapter 8

Blogs and Websites

One of the great things about the Internet is that information is constantly being added to and updated. One of the not so great things is that neglected sites may become, at best, out-dated, or at worst, deleted. A rider to the following list of links is that they were active and accessed in January 2020. If you find that any of these links have subsequently been deleted, it is worth trying the repository for deleted pages known as the *Wayback Machine* (**archive.org**).

There are a number of online sites dedicated to, or referencing, the history and genealogy of city dairymen. They are listed here in alphabetical order, according to title. (The links are given without the https or www prefixes.)

Argyle Dairy
aaahs.org.uk/files/Argyle%20Dairy.pdf
An essay by Sandra Marie Lewis describing the history of the Argyle family and the Argyle Dairy in Abingdon, Berkshire.

Ashbourne Heritage Society
ashbourneheritagesociety.org.uk/trades/
The website of the Ashbourne Heritage Society describes trades carried out by the Titterton family. Joshua Titterton was a cowkeeper in Stockport.

Aunt Kate
auntkatefirmin.wordpress.com/2014/07/05/thomas-hall-cow-keeper
A genealogy blog about the Firmin, Hall and Kenning families. It includes an intriguing investigation into the life of cowkeeper Thomas Hall, who moved from the village of Barby, in Northamptonshire, to keep cows in London.

Bartonsham History Group
bartonshamhistory.org.uk/bartonshamdairy.html
The Bartonsham History Group's website describes the history of the Matthews family and their operation of Bartonsham Dairy, Hereford. The narrative includes references to other city dairies in the area.

Barton-upon-Humber
bartonuponhumber.org.uk/Stories/barton40s.htm
This local history website provides an account, written by Terry Clipson, of the cowkeepers of Barton-upon-Humber, north Lincolnshire, in the late 1940s.

Brighton and Beyond
cowleyfamily.org.uk/cowley_farmers.html
Brighton and Beyond is a history of the Cowley family written by Peter Cowley. The Cowleys were dairymen and farmers in the Brighton area and Peter's account of his family's history includes a collection of old photographs and a number of links to other websites with related content.

British Film Institute
player.bfi.org.uk/free/film/watch-leaving-of-the-cows-1975-online
Leaving of the Cows is the British Film Institute's record of the last city cowkeeping family, the Capsticks, moving their cows out of Liverpool in 1975.

British Land
locallocalhistory.co.uk/brit-land/food/page05.htm
Although this is a local history site, it includes a short article on the typical London milkhouse with reference to the Drewell, Veale and Morrison families.

Brixton Buzz
brixtonbuzz.com/2021/03/brixton-history-avenue-dairies-in-elliot-road-sw9/
Brixton Buzz is a news, events and features website for the Brixton area. It includes a local history article (by contributor 'Puddy Tat') on the Avenue Dairies in Elliot Road, and the family history of dairyman, William Robert Berkshire.

The Brockbanks of Crosthwaite
crosthwaiteandlyth.co.uk/genealogy/thebrockbanksofcrosthwaite.html
Jean Abbey provides a detailed history of the Brockbank family of Crosthwaite, some of whom became dairymen in Liverpool.

Bucks Free Press
bucksfreepress.co.uk/news/18203057.horse-drawn-link-benny-hill-marlows-eddie-price/
This local news and features website includes an article by Michael Eagleton, describing the horse-drawn link between Benny Hill's famous milkman, Ernie, and Marlow's popular local dairyman, Eddie Price.

Dairy Days
blog.yorkshiredales.org.uk/category/wensleydale-dairy-days
This National Lottery-funded project, undertaken by the Yorkshire Dales National Park Authority, includes a number of oral histories about dairying in Wensleydale. It also includes references to Wensleydale families who relocated to Liverpool to become cowkeepers.

Blogs and Websites

Dave Joy – Author
davejoy-author.com
My website focuses on the cowkeepers of Liverpool. It contains lists transcribed from census records and trade directories as well as lists of prizewinners at the various local and county shows. The site also includes a number of family histories, memoirs and reminiscences, illustrated with photographs, maps and newspaper articles.

The Doric Columns
mcjazz.f2s.com/AberdeenDairies.htm
The Doric Columns website describes the many dairies in Aberdeen and the families who ran them. It includes many old photographs and an alphabetical list of dairymen, by surname.

Epsom and Ewell History Explorer
https://eehe.org.uk/
This local history website includes an account of the extensive dairy businesses of the Curtis family of Balham, Epsom, Ewell and Effingham from the mid-1850s to the mid-1950s.

Every Barn Tells a Story
everybarn.yorkshiredales.org.uk
Through this National Lottery-funded project, the Yorkshire Dales National Park Authority worked with local people, businesses and visitors to record, interpret and share the history and stories of field barns (cowhouses) in Upper Swaledale.

Fitz-Henry Family History
fitz-henry.blogspot.com/2009/08/miles-fitzhenry-cowkeeper-in-birmingham.html
Jo Fitz-Henry's blog about the Fitzhenry family includes a timeline for Miles Fitzhenry (1825–1893), a Birmingham cowkeeper.

Four Oaks Genealogy
fouroaksgenealogy.co.uk/case-studies-fruitful
Genealogist Linda Newey describes finding her husband's ancestor, John Newey, listed in a Register of Cowkeepers & Dairymen, kept at Worcester City Archives.

Gail Thornton
gail-thornton.co.uk/trade-vehicles/dairy.php
Gail Thornton's pictorial archive of horse-drawn vehicles includes a page dedicated to dairy vehicles; the livery of a number of these vehicles identifies the family owners.

Goods and Not So Goods
igg.org.uk/gansg/12-linind/milk.htm
Although the purpose of this site is to provide an overview of railway freight operations for modellers, in describing lineside industries it also includes a detailed account of the role played by the railways in the transportation and distribution of milk throughout the country.

Headington History
headington.org.uk/history/shops/allsaintsroad_limewalk73.htm
This guide to Headington, Oxford, by Stephanie Jenkins, includes a number of pages on the history of the area. Amongst these is a history of a property at 73 Lime Walk, which was used as a dairy by a succession of owners from 1886 onwards.

Historic London Tours
historiclondontours.com/tales-of-london/f/the-largest-dairy-in-the-kingdom
The Historic London Tours blog, by accredited tour guide, Tom Currie, includes a short history of Laycock's dairy, Islington, claimed to be the largest dairy in the kingdom.

Ian Visits
ianvisits.co.uk/blog/2011/08/09/the-dairy-supply-company-near-the-british-museum
A blog site about the more obscure aspects of London's history. It includes a description and photographs of George Barham's Dairy Supply Company in Coptic Street, London.

London's Milk Supply – George Barham's former Dairy Supply Company in Coptic Street, London. (Author)

Blogs and Websites

Ipswich War Memorial
ipswichwarmemorial.co.uk/frederick-charles-walker
The Ipswich War Memorial website commemorates the life of Frederick Charles Walker, who spent his early life at the family's Walker's Dairy at 48 Sloane Street in Chelsea. It includes images, courtesy of Kensington Central Library.

Jane Austen's World
janeaustensworld.wordpress.com
This page forms part of a more extensive Jane Austen's World blog, designed to bring to life the author's novels. It includes a detailed but charming account of buying milk in St James's Park and the dairymen of Georgian London.

Jane's London
janeslondon.com/2015/10/friern-manor-limited-dairy-farm.html
Jane Parker's blog site on various aspects of London's history includes a page on Friern Manor's old dairy in Stroud Green. Of particular interest are the seven large sgraffito panels depicting various points in the cow-to-customer service provided by the company. The building is now a pub and restaurant.

John and Marion Hearfield
johnhearfield.com/index.html
John and Marion Hearfield's website contains a wonderful collection of essays on a variety of subjects. Of particular interest are the essays about dairies in London in the seventeenth and eighteenth centuries, as they include lists of dairymen's names taken from London newspapers. Also of interest is the essay on the many families who left Swaledale during the 1880s to try their fortunes elsewhere; some of these became city dairymen.

Kirby and West
kirbyandwest.co.uk/history/
A short history of the Kirby and West dairy company, Leicestershire, from 1861 to present day.

Laindon and District Community Archive
laindonhistory.org.uk/content/people/family_memories/slopers_dairy_of_laindon
This community archive website includes a memoir by Peter Sloper describing the history of Sloper's Dairy of Laindon, South Essex – with some lovely family photographs.

The Library Time Machine
rbkclocalstudies.wordpress.com/2015/10/08/milk/
Dave Walker is the Local Studies Librarian for the Royal Borough of Kensington and Chelsea. This blog describes the history of the dairies in the borough and includes references to a number of dairying families.

Old Church Street, Chelsea – A former dairy in Old Church Street, now a residential property. (Author)

Local Drove Roads
localdroveroads.co.uk/taffy-the-milk
Bruce Smith's website is about the historic drover routes of Britain and some of the families who used them. It includes a page on 'Taffy the Milk', about the Welsh drovers who became London dairymen.

London Details
baldwinhamey.wordpress.com/2013/08/05/dairy-supply-company
The London Details blog includes a page about George Barham (1836–1913), who went on to establish the Dairy Supply Company in London's Coptic Street.

Mal's Rambles & Ramblings
malspond.com/?page_id=1533
Mal's blog site includes articles on the occupants of Everton cemetery. One such occupant was Thomas Read Mansergh who kept cows in Bootle during the late 1800s and early 1900s.

Meet the Grahams

grahamsfamilydairy.com/meet-grahams/grahams-family-story

A photographic history of the Graham's family dairy in Bridge of Allan, Stirlingshire.

Memoirs of a Metro Girl

memoirsofametrogirl.com/2018/11/14/wrights-dairy-cow-heads-chelsea-history-kings-road-old-church-street/

This blog by Metro Girl is aimed at both residents and visitors to the capital and includes various posts on aspects of London history. This post describes the history of Wright's Dairy in Chelsea and the surviving properties in Old Church Street and in King's Road.

King's Road, Chelsea – A former dairy in King's Road, now a mobile phone shop. (Author)

Merseyside Roll of Honour
merseysiderollofhonour.co.uk/obits/notcwgc/pawson.php
The Merseyside Roll of Honour website is dedicated to those who lost their lives during the First World War. As well as those who fought, it also includes information about their families, such as the cowkeeping Pawson family, originally from Wharfedale.

Milk Bottle News
milkbottlenews.org.uk
This site describes itself as a UK newsletter for 'Milk Bottle and Dairyana Collectors everywhere'. As well as the newsletter, the site also includes fascinating features, photographs of family and corporate dairy collectables and an extensive list of links to other dairy-related websites.

Mr Seel's Garden
mrseelsgarden.org
Mr Seel's Garden was an academic and community research project, looking at the history (and future) of locally produced food in Liverpool. In addition to an item about the city's cowkeepers, the website also includes an interactive map showing the location of many family-owned dairies, accompanied by local people's anecdotal recollections of when these businesses were active.

Museum of Soho
mosoho.org.uk/dairy.html
The Museum of Soho is a virtual museum with a physical collection. The museum holds the archives of the former Oxford Express Dairy on 26 Frith Street, once operated by the Pugh family who originated from the county of Ceredigion in west Wales. The website features an article, 'A Welsh Dairy in Soho', by Dr Joan Navarre, illustrated with photographs of the museum's objects collection.

My West Ealing
mywestealing.org.uk/history/jobs-dairy-1920-1987/
A community website for the London Borough of Ealing, it includes a history of the Roberts family and their dairy business, Job's Dairy, 1920–1987.

On London – For the Good City
onlondon.co.uk/vic-keegans-lost-london-153-the-cows-of-st-jamess-park/
This site includes instalment number 153 in Victor Keegan's series 'Lost London' – The Cows of St James's Park.

Only in the Dales
blog.yorkshiredales.org.uk/wensleydale-cowkeepers-in-liverpool/
This website, by the Yorkshire Dales National Park Authority, includes a blog, by Interpretation Officer Karen Griffiths, about 'Wensleydale Cowkeepers in

Blogs and Websites

Liverpool'. It is based on a small collection of old photographs, kept at the Dales Countryside Museum, Hawes, featuring the Bargh family.

Pratt/Hall Family
mcmullin.plus.com/Pratt/ind5657.html
Eric and Hazel McMullin's blog about their Hall ancestors includes a timeline for William Hall (1798–1867), who kept cows in Birmingham.

Primrose Hill
primrosehillhistory.org/?p=1067
This history of the Primrose Hill area of London includes that of Primrose Dairy, 25 Princess Road. Being a dairy for over 120 years, it has the longest history of any of the shops in the area and was home to a succession of dairymen.

Rambling London Tours
ramblinglondontours.com/2021/11/15/welfords/
Blue Badge Tour Guide for London, Amber Tallon, tells the story of Richard Welford & Sons and illustrates the history of Warwick Farm Dairies in Maida Vale.

Sainsbury's
sainsburys.lgfl.org.uk/milk.htm
This site provides a short history of the Sainsbury family and the founding of the J. Sainsbury business in 1870s London (including references to various employees). Interestingly, it espouses the virtues of their 'Railway Milk' over that supplied by the local cowkeepers.

A Sense of Place
asenseofplace.com/2014/05/12/the-cowhouses-of-liverpool
A Sense of Place is Ronnie Hughes's blog on many aspects of the history and community of Liverpool. It includes a page on The Cowhouses of Liverpool, inspired by the book *Urban Cowboys* by Duncan Scott, with references to the Capstick and Harper families, amongst others.

Spitalfields Life
spitalfieldslife.com/2010/04/12/jones-dairy-henry-jones-family
Spitalfields Life traces the history of Jones Dairy, located in Middlesex Street. Henry Jones, originally from Aberystwyth, moved to London and opened up the first Jones Dairy in 1877.

Steve Banks
steve-banks.org/images/historical/milk/lmsj_milk_pdf.pdf
In this fascinating article, Steve Banks provides an overview of the history of the transportation of milk by rail, with specific reference to the London, Midland and Scottish (LMS) railway company.

The Story of Dorset Dairies
eastleighhistory.org.uk/sites/default/files/document/OP28%20-%20 Story%20of%20Dorset%20Dairies.pdf
Courtesy of Eastleigh & District Local History Society, Margaret Batstone provides a history of her ancestors, the Hann family, and their dairy business in Dorset.

Susanna Ives
susannaives.com/wordpress/2012/03/buying-bread-and-milk-in-18th-and-19th-century-london/
Susanna's blog about buying bread and milk in eighteenth and nineteenth century London includes a detailed account of how milk was sold, fresh from the cow, in St James's Park.

Twickenham Park
twickenhampark.co.uk/josiah%20clarke%20and%20sons%20richmond.html
The Twickenham Park Residents Association's website traces the history of the Clarke family's dairy business, in Richmond and East Twickenham, from its beginnings in 1890, through to its takeover by Express Dairies in 1960.

Wagging Tales
travelswithadog.wordpress.com/2016/04/07/the-all-but-lost-dairy/
The Wagging Tales website gives a canine-eye view of the history of the dairy at Warwick Farm, Paddington. It was established in 1845 as J. Welford & Sons Ltd.

Walthamstow Memories
walthamstowmemories.net/pdfs/Bill%20Bayliss%20-%20Hichman.pdf
Daniel Quinn's website includes an article by Bill Bayliss about Hitchman's Dairies and the family history of dairyman John Hitchman.

The Welsh Connection
blipfoto.com/entry/2068642453384072348
This blipfoto page, by 'ceridwen', is inspired by an unusual artefact and contains a short reference to E. Evans & Son, Dairymen and Cowkeepers, Alexandra Dairy, 11 Downham Road, Dalston N1.

Wolverhampton History & Heritage – Darlaston Green Dairies
historywebsite.co.uk/articles/DarlastonGreen/dairies.htm
Peter J. Carter and Dennis Parker's detailed investigation into the urban dairies of Darlaston Green during the 1900s includes histories of the following local dairying families: Small, Worral, Holland, Foster and Andrews.

Blogs and Websites

Wolverhampton History & Heritage – Midland Counties Dairy
historywebsite.co.uk/articles/Dairy/Dairy.htm#menu
Using the scrapbook of George Cartwright (a former employee), Bev Parker traces the history of the White family and the Midland Counties Dairy, Wolverhampton.

A Wrathall Family History
wrathall.org/wrathall/james/england/edward-history.html
The Wrathall family originated in the western dales of Yorkshire and at least one branch of the family became dairymen in Liverpool.

Chapter 9

Tools of the Trade

Vehicles

The evolution of milk delivery vehicles was driven by the need to carry more milk, as round size increased in a competitive market. The traditional yoke and pail was succeeded in the cities by handcarts and prams. These were succeeded in turn by a variety of horse-drawn vehicles, better suited to covering the greater distances involved.

For the city dairyman, the vehicle of choice became the horse-drawn, two-wheeled milk float. Indeed, many cowkeepers continued to use a milk float even after their cows were gone and they were delivering pre-bottled milk to their customers. Others moved with the times and replaced their horse and cart, first, with a variety of petrol-driven vehicles, but ultimately with an electric (battery) vehicle, which continued to be called a 'milk float'.

Left and opposite: Delivery Vehicles – As milk delivery vehicles evolved, many continued to advertise the dairy by displaying name and address information. Photo credits: Joy's (Author); Morton's (courtesy of Dave Morton); Taylor's (courtesy of Kate Thexton); Capstick's (courtesy of Ann Osborne); Greenbank's (courtesy of Ray Smyth); Metcalfe's (courtesy of Karen Stanley)

Tools of the Trade

The value of these vehicles to the family historian is that, in the interests of good enterprise, dairymen emblazoned their vehicles with the family name, their occupation and the address of the dairy; their vehicles were mobile adverts for the family business. As a result of this, photographs of delivery vehicles not only offer

Fastest in the West? – Vintage milk delivery vehicles can be found in transport museums. Museum of Liverpool Life. (Author)

a glimpse of bygone practices but also provide a useful source of name and address information.

Such vehicles feature in the collections of many transport, agriculture and heritage museums throughout the country. On display at the Museum of Liverpool Life is a typical horse-drawn milk float from about 1890. It was made by Pickering Brothers at the city's Windsor Carriage Works, then refurbished in 1965 by Mr B. Lucketti. By way of contrast, The Transport Museum at Wythall in Worcestershire, claims to have the largest collection of battery-powered electric vehicles in the world, most of which are milk floats.

Milk Bottles and Tops

Milk bottles were first introduced into this country by the Express Dairy Company in the 1880s; by the 1920s they had become the accepted means of packaging milk for sale. The independent dairymen followed the example of the corporate dairies and procured milk bottles inscribed with the name and address of their businesses. This was done in part to advertise the business, but it was also done to establish ownership, as all bottles were collected, washed and used again.

Foremost among UK milk bottle collectors is Mark Hudson, with a collection of over 2,000 bottles. In a three-part article for *Antique Bottle Collector* magazine

(2010), Mark describes how the process of inscribing milk bottles developed over the centuries. Before the 1930s, names were embossed on the glass using a slug plate. The name was impressed on the slug plate, which was then inserted into the mould used to make the bottle, and produced raised lettering on the surface of the glass. This type of embossing proved to be expensive for the small dairy operators and a cheaper alternative was available in the form of acid etching or sandblasting on to ready-made bottles, using a stencil. However, as technology improved, embossing was replaced by pyroglazing, also known as Applied Colour Lettering. This process involved applying heated enamel to the glass surface through a silk screen; it greatly increased the diversity of design and colour of the labelling (Hudson, 2010).

Milk Bottles – Milk bottles were at first embossed (left) and later pyroglazed (right) with the name of the dairy as much to facilitate return for re-use than to promote the business. (Author)

By far the most common size of milk bottle in Mark's vast collection is the familiar pinta (one pint). However, when the 1921 Education Act expanded the powers of local authorities to include milk in their provision of free school meals, dairies responded by producing a-third-of-a-pint-bottles to supply this market. The abundance of this size of milk bottle increased when the 1946 School Milk Act specified that all school children under the age of 18 must be issued with a third of a pint of milk.

Although milk bottles represented a not-too-small investment on the part of the dairyman, their re-usability made them worth it. Unfortunately, securing this investment by retrieving milk bottles for re-use proved to be somewhat problematic, with them either being used by another dairy or being utilised by housewives for a different purpose around the home. Retrieval of milk bottles was still a problem in 1961 as the following lament in the *Liverpool Echo* of 24 October illustrates:

> At least 300,000,000 milk bottles are lost or broken in England and Wales every year and the figure is rising annually. The annual cost of replacing them is almost £6,000,000. Obviously, bottles will get broken and cracked. They also get commandeered for other purposes, such as flower vases and paint containers. People forget about them and then suddenly cover the front doorstep with a dozen

or so, presenting the milkman with something of a problem. The heart-cry of the milk distributors is: Please rinse your bottles and leave them out for us to collect every day.

Their popularity and utilitarian nature meant that many milk bottles never found their way back to the dairy. Consequently, today, in addition to seeing vintage milk bottles in museums, there is also a lively trade online. A quick search of the Internet will identify dozens of bottles for sale or auction at a reasonable price. Many of these carry the family or dairy name, often with the full postal address and even with the telephone number. For the collector, *Milk Bottle News* is a quarterly newsletter that can be viewed online (**milkbottlenews.org.uk/index.html**).

Not surprisingly, Mark Hudson also has a collection of the various tops that were used to seal milk bottles. Although early versions took the form of glass or metal plugs, once materials such as cardboard or foil were used, it became possible to imprint these seals with information about the dairy. Waxed cardboard discs were printed with information such as the name and address of the dairy, the type of milk contained in the bottle, reminders to wash and return the bottles, or even Christmas greetings. Similarly, when foil caps replaced cardboard discs, these could be stamped with the name and address of the dairy during the manufacturing process. Thomas Harrison Burns, a dairyman in Liverpool during the 1930s, had the following information stamped on his milk bottles' foil caps:

Accredited Milk
Produced & Farm Bottled
By T.H. Burns
36 Bedford Road, Walton
TUESDAY

The day of the week was included to indicate when the milk had been bottled; this provided the customer with some indication as to the freshness of the contents.

Milk Bottle Tops – Cardboard 'pogs' (left) and foil seals (right) were often printed or stamped with the name, address and telephone number of the dairy. (Pogs, courtesy of Mark Hudson; Foils, Author)

Tools of the Trade

Bespoke Business Stationery

The business's stationery included letterheads, invoices and business cards; by its very nature such paperwork carried a great deal of information. Obvious information was the name, address and telephone number of the business. But the

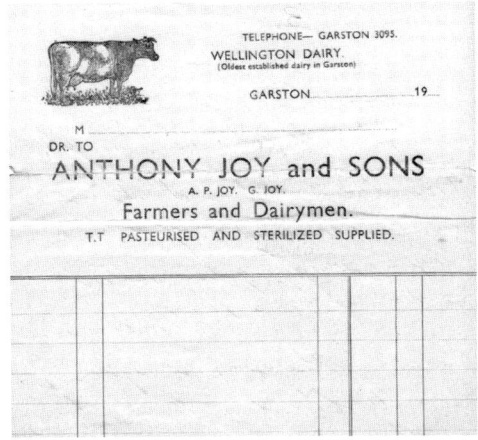

Business Stationery – Dairies used a variety of bespoke business stationery. A. Joy & Sons, Farmers and Cowkeepers. (Author)

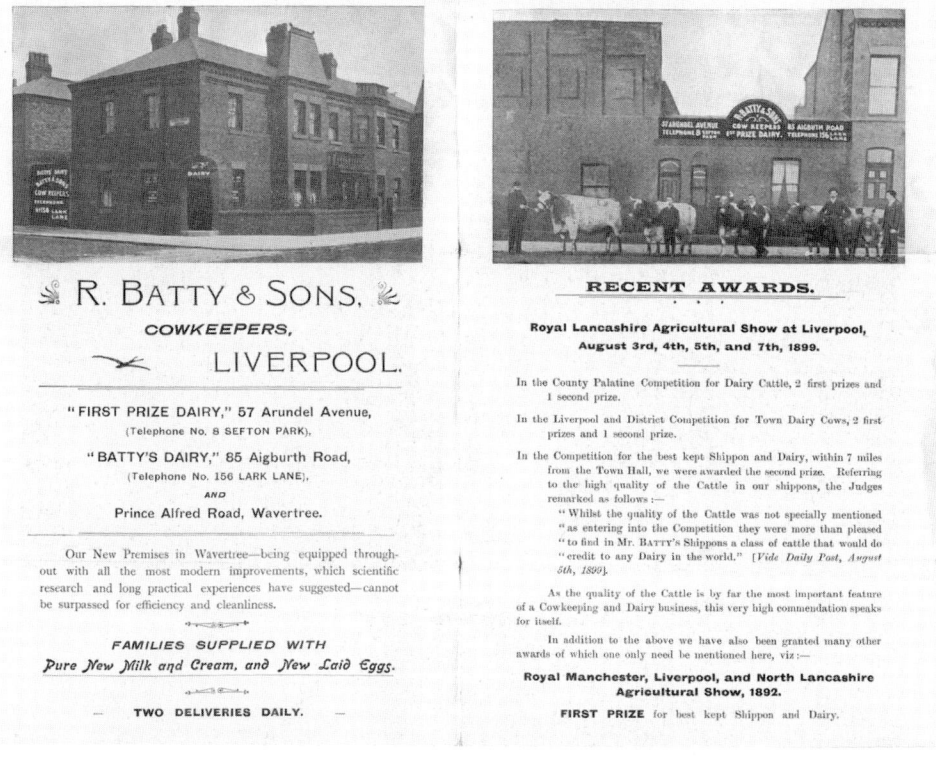

Dairy Leaflet – Dairies produced promotional literature targeted at prospective customers. Batty's Dairy, Arundel Avenue, Liverpool. (Courtesy of Brian Snelson)

dairyman would also take the opportunity to pledge to the customer the quality of their produce and the reliability of their service: they would extoll their 'fresh', 'pure' and 'health-giving' milk and they would invite the customer to enter their premises and inspect it for themselves.

This exaltation of the family business was amplified even more on handbills that were posted through letterboxes or handed out to potential new customers. They would unashamedly list in great detail the many prizes and awards bestowed upon the business, all done with the aim of gaining further competitive advantage and garnering more customers.

Hand Tools and Equipment

Much of the equipment and many of the tools used in the cowkeeping profession were similar to those being used in pastoral farming and include milking stool, milk pail, butter churn, measuring ladle, pasteuriser, cooler, bottles, bottle washer, crates, muck crome, hay rake, pitch fork, mangel knife, hand barrow, etc. These and many other tools of the dairyman can be seen in rural museums throughout

Museum Pieces – Hand tools and dairy equipment can be seen on display in agricultural museums across the country. (Author)

the country. The British Agricultural History Society (**bahs.org.uk**) lists some 120 rural museums, living villages and similar places of interest across the UK.

Competition Trophies

Engraved silver cups, goblets and trays; medals, rosettes and certificates – at some point in time, all will have taken pride of place in the dairy window or hung on the walls inside the shop, extolling the virtues of the family's business and the quality of their produce. As time passed they will have migrated on to someone's mantelpiece as mementos, perhaps eventually being packed away in a box as a family heirloom. However, as well as stating the source, the occasion and the reason for the award, the inscriptions on these trophies can also provide valuable name and date information.

In 1885, cowkeeper Henry Wolfenden entered a number of classes at the 29th annual show of the Ormskirk, Southport and Bootle Agricultural Society, held at Marsh Lane, Bootle. His success at the show resulted in Henry being presented with a silver goblet, now in the possession of his great-granddaughter, Meryl Auty. The trophy has been intricately engraved and carries four separate inscriptions as follows:

- Ormskirk, Southport and Bootle Agricultural Society
- Awarded to Mr Henry Wolfenden of Waterloo
- For the Best Dairy Cow in Premiums Nos 20 & 21 – Robert Mawdsley, Secretary and Treasurer
- Show held at Bootle Wednesday 29th July 1885.

Trophies – Competition trophies can carry name, place and date information: (left) Henry Wolfenden, Dairyman. (Courtesy of Meryl Auty); (right) Charles Blackburn & Sons, Dairyman and Dairy Vessel Manufacturer (Courtesy of Tricia Henton)

Tools of the Trade

Amongst a collection of family heirlooms, Tricia Henton came across a silver medal in an elegant presentation case, inscribed with the following information:

Awarded to
C Blackburn & Sons
for best collection of
Butter Making Dairy Vessels
Liverpool Show
1899

By cross-referencing this information with the national newspaper archive, Tricia discovered that the show in question was that of the Royal Lancashire Agricultural Society, held in Liverpool in 1899, and that her ancestors, who had a stand there, were much more than just cowkeepers and dairymen:

> A double interest attaches to the stand (248) of Messrs C. Blackburn and Sons of 5 and 7 Oldham Street (off Renshaw Street), Liverpool, the exhibitors having for the last forty years carried on the dairy business, while for the past twenty years they have been inventors and makers of articles for the use of cowkeepers and retail dairymen. The front object of their interesting stand is a 'Fram' cream separator, a self-contained machine, new this year, which they have adopted for use in their own business. It works admirably, and requires no fixing. Next in order of importance stands Blackburn's patent milk filter and refrigerator, a contrivance which enables the cleansing of milk and its cooling, so that it will keep for 24 hours, thus suggesting the possibility of avoiding one if not both the Sunday deliveries. The Wedgewood pottery for dairy use to be seen on this stand has attracted many purchasers, and the metal accessories of the dairy, including the railway milk tankards, a capital line, make the display very complete.
> (*Liverpool Mercury* – Friday, 4 August 1899).

For the design and quality of their 'collection of most improved Dairy Vessels for butter making and other dairy work', Charles Blackburn and Sons were awarded the society's silver medal.

Milk Cans

In his book, *Milk Cans: A Celebration of Their History, Use and Design*, Ian Spellerberg (2018) defines the term 'milk can' as 'a container (usually with a lid) commonly made of metal and used for carrying or transporting milk or cream'. Although these metal cans (tinned or galvanised, iron or steel) came in many shapes and sizes, the most common to be found in the city dairies were: the large 17-gallon 'churn' used for transporting milk in bulk via road or rail; the similarly large 'kit' that was pushed or pulled around the streets and from which milk was dispensed using measured ladles; and the smaller 'handcan', used for doorstep delivery or in the kitchen.

Most milk cans were stamped, both on the body and on the lid, with the name of the manufacturer (e.g. the London Dairy Supply Company) as part of the manufacturing process. But many were subsequently inscribed with the name of the local dairy using the vessel (e.g. 'Primrose Dairy, Hayle' or 'Totness Dairy'). This was in accordance with Article 29 (1) of the 1926 Milk and Dairies Act, which stated: 'The name and address of the owner shall be permanently marked on the churn, vessel or other receptacle, or on a plate or plates of metal properly soldered or otherwise securely affixed thereto.'

Occasionally, a dairy would have a special can manufactured, decoratively inscribed with its full name and address; these were used for show rather than being put to daily use on the milk round. Another occurrence was for replica cans to be made out of pottery and put on display in the dairy window; these would also be adorned with the identity of the dairy.

The kits and handcans became redundant with the introduction of the glass milk bottle, and the traditional metal milk churns were retired when glass-lined rail and road tankers became the norm for transporting milk in bulk.

Milk Cans – Milk cans were often engraved with the name and address of the dairy, as well as that of the manufacturer. (Author)

Chapter 10

Buildings and Architecture

The two buildings that were key to a successful cowkeeping business were the milkhouse and the shippon. In some instances, these two buildings were part of the same property, whilst in others they were on separate properties, usually adjacent, sometimes forming two sides of a street corner location. Premises used for a cowkeeping business may have come into being through one of three ways: original, converted or purpose-built.

Original
First, there was the farm on the edge of a town or city that, as the city expanded, lost its fields and became absorbed into the metropolis. To begin with, the farmer may have been able to herd his cows to and from pastures further afield on a daily basis. But as the city continued to expand, and the fields were pushed further away, this would have proved to be impractical. Eventually, the building became

Architectural Clues – There are architectural and signage clues that a building had a previous existence as a city dairy. (Author)

isolated from suitable grazing and the cows were kept on site as a 'flying herd', and farming became cowkeeping. Businesses being operated from these buildings often incorporated the name of the original farm in the name of the new dairy business, for example: Orchard Farm Dairy.

Converted
Second, there was the city centre building that was converted to make it suitable for the keeping of cows. This is the typical end-terraced property that was so popular with the early cowkeepers. The cows, usually between six and twelve in number (depending on the space available), may have been kept in a shed or shippon in what was the backyard of the house or may have been kept in an adjacent property previously used for a different kind of business, such as a carter's stables or a merchant's store.

Purpose-built
Finally, there was the designed and built for purpose milkhouse, many of which were included in the newly expanding suburbs of the cities. These combined milkhouse and cowhouse on a single site and had a sizeable yard, enclosed by all the outbuildings and 'modern' facilities necessary to support herds of thirty or more cattle and meet the exacting health and hygiene standards of the day.

Many of these building have been lost, either to Second World War bombings or to inner-city redevelopment. However, plenty of examples have survived – especially in the suburban areas. Milkhouses were designed for living in and were easily converted for full-time accommodation purposes. Both the shippon and the associated yard would have been designated for 'industrial' or 'trade' use. As such, they were in demand by trades and services needing to be close to their customers, and they seem to have been particularly popular with the auto trade or are being used as warehouses.

Even though the function of these properties may now have changed, there remain clues as to their previous use.

The Milkhouse

Milkhouses came in all shapes and sizes: large, medium or small; terraced, semi-detached or detached; adapted for use or purpose-built. An obvious clue with regard to identifying a former milkhouse is its situation – at the end of a terraced street. It could be slightly larger than the other houses on the block, having been extended in the past and it may still have some associated outbuildings. There may be a single entrance at the front that was used by both family and customers, but often the shop had its own separate entrance – especially if the building is situated on a street corner.

It was common practice to paint a large sign on the gable end of the property, proclaiming the name and nature of the business. This signage outlasted many of the businesses and some can still be discerned today as ghost signs. Purpose-built properties had more permanent signage in the form of ornamental stonework included in the exterior fabric of the building. Some of these featured the name of the family business or just had the word 'DAIRY' in bold capitals, whilst others included the images of cows sculpted from stone. Examples of other, less obvious, clues are the cow images included in ornamental metalwork such as the weather vane attached to a rooftop or the doorknocker in the form of a cow's head.

If you are able to see inside the building, you may find clues there too. Milkhouses were subject to inspection and had to demonstrate the highest standards of hygiene before being deemed fit to receive a licence to sell milk. Paper copies of licences would be framed and hung in a prominent position on the dairy wall or displayed in the shop window. Some cowkeepers who were confident of renewing their licence would have a metal plate made up on which it was permanently emblazoned that they were 'Licensed to Sell Milk'. Similar displays were also made of trophies and certificates, won at the local or county shows.

Interior Hygiene – Easy-to-clean, tiled surfaces are a good clue that the building was once used for the sale of milk. (Author)

One of the requirements of a milk licence was that all surfaces must be scrubbed daily. To facilitate this task, it was common for all rooms associated with the sale of milk to have tiled walls and floors, and many of these features were so robustly constructed that they have stood the test of time. For similar reasons, work surfaces such as sales counters and window displays were also stone-built or tiled. Interior tiled surfaces such as these are a good clue that the building was once used for the sale of milk.

Another clue in the décor of the property is the presence on the walls of whitewash (or quick-lime). To reduce the risk of contamination through dust and debris, there was a requirement for all walls with exposed brickwork to be whitewashed on a regular basis. This also included the exterior walls in the yard.

The Yard

The yard may be located adjacent to the milkhouse, or located to the rear and accessible down a side passage. Its original surface would have been quarried stone or cobbles, the entrance often laid with two parallel lines of long stones to give extra support to the horse-drawn wheeled vehicles and prevent rutting. A later modification was to replace the rough-hewn stone with regularised blocks of stone setts. If they have not been hidden beneath a layer of concrete, these early surfaces may still be visible today.

Brick middens would have been easily demolished once they became redundant. And it is likely that any pits originally used as middens have since been filled in, but might be evidenced by differences in the surface finish.

The Cowhouse or Shippon

Of the various outbuildings associated with the yard, the most important was the shippon. Shippons were subject to their own inspection and licensing regime, aimed at ensuring the safety of the workers, the health of the animals and the quality of the milk. Once a licence was obtained, a sign had to be placed somewhere on the building declaring how many cows the premises were licensed to keep.

Though the original design of these city shippons may have been based on the traditional cowhouses back on the farm, as standards in the city improved, so the licensing regime required changes to be made to their design and layout. Consequently, the clues to the previous use of these buildings are a mixture of the ancient and the relatively modern.

Inside the former shippon, it is unlikely that the original floor will have survived as its combination of kerbs and gullies would make it unsuitable for any other use; more than likely, it has been concreted over. However, there may be evidence on the internal walls of the original fittings and fixtures, such as holes where the boskins had been bolted in place, or a tethering ring, or the remains of a drinking trough.

Buildings and Architecture

Former City Dairy – The typical layout of a former city dairy included milkhouse, cowhouse and yard, with many features still visible today. 1–3 Neilson Road, Liverpool. Access courtesy of Jim Davies. (Author)

The walls may also show signs of the former ventilation system, which was simple but effective. Ventilation was necessary because the digestive system of cattle produces heat – lots of it. This warm, moist air rises to the ceiling. It cannot be vented into the hayloft, above, as the warmth and moisture would spoil the hay. So, windows or vents – or a combination of the two – were installed high in the outer walls, just below the level of the ceiling. A parallel line of intervaled vents, installed lower down the wall, enabled cooler air to be drawn in from the outside. These lower vents were not at ground level as the cold air might chill the cows' legs; rather, they were at 'schoolboy' level – just the right height for curious schoolboys to peer through and see the beasts inside. Simply knocking out single bricks at regular intervals could create crude vents, but more often they were purpose-built airbricks with tiled vent covers. The heat produced by the cattle was what drove the system and windows could be opened or closed to provide a degree of regulation.

Vents would also be installed in the end gables to the hayloft, as a good circulation of fresh air helped to keep the hay fresh. Vent holes could take the form of single slots or could be arranged to form interesting patterns, such as diamonds or triangles.

Other clues as to the building's former use might be a redundant muck hole, located at ground level, through which the cow muck was once shovelled out of the building into the nearby midden. Or, as with the milkhouse, an exterior wall of the shippon might show the ghostly remains of a painted sign, advertising the name of the business.

PART THREE

Case Studies

The following case studies have been selected to illustrate the range of source material that can be used to inform the history of an ancestor who was a dairyman. The case studies have a hierarchical relationship, working down from county to district to local/family level. Each level has its own challenges for the family historian. For example, whereas the papers of The Royal Lancashire Agricultural Society have been preserved and are fully catalogued as part of the National Archives, those of the Liverpool & District Dairy Farmers' Association remain elusive. Fortunately, the activities of the latter organisation and its members can be identified from other sources.

Chapter 11

The Royal Lancashire Agricultural Society

Many dairymen in the towns and cities of Lancashire were paid-up members of the county agricultural society. They participated in the society's many activities, including the annual agricultural shows – especially on those occasions when the show came to their town.

The Royal Lancashire Agricultural Society (RLAS) has an interesting pedigree. The Manchester Agricultural Society (instituted in 1767) and the Liverpool Agricultural Society (instituted in 1830) merged to form the Manchester and Liverpool Agricultural Society, instituted in 1847. This then merged with the North Lancashire Agricultural Society (also instituted in 1847) to form the Royal Manchester, Liverpool and North Lancashire Agricultural Society, instituted in 1874. Finally, this became the Royal Lancashire Agricultural Society in 1893.

The aim of the RLAS was stated as 'the encouragement and general advancement of the science and practice of agriculture'. It fulfilled this aim through competition, demonstration and the dissemination of information; specifically, by holding shows and awarding prizes, and by publishing its journal. Its structure involved a central council with a number of committees, and it divided itself into three geographical divisions, each electing representatives to the council.

By 1925, the main committees, and their duties, were: a Finance and General Purposes Committee, to examine accounts, sign cheques and consider contracts; a Works Committee, to prepare the Show Yard for the annual show; a Catering Committee, to make arrangements for all catering in the Show Yard; a Programme and Prize List Committee, to prepare draft prize lists, plus lists of Judges and Stewards and generally to consider all matters connected with the annual show.

The importance of this structure to the family historian is that it presented countless opportunities for society members to take up positions of responsibility and thereby have their names recorded in the various committee minutes and society records.

Archived Records

The records of RLAS are kept at the Lancashire branch of The National Archives, located in Preston and provided by Lancashire County Council. This collection covers the period 1831–1988 and includes material on every aspect of the society's work. To illustrate the breadth of information available, the following is a complete list of all records along with their relevant reference numbers:

DDX 1795/1 Minutes of Council and Committees
DDX 1795/1/1 Council
DDX 1795/1/2 Finance and General Purposes Committee
DDX 1795/1/3 Show Yard Committee
DDX 1795/1/4 Works Committee
DDX 1795/1/5 Catering Committee
DDX 1795/1/6 Dairy Show Committee
DDX 1795/1/7 Horticultural Committee
DDX 1795/1/8 Judges Selection Committee
DDX 1795/1/9 Scrutiny Committee
DDX 1795/1/10 Annual General Meeting: printed agenda with annual report
DDX 1795/2 Financial records
DDX 1795/3 Secretarial files
DDX 1795/4 Show records
DDX 1795/4/1 Show catalogues
DDX 1795/4/2 Supplementary and dog show catalogues
DDX 1795/4/3 Prize schedules: livestock
DDX 1795/4/4 Prize schedules: dog show
DDX 1795/4/5 Prize schedules: miscellaneous
DDX 1795/4/6 Claims books
DDX 1795/4/7 Award books
DDX 1795/4/8 Showground plans
DDX 1795/4/9 Photographs
DDX 1795/4/10 Miscellaneous show records
DDX 1795/5 Publications
DDX 1795/5/1 Journal of the Royal Lancashire Agricultural Society
DDX 1795/5/2 Miscellaneous publications
DDX 1795/6 Newspaper cuttings

Annual Journals

Of particular use to the family historian are the bound Journals (Ref: DDX 1795/5/1) produced and published by the society each year. This collection includes copies of journals covering the period 1882 to 1955. Each annual journal is crammed with information about the society, its members and the current state of the industry, including the following:

- **Local Committee** – names and positions of the members of the local committee responsible for organising that year's show.
- **Officers of the Society** – giving names and positions.

- **Awards for Best Farm/Crops** – naming the winning farmers and describing their farms and their practices.
- **Rewards to Servants and Labourers** – details of awards to long-serving and/or exemplary agricultural labourers, nominated by their employers.
- **Show Prizes** – listings of the entries and winners in all classes at the previous year's show. In some years there were up to 500 classes. The names of the judges of the various classes are also given. Many of the journals are illustrated with photographs of the prizewinning cows and their owners.
- **In Memoriam** – obituaries of prominent members of the society.
- **List of Society Members** – at its peak the society had nearly 3,000 members. The lists include the names and addresses of the members of the society, presented in alphabetical order by surname.
- **Adverts** – as a means of generating an income, the journals carried adverts for agriculture-related businesses, up to fifty pages with one advert per page. They included the names of the proprietors and the addresses of their businesses.

Another feature of these journals is the inclusion of essays written by society members on various aspects of agriculture. The 1883 journal includes a review of the previous year's show, which was held in Liverpool. That year, a special prize was offered for the best essay on the subject of 'The Management and Working of the Liverpool Town Dairies'. The prize was awarded to Mr Frederick Stoner, whose essay provides a detailed account of the practices of the day as carried out by the city's dairymen.

County Archives – Journals of your local county agricultural society may be found at the county archives. (Author)

Chapter 12

Liverpool & District Dairy Farmers' Association

The Liverpool Cowkeepers' Association came into existence on 28 September 1865. However, as the city expanded, the association's membership also expanded and this wider catchment area was recognised in 1873, when the organisation relaunched itself as 'The City of Liverpool & District Cowkeepers' Association'. Later, in 1935, the association changed its name once more, becoming 'The Liverpool & District Dairy Farmers' Association'. Under whichever title, this organisation served its members and the people of Liverpool for over 100 years. The association's books were eventually closed on 25 April 1975 by the then secretary, Mr Thomas Hogg.

Although this district association was properly constituted, with minuted meetings and regular events, its papers were never archived in any of the expected places. However, it is possible to trace the activities of the association and its members using other sources.

Members' Handbook

Each member of the association was issued with a handbook, which contained the objects and rules of the association and also served as their certificate of membership. Illustrated is a copy of the handbook published in 1919, when the association was called 'City of Liverpool & District Cowkeepers' Association'; this copy was issued to Mr S. Metcalfe of Lower Breck Road. It is pocket-sized (3½ inches by 5 inches) with a blue outer binding. On the first page is a list of the officers of the association, which includes their names, addresses and, in some cases, their telephone numbers. A full transcript of the contents is included at Appendix C.

Membership was subject to payment of a one-off entrance fee (set at £5 when the association was launched in 1865) and of an annually reviewed subscription. Admittance to the association was also subject to the cowkeeper's herd being examined and passed fit by a veterinary surgeon appointed by the association. This was one of many inspections to which the Liverpool cowkeepers were subject.

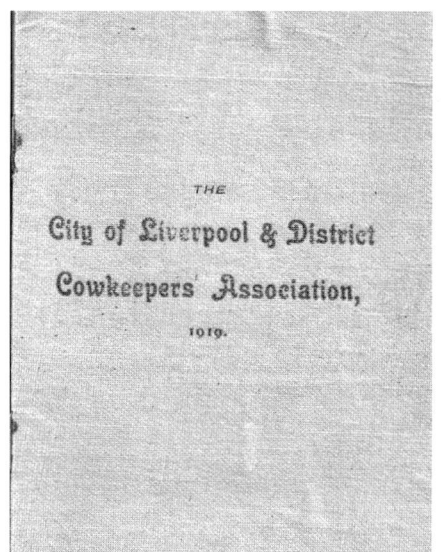 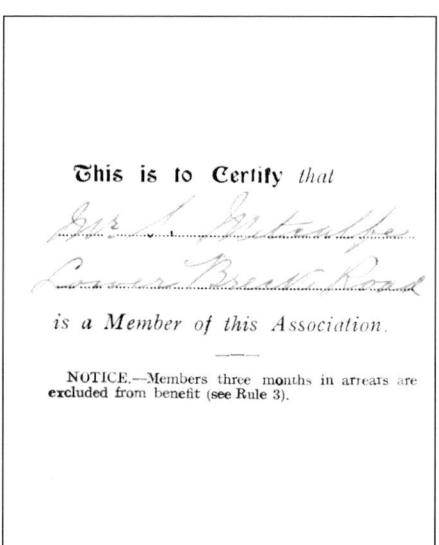

Cowkeepers' Association Rules – Many city dairymen were members of their local cowkeepers' association and had to abide by the association's rules. (Courtesy of Bill Frith)

Local Licensing

Liverpool was the first city to introduce licensing and inspection of cowkeeping premises, via the 1867 Liverpool Improvement Act. Subsequent legislation served to drive continuous improvement in the method of inspection and in the standards being practised.

The city cowkeepers were subject to two types of licensing: a licence to keep cows and a licence to sell milk. Both licences were issued subject to the premises and practices passing quite rigorous inspections, carried out four or more times per year by the officials of the Liverpool Health Committee. The licence for keeping cows applied to the shippon and that for selling milk applied to the milkhouse.

Once a licence was issued, the onus was on the holder to erect a notice stating that the premises in question were 'Licensed for the Sale of Milk' or were 'Licensed to Keep [number] Cows'. Indeed, it was in the dairyman's best interest to erect such notices in order to advertise and reassure their customers of the quality of their produce. It was common practice for the licence document to be framed and put on display in the dairy. Information contained in the document included: name and address of licensee; description and address of licensed premises; and, in the case of shippons, the maximum number of cows that could be kept there.

On 5 April 1971, cowkeeper Henry Winn of 325–327 Smithdown Road, was granted a licence, under the 1921 Liverpool Corporation Act. The licence permitted Henry to keep (up to) twenty-six cattle in the 'cowsheds' on his property until 31 December 1971, after which time he would have to apply to the town clerk to have his licence renewed.

Liverpool & District Dairy Farmers' Association

CITY OF  LIVERPOOL

No. 12

LIVERPOOL CORPORATION ACT, 1921

The LORD MAYOR, ALDERMEN, and CITIZENS of the CITY OF LIVERPOOL Do HEREBY, in pursuance of the Liverpool Corporation Act, 1921, LICENSE certain premises situate No. 325/327, Smithdown Road, Liverpool, 15.

Consisting of Cow sheds

For the keeping therein of 26 Cattle

by Henry Finn,

of 325/327, Smithdown Road,

LIVERPOOL, 15.

until the 31st December, 1971.

This Licence is not transferable to any person and is granted subject to the requirements of the said Lord Mayor, Aldermen and Citizens.

Dated this 5th day of April, 1971

Town Clerk.

IMPORTANT:— This licence must be returned for renewal one month before the date of expiry, or when a change in name or holder occurs, to:—
The Medical Officer of Health,
Health Department,
Hatton Garden, Liverpool, L3 2AN

Cowkeeping Licence – All city milkhouses and cowhouses were subject to a regime of inspection and licensing. (Courtesy of Sedbergh & District History Society)

The City Dairy: A Social and Family History

Following the introduction of the Milk and Dairies Order of 1926, the City Council issued all Liverpool cowkeepers with a varnished notice as an aid to clean milk production (Jones, 1927).

Aids to Clean Milk Production
The Milker

- *Milk only with clean, dry hands.*
- *Do not put the fingers into the milk or cans.*
- *Do not handle milk or cows if you have recently had an infectious disease.*
- *Wear a clean overall during milking.*

The Cow

- *Groom daily and let the dust settle before milking.*
- *Keep the hair at the end of the tail and on the udder clipped.*
- *Clean the udder and teats with a wet cloth just before milking.*
- *Do not feed hay during milking – it creates dust.*
- *Milk a case of Garget LAST, into a vessel not used for dairy purposes, and containing a little disinfectant. Do not milk it on the floor.*
- *Put animals which are unwell by themselves.*
- *Reject the fore milk.*

The Cowshed

- *Keep as clean as possible throughout.*
- *Empty the midden as often as possible.*
- *Use only dry, clean bedding.*
- *Keep the feeding material as far away as possible from the milking shed and milk.*
- *Admit as much fresh air as possible.*

The Milk And Utensils

- *Keep dogs, cats, chickens, flies etc. away from the milk.*
- *Covered milking pails should be used.*
- *Wash out the pails with cold water as soon as they are finished with.*
- *Then SCALD them thoroughly and leave them to dry, mouth downward, in a clean place.*
- *Cool the milk away from the cowshed and keep it cool.*
- *Clean the milking stool.*

REPORT ABNORMALITIES OF UDDER AND HEALTH.

T. Eaton Jones, F.R.C.V.S.,
Chief Veterinary Officer.
Veterinary Department,
30 Hatton Garden,
Liverpool.

Records of the numbers of such licences issued were included in the reports of the city's Medical Officer of Health, presented annually to the Health Committee.

The Liverpool & District Cowkeepers' Association worked closely with the authorities to improve conditions and practices in order to guarantee for the city a supply of the purest milk. Following the introduction of the Milk and Dairies Order of 1926, the city council issued all cowkeepers with a varnished notice as an aid to clean milk production (Jones, 1927).

Newspaper Coverage

The British Newspaper Archive (**britishnewspaperarchive.co.uk**) has a number of Liverpool-based newspapers, searchable online. Although more editions are constantly being added to this archive, the collection (as at May 2022) includes the following:

Title	Issues	Pages	Period Covered
Liverpool Albion	1,203	19,522	1828–1882
Liverpool Chronicle	58	464	1767–1768
Liverpool Daily Courier	1,798	16,770	1870–1910
Liverpool Daily Post	19,133	169,287	1855–1950
Liverpool Echo	35,887	639,988	1879–1999
Liverpool Evening Express	45,795	27,564	1874–1955
Liverpool Journal of Commerce	22,103	200,200	1861–1940
Liverpool Mail	2,487	19,934	1836–1880
Liverpool Mercantile Gazette	2,356	9.456	1822–1875
Liverpool Mercury	15,294	122,405	1811–1900
Liverpool Standard	1,759	16,996	1832–1856
Liverpool Telegraph	81	540	1836–1838
Liverpool Weekly Courier	1,639	13,182	1867–1903

As mentioned earlier, coverage of the association's annual cattle shows by local newspapers included lists of prizewinners, and as such provides a name-rich source for the family historian. By way of illustration, a selection of these lists is included at Appendix D.

The local newspapers also reported on many other aspects of the association's business, especially when there was a degree of debate, controversy or scandal involved – no surprises there, then! In the absence of official documents, these newspaper reports reflect the rise and fall of the association and, indeed, of the dairying way of life in Liverpool:

The City Dairy: A Social and Family History

'**Now Judging**' – Local cowkeepers' associations held their own annual cattle shows. (Courtesy of Roy Thwaite)

Liverpool Mercury and Liverpool Daily Post – Friday, 29 September 1865
Both papers reported the first meeting of the association. The purpose of the meeting was 'to consider the propriety of establishing an association for insurance against the loss of cows by disease or accident, and the regulation of the price of milk according to the current cost of provender, etc.'. It was reported that at that time Liverpool had 338 cowkeepers, owning 2,460 cows. Along with some basic rules of governance, it was agreed that the organisation be named 'Liverpool Cowkeepers' Association'.

Liverpool Mercury – Monday, 25 September 1882
Mr Carr opened his and Liverpool's first Auction Yard, in Breck Road, for dealing with the city trade in dairy cattle. Several of the city's leading agriculturalists and tradesmen were named as being present at the inauguration.

Liverpool Mercury – Wednesday, 3 January 1883
The association made representation to the Markets Committee of the City Council regarding various aspects of the operation of the Haymarket in the city centre. Mr John Hoggarth, the secretary of the association, submitted the written representation.

Liverpool & District Dairy Farmers' Association

Liverpool Mercury – Thursday, 27 February 1890
The chairman of the association, Mr John Verity of 42 Almond Street, wrote to the newspaper on behalf of the membership, after a Milk Dealer in the city was found guilty of watering his milk and in defence had claimed that all Liverpool's milk dealers carried out this practice. Mr Verity pointed out that there was a distinct difference between a 'Milk Dealer' who 'merely retails country milk' and a 'Cowkeeper' who sells milk from his own cows and has no reason to compromise the quality of that milk by adding water.

Liverpool Mercury – Thursday, 5 October 1899
A meeting of the association took place where it was agreed to find from amongst their membership a candidate to stand for election to the city council.

Liverpool Echo – Tuesday, 24 February 1914
Mr T. Backhouse, secretary, describes how the Liverpool & District Cowkeepers' Association were co-operating with the authorities in their efforts to prevent the spread of foot-and-mouth disease.

Liverpool Echo – Wednesday, 10 February 1915
Despite the many problems associated with trading during wartime, the district cowkeepers' association decided to 'put patriotism before profit' and announced that the price of milk would remain at 4d per quart.

Liverpool Daily Post – Thursday, 8 July 1915
The Liverpool Cowkeepers' Association announced that, due to the wartime shortage of labour, milk would be delivered only once, rather than twice, per day.

Liverpool Daily Post – Thursday, 27 January 1916
Due to the price of feeding stuffs and the scarcity of good cattle, the Liverpool & District Cowkeepers' Association gave warning of the need to increase the price of milk from 5d to 6d, per quart.

Liverpool Echo – Friday, 28 December 1917
The Food Control Committee of Liverpool Council gave notification that they had fixed the price of milk for January as follows: 3d per quart, 4d per pint, 2d half-pint and 1d per gill.

Lancashire Evening Post – Wednesday, 11 December 1935
The annual Christmas Cattle Show traditionally organised by the Liverpool & District Cowkeepers' Association, was held for the first time under the organisation's new title: the Liverpool & District Dairy Farmers' Association.

Liverpool Evening Express – Friday, 10 March 1939
The Liverpool & District Dairy Farmers' Association passed a resolution supporting the National Federation of Milk Producer-Retailers in the dispute with the Milk

Marketing Board over the payment to the board of levies and the filling in of record and return sheets.

Liverpool Echo – Friday, 21 February 1941
Liverpool's 'unique company of cowkeepers' were alarmed over the rationing of feeding stuffs and were sending a deputation to the Food Ministry Office at Hutton, near Preston.

Liverpool Daily Post – Tuesday, 4 November 1941
Liverpool's dairymen wrestled with the 5 per cent cut in milk supplies, which had just been introduced.

Liverpool Echo – Thursday, 4 February 1943
The Dairy Farmers' Association agreed to approve the new rationalisation scheme for milk deliveries, providing that the trading interests of producer-retailer were safeguarded after the war.

Liverpool Echo – Friday, 15 November 1968
Milkman and former cowkeeper and farmer, Mr Miles Capstick of Sandy Lane Farm, Fazakerley, retired after forty-seven years in business.

Liverpool Echo – Friday, 22 November 1968
Milkman John Davies retired and left the dairy at 88 Ash Grove, Wavertree, which his father had bought in 1885.

Liverpool Daily Post – Friday, 22 January 1971
One of the city's oldest dairy firms, Thwaite's of Edge Hill, closed for business in the face of extensive redevelopment planned for the area.

Liverpool Echo – Wednesday, 1 March 1972
After 120 years in existence, members of the Liverpool Dairy Farmers' Association met to discuss winding-up the organisation.

Liverpool Echo – Tuesday, 28 January 1975
Joe Capstick of 4 Marlborough Road, Tuebrook, was now the last of the city's cowkeepers. His teenage son, Maurice, expressed his love of the job and his desire to continue with the family business.

This final article pre-empted the end of cowkeeping in the city. Later that year, the Capstick family moved their cows out of their city dairy and relocated their business to Brantbeck Farm, near Lancaster. The family's original cine footage of the move – called '*Leaving of the Cows*' – can now be viewed for free on the website of the British Film Institute (**bfi.org.uk/search?q=leaving-of-the-cows-1975**).

Chapter 13

A Dairy Dynasty

The migration of rural farmers to the cities was not a one-off event, limited to a single family. As word spread through the village that city cowkeeping was proving to be a profitable business, other families were persuaded to try their luck. And so, a chain migration occurred between a specific rural area and a specific city. One example of such a migration is that which took place between the rural town of Sedbergh (and its surrounding countryside) and the city of Liverpool.

From this Sedbergh–Liverpool connection emerged a succession of prominent city dairymen, initially drawn from four Sedbergh families: Nelson, Greenwood, Harper and Mason.

- **James Nelson** (1812–1895) married Margaret Sedgwick (1813–1885) in Dent, in 1834. They lived at Greenwood Haw, where James farmed 26 acres. They went on to have fourteen children. The Nelson cowkeeping dynasty in Liverpool is descended from two of these fourteen children: George and Agnes. George remained in the Sedbergh area, but a number of his children relocated to Liverpool. Whereas, his younger sister, Agnes, undertook that relocation herself and her children were born in the city.
- **Fawcett Greenwood** (1810–1889) married Ann Whitfield (1813–1866) in Dent, in 1834. Of their nine children, it was two of their daughters, Jane and Dorothy, who went on to marry and move with their respective families to Liverpool and became cowkeepers.
- **Richard Harper** (1815–1889) married Elizabeth Capstick (1819–1884) in Garsdale, in 1838. They had eleven children and three of these, John, Rowland and Rosamond, relocated to Liverpool to become cowkeepers.
- **Thomas Mason** (1825–1901) married Jane Lambert (1831–1917) in Sedbergh, in 1850. Three of their eight children, Lawrence, Agnes and Sarah Jane, became Liverpool cowkeepers.

The history of these four families is illustrated below in the form of a number of timelines. As well as demonstrating the chain migration that is so typical of the first generation of dairymen, these timelines also illustrate the tendency of the second-generation to marry within the city dairy community. In this way, matrimonial links expanded the dynasty, bringing many other dairying family names into the frame, including Dinsdale, Tennant, Metcalfe, Chapman, Moore, Fawcett, Thwaite and Raw.

The Nelson-Greenwood-Harper-Mason Dairy Dynasty

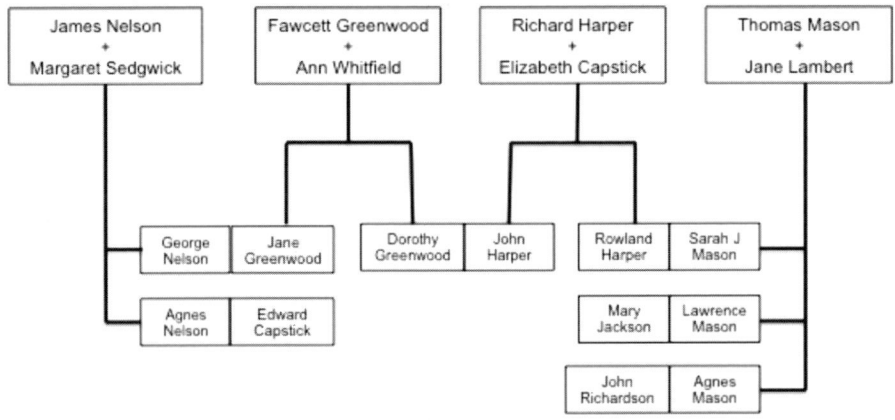

Timeline 1

The Family of George Nelson (1841–1894) and Jane Greenwood (1850–1926)

George and Jane married in June 1868, in Dent. They had ten children, all born in and around Sedbergh. Although George and Jane never left the Sedbergh area, five of their children moved to Liverpool to keep cows: James, Fawcett Greenwood, Ann, Mary Jane and Elizabeth Alice.

Year	Source	Event
1888	England and Wales Marriage Index	Marriage of **James Nelson** to **Agnes Dinsdale,** in Sedbergh.
1894	England and Wales Death Index	Death of George Nelson.
1900	England and Wales Marriage Index	**Fawcett Greenwood Nelson** marries **Frances Tennant** in Liverpool.
1900	Liverpool, England Electoral Register	**William Metcalfe** living at 4–6 Laith Street, described as House and Shippon.
1901	Gore's Directory of Liverpool	**Fawcett Nelson.** Cowkeeper. 1 Newcombe Street.
1901	England and Wales Census	31 Broadgreen Road, Liverpool. **James Nelson** (32) – Cowkeeper. Agnes (34) – wife. Sedbergh-born children: Jane (11), Mary Elgin (9), Margaret Agnes. (6) and George J. (4). Also, James's sister, **Elizabeth Nelson** (17) – domestic servant.

A Dairy Dynasty

Year	Source	Event
1901	England and Wales Census	1 Newcombe Street, Liverpool. **Fawcett Greenwood Nelson** (30) – Cowkeeper. Frances (23) – wife. Edward Roberts (19) – Cowman. Margaret Tenant (14) – Domestic Servant.
1901	England and Wales Census	39 Lower Breck Road, Liverpool. **Mary J. Nelson** working as a Domestic Servant for Sedbergh-born Cowkeeper, John J. Close.
1901	England and Wales Census	**William Metcalfe** working for his brother-in-law, Richard McLeod, as a Cowkeeper at 6 Laith Street, Liverpool.
1904	England and Wales Marriage Index	**Ann Nelson** marries **William Metcalfe** in Liverpool.
1904	England and Wales Birth Index	James and Agnes's son, **William Dinsdale Nelson**, born in Sedbergh.
1906	England and Wales Marriage Index	**Mary Jane Nelson** marries **James Chapman** in Liverpool.
1906	England and Wales Marriage Index	**Elizabeth Alice Nelson** marries Sedbergh-born **Richard Fawcett** [son of Cowkeeper William Fawcett and Margaret Sedgwick of 23–25 Rothwell Street] in Liverpool.
1911	England and Wales Census	**James Nelson** and family had returned to Sedbergh and were living at Hobson's Farm, Cowgill, Dent, Sedbergh.
1911	England and Wales Census	40 Coronation Road, Liverpool. **Fawcett Greenwood Nelson** (33) – Cowkeeper. Frances (33) – wife. George Nelson (9) – son. John E. Molyneux (22) – Cowman.
1911	England and Wales Census	2 Vicar Road, Liverpool. **William Metcalfe** (34) – Cowkeeper. Ann (34) – wife. Liverpool-born Children: Jane (5), George W. (4), Elizabeth (2) and Annie (1). Also: Lydia Winn (20) Dairymaid, Birkenhead, and Eustace W. Mawer – Cowman, Rawdon, Yorks.
1911	England and Wales Census	25 Warbreck Moor, Liverpool. **James Chapman** (30) – Cowkeeper and Dairyman. Mary Jane (29) – wife. Liverpool-born children: Margaret (3) and George Nelson (2).
1911	England and Wales Census	8 Cowl Street, Liverpool. **Richard Fawcett** (28) – Cowkeeper. Elizabeth (27) – wife. Liverpool-born children: William (3), Margaret (2) and George (4 months).

141

The City Dairy: A Social and Family History

Year	Source	Event
1914	Liverpool Electoral Register	**Fawcett G. Nelson**. 40 Coronation Road. Shippon.
1918	Gore's Directory of Liverpool	**Fawcett Greenwood Nelson**. Dairyman. 40 Coronation Road.
1918	England and Wales National Probate Calendar	Death of **Fawcett Greenwood Nelson**. 40 Coronation Road. Cowkeeper and Dairyman. To James Wilson and Richard Tennant, Cowkeepers and Dairymen.
1918	*Liverpool Echo* 7 May	**Fawcett Greenwood Nelson** late of 40 Coronation Road, Great Crosby, Cowkeeper and Dairyman, deceased – All Creditors… to furnish forthwith particulars in writing to H.J. Sharman, Solicitor, 60 Castle Street, Liverpool.
1918	Gore's Directory of Liverpool	**William Metcalfe**. Dairyman. 2 Vicar Road.
1918	Gore's Directory of Liverpool	**Richard Fawcett**. Dairyman. 6–8 Cowl Street.
1925	Liverpool Electoral Register	6–8 Cowl Street. **Richard Fawcett** and **Elizabeth Alice Fawcett**.
1926	Kelly's (Gore's) Directory of Liverpool	**William Metcalfe**. Dairyman. 142 St Domingo Vale and 2 Vicar Road.
1926	Kelly's (Gore's) Directory of Liverpool	**Richard Fawcett**. Dairyman. 6–8 Cowl Street.
1926	Kelly's (Gore's) Directory of Liverpool	**Mrs Elizabeth Fawcett**. Dairyman. 2 Godfrey Street.
1928	England and Wales Marriage Index	**William Dinsdale Nelson** marries **Phyllis Harper** [daughter of Richard Harper and Agnes Thwaite] in Sedbergh.
1929	England and Wales National Probate Calendar	Death of **Ann Metcalfe** [née Nelson]. Probate to William Metcalfe, Dairyman, 2 Vicar Road.
1929	England and Wales Death Index	Death of **James Chapman** of 12 Warbreck Moor, Liverpool.
1930	England and Wales National Probate Calendar	Death of **Elizabeth Alice Fawcett** of 8 Cowl Street. Probate to **Richard Fawcett**, Cowkeeper.

A Dairy Dynasty

Year	Source	Event
1933	England and Wales Marriage Index	**Annie Metcalfe** [daughter of William Metcalfe] marries **Thomas Andrew Harper**, in Liverpool.
1934	England and Wales National Probate Calendar	Death of **George William Metcalfe** of 2 Vicar Road, 24 December 1933. Probate to [father] **William Metcalfe**, Cowkeeper.
1938	Kelly's Directory of Liverpool	**Wm. Dinsdale Nelson**. Dairyman. 50 Sutton Street.
1938	Kelly's Directory of Liverpool	**Richard Fawcett**. Dairyman. 6–8 Cowl Street.
1938	Kelly's Directory of Liverpool	**Wm. Metcalfe**. Dairyman. 142 St Domingo Vale.
1939	Liverpool Electoral Register	**William Metcalfe**, 142 St Domingo Vale.
1939	England and Wales Register	50 Brainerd Street. **William D. Nelson** – Dairy Farmer. Phyllis Nelson – Domestic and Shop duties.
1939	England and Wales Register	2 Vicar Road. **Thomas A. Harper** – Dairy Farmer. **Annie Harper** and David W. Harper [b. 9 Jan. 1938]
1942	England and Wales National Probate Calendar	Death of **William Metcalfe** of 142 St Domingo Vale, Liverpool. Probate to Richard Fawcett, Cowkeeper, and Robert Allen, Farmer.
1955	Kelly's Directory of Liverpool	**Richard Fawcett**. Dairyman. 8 Attwood Street.
1955	Kelly's Directory of Liverpool	**Thomas Andrew Harper**. Dairyman. 2 Vicar Road.
1962	West Yorkshire Electoral Register	**William Dinsdale Nelson** and Phyllis Nelson living at Beecroft Hall, Horton-in-Ribblesdale.
1963	England and Wales National Probate Calendar	Death of **Richard Fawcett** of 21 Stockbridge Street, Liverpool. Probate to William Fawcett, Storekeeper and William Richard Sedgwick, Dairyman.
1964	Kelly's Directory of Liverpool	**Thomas Andrew Harper**. Dairyman. 2 Vicar Road.
1965	England and Wales National Probate Calendar	Death of **Annie Harper** [née Metcalfe] of 2 Vicar Road. Probate to **Thomas Andrew Harper**, Dairyman.
1968	England and Wales Death Index	Death of **Mary Jane Metcalfe** [née Nelson], Liverpool.

Year	Source	Event
1974	Kelly's Directory of Liverpool	**Thos. Andrew Harper**. Dairies. 2 Vicar Road.
1986	England and Wales National Probate Calendar	Death of **Thomas Andrew Harper**. 2 Vicar Road.

Timeline 2

The Family of Edward Capstick (1854–1933) and Agnes Nelson (1853–1929)

Edward Capstick had Liverpool cowkeeping in his blood. He was the son of James Capstick and Mary Dent. At the time of their marriage, Mary was the widow of Thomas Harper, who had kept cows at 18 Roscoe Street. James and Mary continued the business at Roscoe Street – where Edward was born, in 1854 – before returning to their common birthplace, Garsdale.

Edward and Agnes married in October 1875, in Garsdale. They had seven children: James (b. 1876, Sedbergh); Mary (b. 1878, Sedbergh); Margaret (b. 1880, Liverpool); Rose (b. 1887, Gargrave); Edward (b. 1890, Liverpool); James (b. 1892, Liverpool); and Alice (b. 1893, Liverpool).

It is likely that they moved to Liverpool sometime between 1878 (when their daughter, Mary, was born in Sedbergh) and 1880 (when their daughter, Margaret, was born in Liverpool).

Year	Source	Event
1881	England and Wales Census	38 Coleridge Street, Liverpool. **Edward Capstick** (26) – Cowkeeper. Agnes (27) – wife. Children: James (4), Mary (2) and Margaret (1). Also Eliza Johnson (17), Domestic Servant, and John E. Crosse, Cowman.
1881	*Liverpool Mercury* 28 July	WANTED – a young man. Age 18 or 20. Must be a good milker. Apply **Edward Capstick**, Cowkeeper, 38 Coleridge Street.
1882	*Liverpool Mercury* 16 December	Liverpool Cowkeepers' Association, first annual show. Committee member: **Edward Capstick**
1883	*Liverpool Mercury* 19 December	Liverpool Cowkeepers' Association second annual show. 1st prize for Best Fat Cow exceeding 32 scores: **Edward Capstick**, Coleridge Street.
1884	*Liverpool Mercury* 3 January	**Edward Capstick** of 38 Coleridge Street fined 20s and costs for selling adulterated milk.

A Dairy Dynasty

Year	Source	Event
1885	Liverpool Electoral Register	**Edward Capstick**. 38 Coleridge Street. House and Shippon.
1891	England and Wales Census	1 Neilson Road, Liverpool. **Edward Capstick** (36) – Cowkeeper. Agnes (36) – wife. Children: James (14), Mary (12), Maggie (10), Rose (4) and Edward (10 months). Also, Josh Bingley (19), Cowman, and visitor John Harper (41).
1894	Kelly's Directory of Liverpool	**Edwd. Capstick.** Cowkeeper. 20 Hesketh Street.
1900	Gore's Directory of Liverpool	**Edward Capstick**. Cowkeeper. 27 Aigburth Road.
1901	England and Wales Census	27 Aigburth Road, Valley Fields Farm and Dairy, Liverpool. **Edward Capstick** (46) – Farmer. Agnes (47) – wife. Children: Mary (22), Margaret (20), Rose (14), Edward (11), James (9) and Alice (8).
1908	Liverpool Church of England Marriages and Banns. St Anne's, Aigburth.	Marriage of Margaret Capstick of Valley Field, Aigburth (Father: Edward Capstick, Farmer) to **John Creighton Dugdale** Dairyman, of 16 Bridge Road, Mossley Hill (Father: Joshua Dugdale, Farmer). [Joshua Dugdale had been a Cowkeeper at Marlborough Road, Liverpool.]
1911	England and Wales Census	1 Great George's Road, Waterloo, Liverpool. **John Creighton Dugdale** (30) – Cowkeeper. Margaret (30) – wife. Also, Mary Rowlands (32), widow, and John Nelson (19), Cowkeeper and Float Driver.
1911	England and Wales Census	42 Handfield Road, Waterloo, Liverpool. **Agnes Capstick** (58) – Cowkeeper. Children: Rose (24), Dairy Work, Edward (20), Working in Shippon, and James (19), Working in Shippon. Also, grandson, Joseph Creighton Dugdale (3). [Edward was visiting daughter, Mary, in Yorkshire.]
1918	Gore's Directory of Liverpool	**Edward Capstick**. Cowkeeper. 117–119 Handel Street.
1926	Kelly's (Gore's) Directory of Liverpool	**Edward Capstick**, Dairyman, 117–119 Handel Street.
1929	UK and Ireland Find A Grave Index	Death of **Agnes Capstick**. 21 November. Buried at St John the Baptist Churchyard, Garsdale

Year	Source	Event
1933	Kelly's Directory of Liverpool	**Edward Capstick**. Cowkeeper. 92 Webster Road.
1933	UK and Ireland Find A Grave Index	Death of **Edward Capstick**. 5 January. Buried at St John the Baptist Churchyard, Garsdale

Timeline 3

The Family of John Harper (1838–1919) and Dorothy Greenwood (1834–1884)

John and Dorothy had five children, all born in or around Sedbergh: Richard, Elizabeth, Fawcett, Annie and Mary. John farmed at Sunny Side, Frostrow, and did not relocate his family to Liverpool until after his wife's death, in 1884.

Year	Source	Event
1886	Lancashire BMD **lancashirebmd.org.uk**	Widower **John Harper** married widow Alice Haresnape [née Metcalfe] at West Derby Registry Office, Liverpool.
1887	England and Wales Marriage Index	Marriage of **Richard Harper** to **Agnes Thwaite**, in Sedbergh
1888	England and Wales Birth Index	Birth of **Richard and Agnes Harper**'s first child, Dorothy Harper, in Liverpool.
1891	England and Wales Census	32 Withers Street, Liverpool. Widower **John Harper** (53) – Cowkeeper. Sedbergh-born children: Elizabeth (26), Fawcett (22) – Cowkeeper's Labourer, Ann (19) and Mary (14). Also, David Burrow (17) – Cowkeeper's Labourer.
1891	England and Wales Census	53 Annerley Street, Liverpool. **Richard Harper** (28) – Cowkeeper. Agnes (24) – wife. Liverpool-born daughters: Dora (3) and Rose M. (1). Also, visitor John Thwaite, farmer from Sedbergh.
1894	Kelly's Directory of Liverpool	**Richard Harper**. Cowkeeper. 53 Annerley Street.
1894	Kelly's Directory of Liverpool	**John Harper**. Cowkeeper. 32 Withers Street.
1894	Liverpool Marriages and Banns – St James Church. August 21.	**Fawcett Harper** (25), Cowkeeper of 32 Withers Street (father: John Harper, Cowkeeper) to **Isabella Eleanor Raw**, spinster of 20 Town Row (father: Robert Raw, Cowkeeper).

A Dairy Dynasty

Year	Source	Event
1898	England and Wales Birth Index	**Richard and Agnes Harper** still in Liverpool at the time of the birth of their daughter, Agnes.
1900	*The Liverpool Cowkeepers* by Patsy Mellor (2012)	**Richard and Agnes Harper** returned to farm near Sedbergh.
1901	England and Wales Census	**John Harper** (62) and Alice Harper (60) had returned to Sedbergh to farm at Gill Farm.
1901	England Select Births and Christenings 1538–1975	Baptism of **John Fawcett Harper**, son of John and Isabella Eleanor Harper, at Princess Avenue Methodist Chapel, Liverpool.
1901	England and Wales Census	104 Berkley Street, Liverpool. **Fawcett Harper** (32) – Cowkeeper. Isabella (28) – wife. Children: Dora E. (5), Bessie G. (4) and **John F.** (2 months). Also, Robert Lunt (19) – Cowman from Liverpool, and Joseph Greenwood (18) – Cowman from Sedbergh.
1911	England and Wales Census	52 Chestnut Grove, Liverpool. **Fawcett Harper** (40) – Dairy Farmer. Isabella E. (38) – wife, assisting in business. Children: Dora Eleanor (15), Bessie Gladys (14), **John Fawcett** (10) and Elizabeth Isabella (5).
1919	England and Wales Death Index	Death of **John Harper**, in Sedbergh.
1926	Kelly's (Gore's) Directory of Liverpool	**Fawcett Harper**, Dairyman, 52 Chestnut Grove.
1932	England and Wales Marriage Index	Marriage of **John Fawcett Harper** to Ethel M. Elwell, in Liverpool.
1934	Liverpool Electoral Register	52 Chestnut Grove. **Fawcett and Isabella Harper** [abode given as Dye House farm, Tarbock]. Also, John and Ethel Harper.
1938	Kelly's Directory of Liverpool	**John Fawcett Harper**. Cowkeeper. 52 Chestnut Grove.
1944	England and Wales National Probate Calendar	**Fawcett Harper** of West View, Castletown, IOM. Died 1 June. Probate to **John Fawcett Harper** (agricultural worker), Simon Thwaite Harper (farmer and auctioneer) and Frederick Handley Raw (farmer).
1965	Liverpool Electoral Register	15 Rose Brae. **John Fawcett Harper**, Ethel Harper, John Elwell Fawcett Harper and Patricia Ann Harper.

Marriage of Fawcett Harper, 1894 – Marriage certificates recording occupations as *Cowkeeper*, illustrate the trend of marriages between cowkeeping families. (Author)

Timeline 4

The Family of Rowland Harper (1858–1924) and Sarah J. Mason (1867–1937)

Rowland and Sarah were married in 1887, in Sedbergh. Their first seven children were all born in Liverpool between 1891 and 1906. They had returned to Sedbergh by the time their eighth child was born.

Year	Source	Event
1891	England and Wales Census	61a High Street, Wavertree, Liverpool. **Rowland Harper** (22) – Farmer. Sarah J. Harper – wife. Daughter: Elizabeth (1 month). Jane Mason (60) – mother-in-law. Farm Servants: Richard Wilson (20) of Meathop and Mary Woof (22) of Witherslack.
1894	Kelly's Directory of Liverpool	**Rowland Harper**. Cowkeeper. 61a High Street.
1899	*Liverpool Mercury* 14 December	Liverpool and District Cowkeepers' Association Annual Show. First Prize for best Fat Cow not exceeding 13cwt and second prize for best Fat Cow 14cwt and upwards – **Rowland Harper**, 52 Chestnut Close.
1899	Journal of the Royal Lancashire Agricultural Society – 1900, pp. 28–29	Annual Show held at Liverpool. First prize for Best Kept Shippon, Milk house, and Shop or Dairy situated within the borough of Liverpool or Bootle – **Rowland Harper**, Chestnut Grove, Wavertree.
1899	England and Wales Birth Index	Birth of son, **Edward Harper**, in Liverpool.

A Dairy Dynasty

Year	Source	Event
1901	England and Wales Census	52 Chestnut Grove, Wavertree, Liverpool. **Rowland Harper** (42) – Cowkeeper. Sarah J. Harper (34) – wife. Children: Elizabeth (10), Richard (8), Thomas (5) and **Edward Harper** (1). Thomas Mason (85) father-in-law and retired farmer. Dairy Hands: George Ellis (22) of Oxenholme, Sam Coupland (19) of Witherslack and James Chesters (17) of Cheshire. Domestic Servants: Jane Richardson (18) of Sedbergh and Betsy Handley (25) of Sedbergh.
1906	England and Wales Birth Index	**Rowland and Sarah Harper** were still in Liverpool at the time of the birth of their daughter, Agnes.
1909	England and Wales Birth Index	The family had moved back to Sedbergh by the time their daughter, Rose, was born [farming at Dove Cote Gill, Dowbiggin].
1924	England and Wales Marriage Index	**Edward Harper** marries Doris Stockdale in Sedbergh.
1932	England and Wales Birth Index	Birth of **Joan Harper** in Sedbergh.
1935	Interview with Joan Fenney, daughter of Edward and Doris Harper, in *Urban Cowboys* by Duncan Scott (2010)	**Edward and Doris Harper** move to Liverpool and take over a purpose-built dairy ['Bower Bank'] on the corner of Rose Lane and Rose Brae.
1939	England and Wales Register	'Bower Bank', Rose Lane, Liverpool. **Edmund Harper** (b. 22 April 1899), Dairy Farmer (Heavy Lifting). Doris Harper (b. 19 April 1898), Unpaid Domestic Duties. Margaret C. Harper (b. 5 February 1925), at school. Thomas R. Harper (b. 24 March 1928), at school. [One other record still officially closed.] Also, Margaret Herd (b. 26 April 1911), Dairy Maid.
1954	Lancashire BMD **lancashirebmd.org.uk**	Marriage of **Joan Harper** and James R. Fenney. All Hallows Church, Allerton, Liverpool.
1964	Kelly's Directory of Liverpool	**Edward Harper**. Dairy. Rose Lane.

149

Year	Source	Event
1974	Kelly's Directory of Liverpool	**Edward Harper**. Dairy. Rose Lane.
1986	England and Wales Death Index	Death of **Edward Harper** in Liverpool.

Timeline 5

The Family of Lawrence Mason (1854–1934) and Mary Jackson (1856–1938)

Lawrence and Mary were married in Sedbergh in 1875 and had four children, all born in Sedbergh between 1878 and 1881. They moved to Liverpool sometime between 1891 and 1895. Two of their sons, Thomas James Mason and Richard Jackson Mason, also became cowkeepers.

Year	Source	Event
1895	Kelly's Directory of Lancashire	**Lawrence Mason**. Dairyman. 60 Chapel Road, Garston.
1899	*Liverpool Mercury* 14 December	Liverpool Cowkeepers' Association Annual Show. First prize for best fat cow not exceeding 14cwt – **L. Mason**, Chapel Road, Garston.
1900	Kelly's Directory of Liverpool	**Lawrence Mason**. Dairyman. 60 Chapel Road, Garston.
1901	England and Wales Census	60 Chapel Road, Garston, Liverpool. **Lawrence Mason** (46) – Cowkeeper. Mary Nelson (44) – wife. Children: **Thomas James** (23), **Richard Jackson** (16) and Charles (12). Also, Domestic Servant, Jane E. Bland (22), from Kentmere and visitor, Sarah A. Levitt (24) from Leeds.
1901	England and Wales Marriage Index	Marriage of **Thomas James Mason** to **Sarah Ann Levitt**.
1904	Royal Lancashire Agricultural Society Annual Journal – list of members	**Lawrence Mason** – 60 Chapel Road, Garston, Liverpool [continued until 1918].

A Dairy Dynasty

Year	Source	Event
1906	England and Wales Marriage Index	Marriage of **Richard Jackson Mason** to Agnes Millakin, in Liverpool.
1911	England and Wales Census	60 Chapel Road, Garston, Liverpool. **Lawrence Mason** (56) – Cowkeeper. Mary Mason (54) – wife, assisting in business. Son, Charles (22) and grandson Lawrence (4). Also, Domestic Servants: Ebeline Ellard (27) and Elsie Ellard (16).
1911	England and Wales Census	2 McBride Street, Garston, Liverpool. **Thomas James Mason** (33) – Farmer and Cowkeeper. Sarah Ann (34) – wife. Daughter: Olive (7). Also, Housemaid, Mary Jane Cragg (24).
1911	England and Wales Census	19 Gladstone Road, Garston, Liverpool. **Jackson Mason** (26) – Dairyman Worker. Mary Agnes Mason (29). Children: Vera (1) and Charlie (3 months), both born in Garston.
1913	England and Wales Marriage Index	Following the death of his first wife, in 1912, **Richard Jackson Mason** married Agnes Goss, in Liverpool.
1920	Liverpool Electoral Register	**Thomas James Mason, Sarah Ann Mason** and Richard Beresford Burrows. Holly Cottage, 10 Woolton Road, Garston.
1926	Kelly's (Gore's) Directory of Liverpool	**Richard Jackson Mason**, Dairyman, 60 Chapel Road, Garston.
1926	Kelly's (Gore's) Directory of Liverpool	**Mrs Sarah Ann Mason**, Dairyman, 10 Woolton Road, Garston.
1933	England and Wales National Probate Calendar	**Richard Jackson Mason** of 60 Chapel Road, Garston. Probate to his widow, Agnes Mason.
1934	England and Wales National Probate Calendar	**Lawrence Mason** of 'Highlands', Pex Hill, Cronton. Died 6 April. Probate to John Husband (Solicitor) and James Gore (Retired Farmer).
1938	Kelly's Directory of Liverpool	**Mrs Agnes Mason**. Dairyman. 60 Chapel Road, Garston.
1939	England and Wales Register	60 Chapel Road, Garston. **Agnes Mason** – Dairy Farmer. Children: Thomas Mason, Ada Mason, Vera Mason and Roger Mason.

'**Cumberland Dairy**' – Thomas James Mason, Cowkeeper and Farmer, was recorded in the 1911 census of Liverpool, living at 2 McBride Street, Garston. (Courtesy of Garston Historical Society)

Timeline 6

The Family of John Richardson (1854–1916) and Agnes Mason (1856–1910)

John and Agnes were married in Sedbergh, in 1881. They had five daughters, all born in Sedbergh between 1883 and 1891: Jane, Agnes, Margaret, Sarah and Isabel. The family were in Liverpool by 1900.

Year	Source	Event
1900	Gore's Directory of Liverpool	**Jn. Richardson**. Cowkeeper. 3 Granville Road, Garston.
1901	England and Wales Census	3 Granville Road, Garston, Liverpool. **John Richardson** (46) – Cowkeeper (own account at home). Agnes (44) – wife. Children: Maggie (16), Sarah A. (13), and Isabella (9).
1901	England and Wales Census	52 Chestnut Grove, Wavertree, Liverpool. **Jane Richardson** (18) working for Rowland Harper, Cowkeeper.

A Dairy Dynasty

Year	Source	Event
1905	Kelly's Directory of Liverpool	**John Richardson.** Cowkeeper. 3 Granville Road, Garston.
1910	England and Wales Death Index	Death of **Agnes Richardson**, in Liverpool.
1911	England and Wales Census	64 Chapel Road, Garston, Liverpool. **John Richardson** (57) widower – Cowkeeper. Daughters: Agnes (27), Margaret (26), Sarah (23) and Isabel (19).
1916	England and Wales National Probate Calendar	Death of **John Richardson**, Cowkeeper, of 64 Chapel Road, Garston, on 3 January. Probate to Lawrence Mason, Farmer.
1926	Kelly's (Gore's) Directory of Liverpool	**Miss Margaret Richardson**, Dairyman, 64 Chapel Road, Garston.

Postscript

Fieldwork: Finding Your Ancestral City Dairy

Once armed with the street address of your ancestral dairy, you can begin tracking down its location. With the changes in the urban landscape that have taken place over the past 100 years, perhaps the property no longer exists. However, it might still be possible to find its original location using either Godfrey's Old Ordnance Survey maps, or the National Library of Scotland's Side-by-Side Geographical Reference Map Viewer, or TheGenealogist's Map Explorer.

If you are fortunate to find that the building in question is still standing, then you can make use of another digital tool to see what it looks like today. The wonder that is *Google Street View* enables you to do this from the comfort of your armchair. However, the view from your armchair is no substitute for getting out there and seeing it for yourself.

But, prepare yourself. For what was once a thriving business property, with all the sights, sounds and smells of a working dairy, is not so any more. It might now be in poor condition or, alternatively, it may have been modernised – altered or extended beyond recognition. But, if you look closely, the clues may be still there.

That end-terraced property has an alleyway down the side, which leads to a larger than normal yard, still surfaced with stone setts – large enough to contain half-a-dozen cows? Or, that property next door that is today a warehouse, a tradesman's workshop or even the local *Kwik-Fit* garage – it's just the right shape and size to have been a shippon, with a herd of twenty or more cows. If you look closely, that gable-end wall has a ghost sign with the word 'COWKEEPER', barely discernible. Or, what about that rather ornate mosaic in the doorway threshold, spelling out the word 'DAIRY' in blue and white tiles? And those carved heads with horns – they definitely look more bovine than gargoyle!

Someone comes out of the house – an elderly gentleman. He notices you studying the building. 'Can I help you?' he asks. You apologise for any inconvenience but explain that you are tracing your family history and believe this might be an old dairy. 'It certainly is,' he replies. 'I used to work here when I was a lad. Would you like to come in and I'll tell you all about it?'

Glossary

Adulteration – usually, adding water to milk to increase the quantity (and, thereby, the profits) but also included such practices as adding chalk or some other substance to give the impression of freshness.

Baulks or *Baux* – a loft for storing hay, traditionally located above the cattle stalls.

Brewery Grain or Brewer's Grain – in the brewing process, grain (usually, barley) is soaked in water until it germinates and is then dried. This 'malted' grain is then milled and steeped in hot water to transform starch into sugar. Whilst the resulting sugar-rich liquid is used to make beer, the residual product is brewery grain – a concentrate of proteins and fibre that is suitable for animal feed.

Boose or bus – cow stall.

Boskin – a stone or wooden panel separating the cow stalls.

Cattleman – one who works with or deals with cattle.

Chain Migration – a process by which migrants from a particular location (e.g. a rural parish) follow others from that location to a particular destination (e.g. a city).

Churn (noun) – a machine for making butter or a large metal container for milk.

Churn (verb) – to produce butter from milk by shaking or other vigorous agitation.

Consumption – see *Tuberculosis*.

Cowhouse (Shippon) – a building in which cows are kept.

Cowkeeperess – female Cowkeeper or the wife of a Cowkeeper.

Cowman – one who tends cows, usually, the employee of a Cowkeeper.

Dairy – specifically, the room in which milk, cheese and butter is prepared and stored, or, more generally, the premises on which milk is produced and/or sold.

Dairying – the business of producing, storing and distributing milk and its products.

Dairyman – one who owns/works in a dairy and sells milk.

Delivery can – a hand-held metal can in which milk was carried and delivered to the doorstep, where it was left for collection later.

Drover – one who drives/herds cattle, usually to market.

Flying Herd – a city-based herd of cattle maintained by buying cows in full lactation and then selling them on once milk production falls (usually below 3 gallons per day).

Foddergang – a passageway connecting the hay store to the cattle stalls.

Fore Milk – the first milk drawn from a cow during milking.

Forkinghole – a hole in the shippon wall, usually high up and located next to the hayloft (or mew), through which hay could be forked into the shippon.

Garget – inflammation of the udder.

Geld – without calf.

Groop – a stone-lined gutter running along the rear of the stalls, designed to collect the muck.

Husbandry (animal) – the care, cultivation and breeding of animals.

Kit – a 7–14-gallon metal can used for transporting milk.

Kitting – the action of serving milk from the kit, often using measured ladles.

Lactation – the production of milk by the cow.

Mangel – short for 'mangold', a variety of beet grown as a feed for cattle.

Manure Pit – a covered hole in the yard in which cow/horse muck was temporarily stored before disposal.

Mew – a room used for storing hay.

Midden – a brick or wooden bay, usually in the corner of a yard, in which cow/horse muck was stored before disposal; alternatively, a covered pit in the floor of the yard.

Milk Can – a metal container (usually with a lid) used for carrying or transporting milk or cream.

Milk Marketing Board – established in 1933 to control milk production and distribution in the UK. It guaranteed producers a minimum price for their milk.

Milk Purveyor – one who deals in milk.

Milk Shop – a premises selling milk not produced on site, usually *Railway Milk*.

Milker – a cow that is producing milk. Often used to describe the productivity of the cow, viz. a 'good milker' is a cow that produces plenty of milk.

Milking Stool – a short, three-legged stool, sat on when milking cows. Known in Yorkshire as a 'coppy'.

Milkhouse – a property in which the family lived and from where they sold milk; usually associated with the keeping of cows on the same, or an adjacent, property.

Molasses – thick, dark brown juice obtained from raw sugar during the refining process (often added to cattle fodder to 'sweeten' it).

Muck Crome – three-pronged rake for spreading or lifting cow muck.

Muck Merchant – one who buys/collects muck from the cowkeepers' premises, transports it (usually via horse and cart) to the countryside for resale to farmers as a fertiliser.

Muck Rake – see *Muck Crome*.

Glossary

Muckhole – a hole in the shippon wall, usually low down and at the end of the gutter, through which muck could be shovelled out of the shippon.

Mucking Out – clearing the shippon or yard of all cow muck using a brush, shovel and barrow; usually transferring it to the on-site midden for temporary storage.

Oilseed Cake – a protein-rich animal feed manufactured from the meal that remains once vegetable oil has been extracted from seeds/plants.

Pasteurisation – a process of treating milk with heat to eliminate harmful bacteria. The milk is usually then cooled prior to sale.

Pennine Dales – defined (by Joan Grundy) as: Westmorland; the West Riding Registration districts of Settle, Skipton and Sedbergh; and Lancashire north of the Lune including east Lancashire from Pendle Forest northwards.

Phthisis – see *Tuberculosis*.

Provender – dry food for cattle and other domesticated animals.

Pudding Round – the midday milk round.

Railway Milk – milk transported into the cities from the rural areas via the rail network.

Rinderpest – cattle plague; caused by the rinderpest virus.

Rudstake – a pole at the head of a stall, to which a cow can be tethered.

Settlestones – large kerb stones at the rear of a stall, which help to form a gutter.

Shandry – a light horse-drawn cart on springs.

Shippon – a building (usually, rectangular in plan) in which cows are kept (cf. Cowhouse). A single shippon has one line of cow stalls facing one of the long walls. A double shippon has two lines of stalls, one along each long wall.

Shorthorn – a breed of cattle developed as a dual-purpose animal that would give a relatively high milk yield but would also fatten easily for the beef market.

Skelbus – a wooden or stone divide, separating the cows from the stored hay.

Tuberculosis – an infectious bacterial disease, usually of the lungs.

Whitewash or Whiting – a type of paint made from lime, chalk and water, used on both internal and external walls in dairies due to its mild antibacterial properties and its ability to bind and seal in dust/dirt particles.

Yard – an enclosed, hard-surfaced space, often with outbuildings on three sides (and a set of gates on the fourth), used variously for exercising cows, loading and unloading, storing materials, garaging vehicles, etc.

Appendix A

Key Dates and Events Affecting City Dairymen

Year	Event
1822	Mr George Coates published the first Herd Book containing 710 bulls and 850 cows; Coates's *Herd Book* became the first pedigree herd book for cattle in the world.
1830	The Liverpool and Manchester Railway became the first inter-city railway in the world.
1839	The English Agricultural Society held its first show.
1844	Manchester became the first city to be supplied with milk via the railways.
1846	The Eastern Counties Railway began carrying milk to supply London.
1860	The Adulteration of Food & Drugs Act gave power to appoint public analysts.
1864	George Barham set up the Express County Milk Supply Company (Express Dairies) to supply London with milk via the railways.
1865	A major outbreak of the cattle plague, rinderpest, occurred and spread across the country.
1870	Water coolers were first used at rural railway stations to prepare milk for transit.
1872	The Adulteration of Food, Drink and Drugs Act made the appointment of public analysts mandatory.
1874	The Shorthorn Society of Great Britain and Ireland was formed.
1875	The Public Health Act provided powers to inspect and seize unsound food, including milk.
1875	The Sale of Food and Drugs Act introduced heavy penalties for adulteration of food including three months' hard labour for a second offence.
1876	The British Dairy Farmers' Association was founded and held its first show, in Islington.

Key Dates and Events Affecting City Dairymen

Year	Event
1878	The Contagious Diseases (Animals) Act made it possible (not compulsory) for local authorities to register all cowkeepers, dairymen and purveyors of milk, to regulate the lighting and ventilation of cowsheds, and to secure the cleanliness of dairies and milkshops.
1878	George Henry Lester of Brooklyn, New York, patented the first glass jar intended to hold milk.
1879	The Dairies, Cowsheds and Milkshops Order required cowsheds to have adequate lighting, ventilation, cleansing, drainage and water supply to the satisfaction of the local authority. Milk from diseased animals could not be used as human food.
1880	Milk bottles were first produced and used by the Express Dairy Company in London.
1885	The Dairies, Cowsheds and Milkshops Order provided further structure for local authorities to register dairymen, cowkeepers and milk purveyors. It specified dairy regulation, providing guidelines for the lighting, ventilation, cleansing, drainage and water supply of dairies and cowsheds.
1894	Anthony Hailwood, a Cheshire dairyman, began the commercial sterilisation of milk in the UK.
1895	The First Royal Commission on Tuberculosis concluded that the consumption of tuberculous milk was a contributory factor to human tuberculosis.
1901	The Royal Commission to Inquire into the Relations of Human and Animal Tuberculosis was set up.
1901	The Sale of Milk Regulations stipulated that milk should contain at least 3 per cent milk fat and 8.5 per cent other. There were no minimum standards of cleanliness.
1906	The Education (Provision of Meals) Act enabled local authorities to offer free school meals.
1909	The British Holstein Cattle Society was formed. (Later to become The British Holstein-Friesian Cattle Society, and then The Friesian Cattle Society.)
1913	The Royal Commission to Inquire into the Relations of Human and Animal Tuberculosis concluded that tuberculosis in humans could be contracted from cattle.
1913	The major London dairies reached agreement that all milk would be delivered to the consumer only in glass bottles, which must be sealed at the dairy.

The City Dairy: A Social and Family History

Year	Event
1915	The National Clean Milk Society was founded (by Wilfred Buckley), with the stated aims of raising the hygienic standard of milk, and of educating the public about the importance of clean milk.
1915	United Dairies was formed following a merger of wholesale and retail milk companies. Often referred to as *The Combine*.
1916	As part of the war effort, the Ministry of Food was created with powers to regulate the supply and consumption of food; this included setting the price of milk.
1917	The Milk (Special Designation) Order introduced the grading of milk.
1920	The Trade Boards (Milk Distributive) Order applied hours and conditions of labour to the sale of fresh milk and all its associated operations.
1920	The National Milk Publicity Council of England and Wales was formed.
1921	The 1906 Education Act, which enabled Local Education Authorities to provide free school meals, was extended to include free milk.
1922	The Milk and Dairies (Amendment) Act outlawed the sale of tuberculous milk and introduced licensed designations, including 'Pasteurised' through the 1923 Milk and Dairies Order, which gave detailed definitions of graded milk.
1925	The Milk and Dairies Act officially adopted the Methylene Blue test for raw and graded milks. The sterilisation of milk vessels and appliances was required. All producers and retailers of milk now had to be registered. The cooling of milk was made compulsory.
1926	The Milk and Dairies Order prohibited the opening of any milk churn on any milk van or on any railway station.
1927	The National Milk Publicity Council of England and Wales publicised a school milk club scheme whereby a third of a pint of milk could be bought for a penny.
1933	The Agricultural Marketing Act created the Milk Marketing Board to control milk production and supply in the UK.
1936	The Milk (Special Designations) Order prescribed five new grades of milk, replacing 'Grade A'.
1937	The Agriculture Act enabled the Ministry of Agriculture's veterinary inspectors to examine and test herds holding accredited licences.
1943	The Ministry of Food introduced arrangements for the rationalisation of milk delivery (zoning) to conserve resources (manpower, fuel, tyres, vehicles etc.) in support of the war effort.

Key Dates and Events Affecting City Dairymen

Year	Event
1944	The Food and Drugs (Milk and Dairies) Act shifted responsibility for cleanliness to the Ministry of Agriculture.
1946	The Free School Milk Act gave every school child under 18 the right to a third of a pint of milk each day.
1949	The Milk and Dairies Act required for the first time that all milk had to be graded.
1949	The Milk (Special Designations) Act introduced the first local option of compulsory pasteurisation of milk.
1959	The Milk Marketing Board launched its 'Drinka Pinta Milka Day' advertising campaign.
1963	The national herd was declared free from tuberculosis and the TT (Tuberculin Tested) designation was dropped from the milk grading scheme.
1968	Free milk was abolished in secondary schools.
1971	Free school milk for children over the age of 7 was ended.
1975	The last known true city cowkeeper, Joe Capstick, of 4 Marlborough Road, Liverpool, moved his cows out of the city and relocated them to a farm near Lancaster.
1993	The Agriculture Act brought about the deregulation of the British milk market.
2002	The Milk Marketing Board was finally dissolved.

Appendix B

List of Historical District Cowkeepers' and Dairymen's Associations

Aldershot, Farnborough & District Dairymen and Cowkeepers' Association
Alfreton & District Cowkeepers' Association
Beverley Cowkeepers' Association
Blackheath Cowkeepers' Association
Blackrock & District Cowkeepers' Association
Bradford & District Dairy Farmers and Cowkeepers' Association
Bristol & District Cowkeepers' Association
Cardiff Dairymen & Cowkeepers' Association
Crosby & District Cowkeepers' and Retail Dairymen's Association
Croydon Dairymen & Cowkeepers' Association
Driffield Cowkeepers' Association
Dublin Cowkeepers' Association
East London Cowkeepers' Association
East Riding & District Cowkeepers' and Dairymen's Association
Edinburgh and Leith Cowkeepers' Association
Farsley & District Farmers and Cowkeepers' Association
Goole & District Dairymen & Cowkeepers' Association
Grantham & District Dairymen and Cowkeepers' Association
Harrogate, Knaresborough & District Milk Dealers' & Cowkeepers' Association
Hull Cowkeepers and Farmers' Association
Kingstown & District Cowkeepers' Association
Kirkby-in-Ashfield Cowkeepers' Association
Leeds & District Cowkeepers' Association
Lincoln Cowkeepers' Association
Lincolnshire Dairymen and Cowkeepers' Association
Liverpool & District Cowkeepers' Association
London Cowkeepers' Association
Malton Cowkeepers' Association
North East of London Cowkeepers' Association
North Staffordshire Dairymen & Cowkeepers' Association
Nottingham Dairymen & Cowkeepers' Association
Ormskirk & District Cowkeepers' Association
Rainford Cowkeepers' Association
Reading & District Dairymen and Cowkeepers' Association

List of Historical District Cowkeepers' and Dairymen's Associations

Sheffield & District Cowkeepers' Association
Spilsby & District Cowkeepers' Association
Waterford Cowkeepers' Association
Wigan Farmers' and Cowkeepers' Association

Appendix C

Rules of The City of Liverpool & District Cowkeepers' Association (1919)

**The City of Liverpool
And District
Cowkeepers' Association
1919**
President:
The Hon. Sir Arthur Stanley, G.B.E., C.B., M.V.O.
Chairman:
Mr. Fredk. Stoner, 29 Beaufort Street, S.
Vice-Chairman:
Mr. John W. Foster, Newstead Farm, Woolton
Secretary & Treasurer:
Mr. Thos. Backhouse, 175 Walton Lane, N.
Telephone 3228 Royal.
Assistant Secretary:
Mr. Samuel Backhouse,
58 Tetlow Street, N.
Solicitor:
Mr. W. Rudd, 10 Dale Street, W.
Veterinary Surgeon:
Mr. Stafford Jackson, 3 Low Hill, E.
Analyst:
Mr. G. Watson Gray, F.I.C., 8 Inner Temple, Dale Street
'UNITY IS STRENGTH'

OBJECTS AND RULES

1. The Association shall be called the City of Liverpool and District Cowkeepers' Association, and shall include all Cowkeepers residing in Liverpool, Bootle, Seaforth, Litherland, Waterloo, Crosby, Aintree, Netherton, Sefton, Maghull, Lydiate, Woolton, Fazakerley, West Derby, Old Swan, Wavertree, Walton, Gateacre, Garston, Speke, Knotty Ash, Roby, Huyton, Prescot, Rainhill and Eccleston. The Objects for which the Association is formed are the following:
    a. To promote and protect the various interests of the Trade or Business of Cowkeepers generally, but more especially within the City of Liverpool and the vicinity.

Rules of The City of Liverpool & District Cowkeepers' Association

b. To promote and support or oppose legislative or other measures affecting the aforesaid interests.
c. So far as lawfully may be to defend and protect the Members in the lawful exercise of their Business.
d. To assist the Authorities to detect and prevent the spread of all contagious disease affecting the cattle.
e. To assist in the prevention of Milk adulteration.
f. To hold and Annual Show of Fat and Dairy cattle. To award prizes thereat, and to do all such acts as are customary in the promotion and carrying out of public cattle shows.
g. To consider all questions which may arise affecting the interests of the Trade, and take such action thereon as may be thought desirable, and, if deemed expedient, to co-operate with other Associations for any of the purposes aforesaid.
h. To acquire a fund for the aforesaid purposes, and to do all such other lawful things as may be considered conducive or incidental to the attainment of the foregoing objectives.

MEMBERS
Their Privileges and Obligations

2. The Association shall consist of Cowkeepers in Liverpool and adjacent districts who shall have been duly elected at a Committee or General Meeting of the Association, and any member may be expelled at Annual or Special General Meeting for any cause which such meeting may consider sufficient provided that seven days' notice shall be given to such member of the proposal to expel, and of the grounds for his expulsion.

   The Committee shall have the power to suspend a member until the then next Annual or Special General Meeting.

   Every member shall upon admission be furnished on application with a copy of the Rules, and shall be bound thereby.

3. Every person on being admitted a member shall pay an annual subscription of 10 shillings, payable on the first day of January in every year, or such other subscription as may be determined upon at an Annual or Special General Meeting of the Association. Any member neglecting to pay his subscription for three months after it shall become due shall forfeit his or her membership, but shall be re-admitted upon paying a fine of 2s 1d, together with arrears, provided, however, that any person ceasing to be a member by reason of such neglect shall not after being re-admitted a member under the provisions of this rule be entitled to receive any payment out of the funds of the Association in respect of any prosecution instituted before the expiration of three months after his re-admission except at the discretion of the Committee, but shall be entitled to all other privileges of the Association.

4. Any new member joining after the first of July in any year shall pay only 5s as his subscription for the then current year. The Committee shall have

power to admit any person who, previous to retirement, had been a member of the Association on payment of such subscription, not being less than 10/- per annum; as honorary member. He shall have the privilege of voting and speaking on all matters brought before the meeting.

5. If the funds of the Association shall at any time be insufficient to meet the expenses thereof, it shall be lawful for the Committee with the authority of a resolution to that effect, passed at any Annual or Special General Meeting, to call upon the members from time to time to contribute rateably such sum as may be decided upon at such meeting.

All moneys which shall become due from any member under these rules, may be used for in the name of the President or Vice-President or Secretary for the time being.

6. Any member who wishes to withdraw from the Association, shall give one month's written notice to that effect addressed to the Secretary of the Association, otherwise he shall be liable to pay his subscription for the year commencing 1st January next ensuing, and a member giving due notice, but using the Association nevertheless, on or after such 1st January shall be liable for payment of his subscription for the current year.

7. No Member who shall cease to belong to the Association, nor the executors or administrators of any deceased member, shall have any claim upon, or be entitled to participate in any effects or property belonging to the Association.

8. No Member shall be able to receive any assistance out of the funds of the Association, in respect of any prosecution instituted before the expiration of one month after he shall have become a member.

MANAGEMENT

9. The affairs of the Association shall be under the management of the Chairman, Vice-Chairman, Treasurer, Secretary and twenty-three other members of the Association, who shall be elected annually and form the Committee of the Association.

The Committee shall meet the second Tuesday in March, June, September and December, in each year, eight to form a quorum; the Meetings to open at 7.45 and conclude at 9.45 p.m.

All questions shall be decided by a majority, and the Chairman of the meeting shall have a second or casting vote in addition to his ordinary vote, when the votes are equal.

An emergency Committee shall be elected annually of officers and members, consisting of five in number, three to form a quorum, and a General meeting of the Association be held in the month of July each year.

The Annual Meeting of the Association shall be held on the second Tuesday in the month of February in each year, at which a report by the Committee of the proceedings of the Association during the past year shall be read; the balance sheet of the Treasurer, duly audited by the Auditors, presented, and the officers and committee elected for the ensuing year. At least five days' notice shall be given, by circular, of the Annual Meeting.

The Chairman and Secretary may convene a special meeting of the Association at any time, and the Secretary shall convene such meeting, when so directed by the Committee, or when so requested, in writing, by any seven members, which request shall state the business to be submitted to the meeting. Such meetings shall be called by circular, in which shall be stated the business to be transacted at such meeting. Three clear days' notice shall be given. Twelve members shall form a quorum.

TRUSTEES

10. There shall be three Trustees to be selected by the Committee for the time being. Every Trustee respectively shall remain in office until death or resignation, or refusal, or becoming incapable to act, or residing abroad for twelve calendar months, or until a general meeting of the members shall think proper to remove him. All the property of the Association shall be vested in the Trustees, who shall hold the same for the general use of the members, in accordance with these Rules, and all securities shall be taken, stocks purchased, and purchases and investments made in the names of such Trustees, or some of them.

    The property, the subject of the trust, may be dealt with by the Trustees at the request of the Committee; the request in writing of three of whom assembled at the Board, and signed by the Chairman of the day, and attested by the Secretary, shall be justification to the Trustees as to any such purchase, sale, investment or disposal. The Trustees and every of them shall be fully indemnified by the association from all liability incurred by them or any of them, from time to time, as such Trustees or Trustee, shall, so far as regards the safety and protection of the person or persons dealing with him or them, absolutely bind the Association and every member thereof.

    Trustees of the Association:
    Mr. FREDERICK STONER, Beaufort Street, S.
JOSHUA BURROW, Garston
JOHN W. FOSTER, Woolton

TREASURER

11. The Treasurer shall receive all moneys belonging to the Association, and shall keep an account of all sums received and paid by him on account of the Association, and when the cash in his hands shall exceed £5, he shall pay the same into such bank as the Committee for the time being shall appoint. He shall submit the accounts and banking book to the Committee for inspection, whenever required by them and shall, prior to the annual meeting, prepare and present to the auditors his balance sheet and vouchers

for audit, and act generally under the directions of the Committee. No money shall be withdrawn from the bank except by cheque signed by the Chairman and Treasurer.

SECRETARY

12. The Secretary shall keep the books and accounts and have the custody of all papers and documents of the Association. He shall collect the subscriptions of the Members, summon all meetings, and take minutes of the proceedings thereat. He shall pay over to the Treasurer all moneys received on behalf of the Association, and attend generally to the affairs of the Association under the direction of the Committee.

SOLICITOR

13. Mr. William Rudd, of 10 Dale Street, Liverpool, is appointed Solicitor to the Association and shall conduct all legal proceedings on behalf of the Association, at the request of the Secretary in writing, for which he will be paid the usual lawful charges.

COMMITTEE

14. The Committee shall watch over the interests and promote the objects of the Association, and for such purposes may expend such portion of the funds of the Association as they may think necessary. They shall cause proper books to be kept, fill up any vacancies in their body, or in the officers, as they arise; audit the Treasurer's balance sheet, and present the same with a report of the proceedings of the Association during the year, to the Annual Meeting, call Special General Meetings of the members whenever they consider it necessary, and do all other acts and things or promoting the objects of the Association which they may deem necessary or desirable, whether provided for in these rules or not.

AUDITORS

15. At the Annual Meeting, two persons (both members of the Association), shall be appointed Auditors of the Accounts of the current year; by whom such accounts shall be audited, previous to their being submitted to the Annual Meeting.

ALTERATIONS OF RULES, AND DISSOLUTION

16. No new rule or alteration of an existing rule shall be made without the sanction of an Annual or Special General meeting of the Association. Three days' notice at least, of such proposed new rule, shall be sent by the Secretary to every member.
17. In the event of dissolution of the Association which may take place, only by resolution carried by a majority of three-fourths of the Members at any Special General Meeting, duly convened for that purpose, of which ten

Rules of The City of Liverpool & District Cowkeepers' Association

days' previous notice has been given, the property of the Association, after liquidation of all liabilities, may be disposed of as may be decided by the resolution to dissolve.

Committee rooms: St. Martin's Hall, Scotland Road.

F. STONER, Chairman
THOMAS BACKHOUSE, Secretary & Treasurer
F. STONER, Trustee
J. BURROW, Trustee
JOHN W. FOSTER, Trustee
Established in 1873
First Rules Printed Sept. 1888
Amended and Reprinted, May 1919.

Appendix D

The Liverpool & District Cowkeepers' Association Annual Cattle Show

Lists of judges and prizewinners as reported in local newspapers

1885 – The Liverpool Mercury, Wednesday, 16 December 1885.

Judges

Fat cattle: **Mr Thomas Walker**, Lancaster, and **Mr William Phillips**, Liverpool. Dairy cattle: **Mr William Carr**, Slaidburn, and **Mr William Morpeth**, Salwick.

Prizewinners

Class 1: 1. **J. Walker**, Castle Street, Woolton; 2. **J. Verity**, 1 Back Mount Vernon; 3. **R. Brownlow**, Mill Street; 4. **T. Lawson**, 3 Dalton Street; 5. **W. Waterworth**, 7 Newton Street.

Class 2: 1. **R. Alderson**, Strand Road, Bootle; 2. **R. Demaine**, Lambert Street; 3. **J. Newsome**, Vine Street; 4. **J. Walker**, Castle Street, Woolton; 5. **H. Snowdon**, Gladstone Road, Seaforth.

Class 3: 1. **M. Burton**, Cockerel Street; 2. **Mrs Woods**, Carr Lane, West Derby; 3. **Mrs Scholes**, Ashfield Street; 4. **William Staunton**, Wren Street; 5. **George Mason**, Almond Green, West Derby.

Class 4: 1. **C. Swinbank**, Albion Street; 2. **John Benson**, Osborne Grove; 3. **Thomas Briggs**, Dryden Street; 4. **Daniel Joy**, Railway Street, Garston; 5. **John Moore**, Candia Street.

Class 5: 1. **J.T. Atkinson**; 2. **J. Walker**; 3. **G. Hutchinson**; 4. **R. Alderson**.

Class 6: 1. **T. Gibson**; 2 **W. Verity**; 3. **W. Davidson**; 4. **T. Briggs**.

Class 7: 1. **G. Windle**; 2. **Mrs Parker**; 3. **W. Waterworth**; 4. **H. Robinson**.

Class 8: 1. **J. Verity**; 2. **M. Whitfield**; 3. **G. Atkinson**; 4. **T. Chapman**.

Class 9. 1. **C. Wolfenden**, Beach Street, Bootle; 2. **R. Wolfenden**, Salisbury Road, Bootle; 3. **R. Burnside**, Larch Lea; 4. **R. Burnside**, Larch Lea; 5. **M. Stoner and Son**, Beaufort Street, Bootle.

The Liverpool & District Cowkeepers' Association Annual

Class 10: 1. **R. Burnside**, Larch Lea; 2. **R. Wolfenden**, Salisbury Road, Bootle; 3. **J. Newsome**, Vine Street; 4. **R. Alderson**, Strand Road, Bootle; 5. **R. Burnside**, Larch Lea.

Special Prizes: **Mrs Holding**, Binns Road; **T. Hindle**, Keble Street, Bootle.

1890 – The Liverpool Mercury, Thursday, 11 December 1890.

Judges

Fat cattle: **Mr Thomas Walker** (Lancaster), **Mr Robert Carr** (Skipton), and **Mr Rt. Harrison** (Burton-in-Lonsdale). Dairy cattle: **Mr John Ellis** (Ripon) and **Mr Edward Mason** (Kendal).

Prizewinners

Class 1: 1. **T. Mansergh**; 2. **W. Waterworth**; 3. **J. Walker**; 4. **J. Newsholme**; 5. **T. Scarr.**

Class 2: 1. **T. Carr**; 2. **C. Swinbank**; 3. **J. Akrigg**; 4. **J. Walker**; 5. **J. Verity**.

Class 3: 1. **F. Stoner**; 2. **W. Culshaw**; 3. **T. Scarr**; 4. **Mrs A. Scholes**; 5. **T. Lawson**.

Class 4: 1. **J. Brown**; 2. **Mrs Manchester**; 3. **G. Hunter**; 4. **J. Moore**; 5. **J. Raw**.

Class 5: 1. **H. Snowdon**; 2. **H. Robinson**: 3. **R. Wolfenden**; 4. **T. M'Manns**.

Class 6: 1. **R. Kitching**; 2. **G. Atkinson**; 3. **W. Culshaw**; 4. **Mrs Parker**.

Class 7: 1. **J. Moore**; 2. **J. Benson**; 3. **G. Joy**; 4. **T. Lawson**.

Class 8: 1. **W. Verity**; 2. **R. Mansergh**; 3. **R. Hitching**; 4. **N. Strickland**.

Class 9: 1. and 2. **J. Wolfenden**; 3. **C. Wolfenden**; 4. **F. Alderson**; 5. **J. Irving**.

Class 10: 1. **J. Wolfenden**; 2. **B. Alderson**; 3. **R. Wolfenden**; 4. **M. Verity**; 5. **T. Lawson**

Class 11: 1. **J. Hogg**; 2. **F. Alderson**; 3. **J. Verity**; 4. **R. Alderson**; 5. **J. Wolfenden**.

Class 12: 1, 2, 3, and 4. **Gregory Verity**, Upton Rocks, near Widnes.

Class 13: 1. **C. Wolfenden**; 2. **E. Alderson**; 3. **R. Wolfenden**; 4. **R. Alderson**; 5. **T. Hindle**.

Class 14: 1. **L. Briggs**; 2. **T. Scarr**

Class 15: 1. **R. Jackson**; 2. **W. Heapy**.

Class 16: 1. **F. Stoner**; 2. **L. Briggs**.

Class 17: 1. **F. Stoner**; 2. **W. Davidson**.

Special Prizes: **T. Snowden, H. Snowden, T. Scarr, W. Davison, N. Strickland, J. Newsham, T. Carr, H. Robinson, G. Bellman, W. Peters, T. M'Manns, F. Stoner, C. Swinbank, J. Walker, W. Culshaw, W. Waterworth, J. Verity, Miles Verity, Thomas Mansergh, J. Wolfenden.**

The City Dairy: A Social and Family History

1895 – The Liverpool Mercury, Thursday, 12 December 1895

Judges

Fat cattle: **W. Carr** (Clitheroe), **J. Howard** (Gargrave), and **J. Irving Richardson** (Kirkby Lonsdale). Dairy cattle: **C. Bousfield** (Kirkby Sowerby) and **W. Morphet** (Preston).

Prizewinners

Class 1: 1. **T. Backhouse**, 58 Tetlow Street; 2. **Mrs Wilson**, 3 Moor Lane, Great Crosby; 3. **Robert Wolfenden**, Salisbury Road, Bootle; 4. **T. Backhouse**; 5. **John Noble**, 5 Tawd Street.

Class 2: 1. **W. Akrigg**, Garston Old Road, Cressington; 2. **E. Alderson**, 29 Browne Street, Bootle; 3. **Robert Jackson**, 19 Leyfield Road, West Derby; 4. **H. Robinson**, 3–5 Knight Street; 5. **R. Greenbank**, Carisbrooke Place, Walton.

Class 3: 1. **W. Lees**, 26 West Derby Village; 2. **R. Batty and Sons**, Aigburth Road; 3. **H. Porter**, 119 South Street, Prince's Park.

Class 4: 1. **M. Whitfield**, 53 Tegid Street, Everton; 2. **T. Backhouse**; 3. **R. Tunstall**, Walton Breck Road; 4. **W. Verity**, 8 Jubilee Street; 5. **Mrs Brownrigg**, West Derby.

Class 5: 1. **J. & R. Atkinson**, Greenbank Dairy, Sefton Park; 2. **R. Batty and Sons**; 3. **G. Woodruff**, Northumberland Street; 4. **Robert Jackson**, 19 Leyfield Road.

Class 6: 1. **T. Mansergh**, Wadham Road, Bootle; 2, **W. Lawson**, 66 Eversley Street; 3. **J. Hogg**, 3 Back Parkfield Road; 4. **T. Hindle**, Keble Road, Bootle.

Class 7: 1. **T. Parrington**, 3 Salop Street; 2. **W. Lawson**; 3. **J. Hogg**; 4. **T. Hindle**.

Class 7a: 1. **T. Parrington**; 2. **J. Moore**, Alwyn Street; 3. **Benjamin Whitehead**, New Road, Tuebrook; 4. **Mrs Manchester**, Burlington Street.

Class 8: 1. **R. Mansergh**; 2. **R. Goth**, Eyes Street, Everton; 3. **T. Balmer**, Hawksworth Street: 4. **W. Beardwood**, Burlington Street.

Class 9: 1. **R. Wolfenden**, Bootle; 2. **F. Stoner**, 29 Beaufort Street; 3. **E. Alderson**; 4. **E. Cave**, Sanderson Street, Everton; 5. **W.T. Dean**, 61 Robson Street.

Class 10: 1. **R. Raw**, Queen's Road, Bootle; 2. **Mrs Prescott**, 8 Rockley Street; 3. **W. Sayers,** Walton Breck Road; 4 and 5. **R. Wolfenden**.

Class 11: 1. **T. Ingham**, Blackburn Grove, Bootle; 2. **R. Raw**; 3. **Mrs Newhouse**, Clarendon Street; 4. **W. Verity**; 5. **R. Batty and Sons**.

Special Prizes: **Gregory Verity**, Upton Rocks, near Widnes; **Thomas Howard**, Woodbine, Bretherton; **T. Clark**, Westfield, Knotty Ash; **G. Ingham**, 4 Church View, Bootle; **F. Stoner**, 29 Beaufort Street; **H. Wolfenden**, Bootle; **T. Backhouse**; **F. Stoner**; **R. Wolfenden**.

The Liverpool & District Cowkeepers' Association Annual

1899 – The Liverpool Mercury, Thursday, 14 December 1899.

Judges

Fat cattle: **W. Carr** (Clitheroe) and **J. Howard** (Gargrave). Dairy cattle: **Ed. Mason** (Watercrook, Kendal) and **Geo. Holden** (Westhoughton).

Prizewinners

Class 1: 1. **R. Raw**, Queen's Road, Bootle; 2. **R. Harper**, 52 Chestnut Grove, Wavertree; 3. **H. Morphet**, Germoyle Road; 4. **R. Tunstall**, 190 Walton Breck Road; 5. **Mrs E. Smith**, Quarry Street, Woolton.

Class 2: 1. **C. Swinbank**, 64 Albion Street, Everton; 2. **G. Joy and Sons**, 2 Carlton Avenue, Smithdown Road; 3. **R. Ellison**, 15 Brook Road, Walton; 4. **R. Batty and Sons**, Arundel Avenue and Aigburth Road; 5. **J. Oversby**, Alexander Road, Great Crosby.

Class 3: 1. **W.T. Dean**, 8 Attwood Street; 2. **J. Furrer**, Moss Farm, Old Swan; 3. **J. Raw**, 76 Candia Street; 4. **R. Batty and Sons**; 5. **W. Ellison**, 24 Upper Stanhope Street.

Class 4: 1. **Mrs S. Brownrigg**, 39 Almonds Green, West Derby; 2. **R. Greenbank**, Bedford Road, Walton; 3. **W.T. Dean**, 8 Atwood Street; 4. **R. Tunstall**, 190 Walton Breck Road: 5. **W. Culshaw**, 49 Marlborough Street.

Class 5: 1. **H. Robinson**, Dickens Street; 2. **T. Backhouse**, Tetlow Street; 3. **J. Hogg**, Back Parkfield Road; 4. **T. Goss**, Langton Road, Wavertree.

Class 6: 1. **L. Mason**, Chapel Road, Garston; 2. **J. and R. Atkinson**, Green Bank Dairy, Sefton Park; 3. **H. Snowdon**, Gladstone Road, Seaforth; 4. **J. Bracken**, Hawksworth Street.

Class 7: 1. **R. Harper**, Chestnut Grove, Wavertree; 2. **W. Fawcett**, Rothwell Street; 3. **J. Wilson**, Wellington Road; 4. **R. Wright**, Victoria Road, Crosby.

Class 8: 1. **J. Noble**, Freeland Street; 2. **B. Whitehead**, New Road, Tuebrook; 3. **J. Irving**, Anthony Street, Everton; 4. **R. Batty and Sons**.

Class 9: 1. **R. Batty and Sons**: 2. **F. Heath**, Mulberry Street; 3. **G. Woodruff**, Northumberland Street; 4. **R. Batty and Sons**; 5. **R. Batty and Sons**.

Class 10: 1. **W. Sayer**, Walton Breck Road; 2. **J. Wolfenden**, Chapel Street, Waterloo; 3. **T. Backhouse**; 4. **J. and R. Atkinson**; 5. **R. Tunstall**, 190 Walton Breck Road.

Class 11: 1. **R. Capstick**, Rathbone Street; 2. **J. and R. Atkinson**; 3. **R. Thwaite**, Annerley Street; 4. **R. Batty and Sons**; 5. **T. Backhouse**.

Class 12: 1. **M. Verity**, Upton Rocks, Widnes; 2. **R. Alderson**, Crow Lane, Newton-le-Willows; 3. **C. Baldwin**, Park Style, West Derby.

Class 13: 1. **R. Scarr**, Ivy Leigh, Tuebrook; 2. **T. Wolfenden**, Chepstow Street; 3. **J. Pemberton**, Travers Farm, Bold.

Class 14: 1. **J. and R. Atkinson**; 2. **R. Batty and Sons**; 3. **J. Heath**, Mulberry Street; 4. **R. Tunstall**. 5. **T. Foster**, Newstead Farm, Woolton.

Class 15: 1. **G. Woodruff**; 2. **Mrs Smith**, Woolton; 3. **F. Stoner**, Beaufort Street; 4. **G. Woodruff**; 5. **N. Strickland**, Mulberry Street.

1906 – The Liverpool Daily Post, Thursday, 13 December 1906.

Judges

Fat cattle: **John Howard**, Pagett Hall, Gargrave; **C. Iveson**, Main Street, Sedbergh. Dairy cattle: **George Holden**, Daisy Hill, Westhoughton; and **E. Mason**, Watercrook, Kendal.

Prizewinners

Class 1: **W. Batty**, 85 Aigburth Road; **Mrs A. Beck & Sons**, 189 Park Road; **R. Pawton**, 99 High Street, Wavertree.

Class 2: **R. Raw & Sons**, Barn Hey Farm, West Derby; **J. Raw**, Goodison Road, Walton; **J. Farrer**, 38 Coleridge Street;

Class 3: **J. Kendal**, 2 Blenheim Road; **Mrs Joel**, Houlding Street, Anfield; **G. Batty**, Macdonald Street, Wavertree.

Class 4: **T. Stockdale**, Smithdown Road; **J. Handley**, 15 Mulberry Street; **G. Mason**, Guildhall Road, Aintree.

Class 5: **Joy Bros**. 362 Smithdown Road; **R. Thwaite**, 35 Annerley Street; **R. Raw**, 20 Queen's Road, Bootle.

Class 6: **W. Batty**; **T. Stockdale**; **W. Brownrigg**, Lyons Street.

Class 7: **J. Nicholson**, 64 Stitt Street, Everton; **E. Williams & Sons**, Willowdale Road, Walton; **J. Capstick**, Chapel Avenue, Walton.

Class 8: **J.R. Dinsdale**, St Oswalds Street, Old Swan; **H. Wood**, Boundary Lane, Everton; **Mrs Williams**, 2 Parkinson Road, Walton.

Class 9: **J. & R. Atkinson**, Heathfield Road, Wavertree; **R. Raw**; **W.T. Dean**; **Mrs M.F. Smith**, 87 Quarry Street, Woolton; **J. & R. Atkinson**.

Class 10: **Joy Bros**.; **G. Mason**; **R. Batty**, Prince Alfred Road, Wavertree.

Special Prizes: **Mrs A. Beck and Sons**; **J. Pemberton**, Travers Farm, Bold; **L. Dilworth**, Ramsbrooke Farm, Halebank; **R. Ball**, Norris Green Farm, West Derby; **J. Ashcroft**, Thorntree Farm, Aughton; **R. Swift**, Door Barn Farm, Aintree; **M. Verity**, Upton Rocks, Widnes; **R. Boyes**, Burton Farm, Kirkby; **T. Hindle**, 79 Keble Road, Bootle; **G. Ingham**, Stanley Road, Bootle; **R. Scarr**, 3 Ivy Leigh, Tuebrook; **W. T. Dean**, Attwood Street; **J. & R. Atkinson**, Heathfield

Road, Wavertree; **T. Chapman,** 79 Tiber Street; **Mrs M.F. Smith; T. Chapman; R. Raw; Mrs Fawcett,** 39 Lothair Road, Anfield; **T. Backhouse,** 58 Tetlow Street; **J.G. Braithwaite; J. Owen,** 20 Newsham Street; **F. Brownrigg & Sons,** 39 Almonds Green, West Derby Village; **W. Capstick,** Mossley Hill; **R. Porter,** 119 South Street; **W. Lewes,** 26 West Derby Village; **R. Thwaite; T.E. Allen,** 4 Whitefield Road, Everton; **T. Shaw,** Maple Grove, Sefton Park; **Mrs Wilson and Sons,** Great Crosby; **E. Williams and Son; W. Mark,** 10 Ledward Street; **J. Raw; J. Capstick; R. Pawson; J. Kendal; Joy Bros; W. Batty; S. Stockdale; R. Fawkes; W. Brownrigg; Mrs Joel,** 1 Houlding Street; **W. Hall; F. Heath ,** Berkley Street; **Mrs M.E. Smith; C.E. Bateman; C.N. Newton; J. Pemberton; Mr J.R. Smith.**

1926 – The Liverpool Echo, Wednesday, 12 December 1926

Prizewinners

Fat Cow (exceeding 14cwt). 1. **Greenwood Blades,** Roby; 2. **Mrs Talbot,** Parliament Street; 3. **John Herd,** Aigburth; 4. **James Dean,** Anfield.

Fat Cow (under 14cwt). 1. **Anthony Joy,** Garston; 2. **J. Handley,** Farnworth Street; **Mrs Mason,** Florist Street; 4. **M. Braithwaite,** Aigburth Vale.

Fat Cow (under 13cwt). 1. **A. Bradbury,** Fielding Street; 2. **James Taylor and Sons,** Tuebrook; 3. **G. Nelson,** Dingle.

Fat Cow (under 12cwt). 1. **Robert Raw,** Bootle; 2. **Edward Hall,** Great Crosby; 3. **James Wolfenden,** Waterloo.

Fat Cow (under 11cwt). 1. **J.A. Eardley,** Waterloo; 2. **T. Culthwaite,** Seaforth; 3. **J. Lancley**.

Cows over 14cwt (not having won in open competition). 1. **T.J. Parrington,** Great Crosby; 2. **M. Whitfield,** Fairfield; 3. **J. Howarth,** Great Crosby.

Cows under 14cwt. 1. **William Herd,** Greta Street; 2. **W. Turton,** Anfield; 3. **James Burton,** Seaforth.

Cows under 13cwt. 1. **G. Bargh,** Walton; 2. **J.A. Eardley,** Waterloo; 3. **Wm. Metcalfe,** Anfield.

Cows under 12cwt. 1. **J. Holgate,** Bootle; 2. **J. Handley,** Farnworth Street; 3. **T.W. Whitfield,** Everton.

Cows under 11cwt. 1. **J. Whitman,** Bootle; 2. **James Robinson,** Doncaster Street; 3. **F. R. Hudson,** Lovat Street.

Cows in calf or milk (not exceeding 11½cwt). 1. **M. Braithwaite;** 2. **G. Batty;** 3. **J. Farrer**.

Cows under 10½cwt. 1. **J. Hird;** 2. **J. Hogg;** 3. **W. Heslop**.

Cows under 9½cwt. 1. **J. Brenchley**; 2. **Mrs Mason**; 3. **R. Batty**.

President's Prize awarded to **J. Greenwood.**

Lord Mayor's Prize awarded to **J. Airey.**

1929 – The Liverpool Echo, Wednesday, 11 December 1929

Prizewinners

Fat Cow (over 14cwt). 1. **Newsham Bros.**, West Derby; 2. **Jas. Dean**, Anfield; 3. **H. Wood**, West Derby; 4. **John Wolfenden**, Bootle.

Fat Cow (under 14cwt). 1. **Jas. Owen**, Everton; 2. **T.J. Partington**, Great Crosby; 3. **M. Braithwaite**; 4. **Jackson Bros.**, West Derby.

Fat Cow (under 13cwt). 1. **J. Hanson**, Great Crosby; 2. **A. Joy**, Garston; 3. **A.H. Hill**. Litherland; 4. **H. Littlefair**, Bootle.

Fat Cows which have not won a prize in open competition:

Under 14cwt 1. **A. Stubbs**; 2. **W. Blades**; 3. **J. Mercer**.

Under 14cwt. 1. **M. Braithwaite**; 2. **G. Stanton**; 3. **G. Batty**.

Under 13cwt. 1. **J. Dean**; 2. **F. Baxter**; 3. **Jackson Bros**.

Town Dairy Cows:

Cows in calf or milk over 12cwt. 1. **T.F. Mercer**: 2. **J. Hird**; 3. **J. H. Moor and Son**; 4. **G. Batty**; 5. **J. Howarth**.

Cows over 11cwt. 1. **J. Hogg**; 2. **J. Berkley**; 3. **E. Mercer**; 4. **Jackson Bros.**; 5. **J. Farrer**.

Cows over 10cwt. 1. **Jackson Bros.** 2. **J. Close and Son**; 3. **E. Hall**; 4. **R. Merton**; 5. **R. Raw**, Bootle.

Cows under 10cwt. 1. **J. Berkley**; 2. **W. Metcalf**; 3. **R. Raw**, Bootle; 4. **J. Farrer**; 5. **Mrs M.J. Mason**.

Best Farmer's Cow:

Best Cow or Heifer. 1. **W.H. Grace**, Halewood; 2. **J.H. Moor and Sons**, West Derby; 3. **Robert Batty**, Grassendale.

Fat Cow under 12cwt. 1. **J. Taylor**, Waterloo; 2. **Mrs M.J. Mason**, Florist Street; 3. **J. W. Wightman**, Bootle.

Fat Cow under 11cwt. 1. **G. Batty**, Aigburth Road; 2. **T.J. Farrington**, Great Crosby; 3. **H. Tasker**, Waterloo.

Best Cow, Farmers' Club. 1. **W.H. Grace**; 2. **Jas. Moor and Sons**, West Derby; 3. **R. Batty.**

Cow in calf. 1. **W.H. Grace**; 2. **R. Raw**, West Derby; 3. **M. Braithwaite**.

Open Class. 1. **T. Mercer**, Litherland; 2. **W.H. Grace**; 3. **John Herd**, Alwyn Street.

Metcalfe Challenge Shield for Best Dairy Cow to **J. Hogg**, Little Parkfield Road.

Silver Cup for Best Dairy Cow awarded to **T.F. Mercer**. Res: **W. Grace**.

1931 – The Liverpool Echo, Wednesday, 9 December 1931

Prizewinners

Fat Cow exceeding 14cwt. 1. **W.H. Prickett**, Edge Hill; 2. **J. Joy**, Garston; 3. **E. Mercer**.

Fat Cow not exceeding 14cwt. 1. **W.H. Prickett**, Edge Hill; 2. **W.H. Hartley**, Tiber Street; 3. **T.J. Partington**, Great Crosby.

Fat Cow exceeding 14cwt (not having obtained a prize in open competition). 1. **H. Hanson**, Great Crosby; 2. **Robert Raw**, Bootle; 3. **Samuel Redfern**, Knotty Ash.

Fat Cow not exceeding 14cwt (not having obtained a prize in open competition). 1. **Robert Wilson**, Mossley Hill; 2. **J. Wolfenden**, Bootle; 3. **Sydney Warburton**.

Cows suitable for town dairies exceeding 12cwt. 1. **Robert Raw**, Bootle; 2. **J.W. Beck**, Fazakerley; 3. **J.W. Law**, Great Crosby.

Cow not exceeding 11cwt. 1. **J. Handley**, Wavertree; 2. **H. Herd**, Princess Park; 3. **J.H. Moore and Sons**, West Derby.

Cows not exceeding 10cwt. 1. **R. Batty**, Grassendale; 2. **W.H. Grace**, Halewood.

Metcalfe Silver Challenge Cup for best Pair of Cows. 1. **A. Handley**; res. **M. Dugdale**.

President's Prize for Best Cow awarded to **J. Herd**.

Bibliography

Almeroth-Williams T. (2013), 'Horses and Livestock in Hanoverian London'. PhD. (History) dissertation. University of York.

Armstrong J. (2007), 'Cowkeepers'. Article published in the *Newsletter*, December, pp. 2–4, of Sedbergh & District History Society.

Atkins P.J. (1977), *London's Intra-Urban Milk Supply, circa 1790–1914*. Transactions of the Institute of British Geographers. New Series, Vol. 2, No. 3, pp. 383–399.

Atkins P.J. (1999), 'Is it urban? The relationship between food production and urban space in Britain, 1800–1950'. Helsinki: Finnish Literature Society. (Downloadable: **dro.dur.ac.uk/10383/**)

Atkins P.J. (2010), *Liquid Materialities: A History of Milk, Science and the Law* Farnham: Ashgate.

Atkins P.J. (2012^1), 'The Charmed Circle'. In: Atkins P.J. (ed.) *Animal Cities – Beastly Urban Histories*. London: Routledge.

Atkins P.J. (2012^2), 'Animal Wastes and Nuisances in Nineteenth-Century London'. In: Atkins P.J. (ed.) *Animal Cities: Beastly Urban Histories*. London: Routledge.

Atkins P.J. (2017), 'The Long Genealogy of Quality in the British Drinking-milk Sector'. *Agrarian History*, 73. December 2017. pp. 35–58.

Burnett J. (1999), *Liquid Pleasures; A Social History of Drinks in Modern Britain*. (Chapter 2. 'Milk: No Finer Investment?') London: Routledge.

Callaghan J. (2011), *Candles, Carts & Carbolic: A Liverpool Childhood Between the Wars*. Lancaster: Carnegie.

Carpenter R.S. (1934), 'Milk for the Family'. Article in *Farmers' Bulletin*, issue 1705, 1934. Washington: U.S. Department of Agriculture.

Carter P.J. and Parker D. (2019), 'Urban Dairy Farms in Darlaston Green in the Early 1900s'. Article in *The Blackcountryman* Vol. 52, No. 3. The Black Country Society.

Collacott B. (2016), *A Brief History of Milk Production: From Farm to Market*. Aldwick: Old Pond Publishing.

Curtler W.H.R. (1909), *A Short History of English Agriculture*. Oxford: The Clarendon Press.

Dickens C. (1851), 'The Cow with the Iron Tail'. Article in *Household Words* Vol. IV. Leipzig: Tauchutz.

Enock A.G. (1934), *This Milk Business: A Study from 1895 to 1943*. London: H.K. Lewis & Co. Ltd.

Bibliography

Finegan F.W. (1994), *A Bit Akin: The Story of a North Craven Farming Family*. Settle: F.W. Finegan.

Fussell G.E. (1952), '"I'm Going A-Milking, Sir," She Said'. Article in *Illustrated Sporting and Dramatic News,* 29 October 1952.

Fussell G.E. (1966), *The English Dairy Farmer, 1500–1900*. Abingdon: Routledge Revivals.

Ginn P. and Goodman R. (2016), *Full Steam Ahead: How the Railways Made Britain*. (pp. 135–150. 'Milk'.). London: William Collins.

Grundy J.E. (1982), 'Origins of the Liverpool Cowkeepers'. Unpublished master's degree thesis. University of Lancaster.

Hallas C. (2004), *The Wensleydale Railway* (4th edition). (pp. 62–68. 'Milk Traffic'.). Ilkley: Great Northern Books.

Hanson J. (1939), *A Rolling Stone: Sixty-Three Years' Retrospective*. Liverpool: Wilmar Bros.

Hayes M. (2015), *The London Milk Trail – The Story of Welsh Dairies in the City*. Gwasg Carreg Gwalch.

Hayes M. (2018), *Cows, Cobs and Corner Shops*. Tal-y-bont: Y Lolfa.

Hearn M. (2013), *Saucy Postcards: The Bamforth Collection*. London: Constable.

Herefordshire Lore (2012), *Milk, Herefordshire*. Little Hereford Histories 1. Hereford: Herefordshire Lore.

Hill H. (1956), 'Liverpool – Last Stronghold of Town Cowkeepers'. Article in *Dairy Engineering*, April 1956 (pp 107–110).

Hindley C. (1881), *A History of the Cries of London: Ancient and Modern*. London: Reeves and Turner.

Hope E.W. (1931), *Health at the Gateway: Problems and International Obligations of a Seaport City*. Cambridge University Press.

Horn A. (2009), *Juke Box Britain: Americanisation and Youth Culture, 1945–1960*. Manchester University Press.

Howell J.B. (1927), 'The Problem of a Clean Milk Supply for London'. Article in *The Veterinary Journal*, Vol. 83, April 1927 (pp. 182–184).

Hudson M. (2010), 'A Milk Bottle Collection …' Three-part article in *Antique Bottle Collector* magazine, issues 40–42, 2010.

Jenkins A. (1970), *Drinka Pinta: The Story of Milk & the Industry that Serves it*. London: Heinemann.

Johnson P. (1991), *The Birth of The Modern: World Society 1815–1830*. London: Harper Collins.

Jones T.E. (1927), 'The Supervision of the Liverpool Milk Supply'. Article in *The Veterinary Journal*, Vol. 83, April 1927 (pp. 178–182).

Joy D. (2014), *My Family and Other Scousers: A Liverpool Boy's Summer of Adventure in '69*. Stroud: The History Press.

Joy D. (2016[1]), 'The Cowkeepers of Garston'. *Past & Present*. Issue 22. May 2016. Garston & District Historical Society.

Joy D. (2016[2]), *Liverpool Cowkeepers*. Stroud: Amberley.

Joy D. (2017¹), 'Life and Death in Bolton Bridge'. Article published in the *Wharfedale Newsletter*. Issue 104. March 2017. Wharfedale Family History Group.

Joy D. (2017²), 'Life and Death in Skipton'. Article published in the *Wharfedale Newsletter*. Issue 105. June 2017. Wharfedale Family History Group.

Joy D. (2018), *The Wright Stuff. George Eric Wright (1890–1916): A Garston Dairyman and an Australian Soldier*. Garston & District Historical Society.

Joy D. (2021), 'The Iron Cow of Liverpool and the Crusade for Clean Milk'. Article published in *Liverpool History*. Journal No. 20 of the Liverpool History Society.

Leigh S. (2004), 'Cows in the City – The Story of Urban Dairies'. Article in *Farmers Guardian*. 20 February 2004.

Mackenzie K.J. (1910), 'The Dual Purpose Cow at Liverpool'. *Journal of the Royal Agricultural Society of England*, Vol. 71, pp. 364–365.

Marriott G. (ed.) 2010, *Those Who Left the Dales*. The Upper Dales Family History Group.

Mathias P. (1952), 'Agriculture and the Brewing and Distilling Industries in the Eighteenth Century'. *The Economic History Review*. New Series, Vol. 5, No. 2, page 249.

Mellor P.J. (1978), 'Cowkeepers From the Pennine Dales'. Article published in *Dalesman* magazine. May 1978.

Mellor P.J. (2012), *The Liverpool Cowkeepers*. Hellifield: P.J. Mellor.

Mingay G.E. (ed.) (1989), *The Agrarian History of England, Vol. 6: 1750–1850*. Cambridge: Cambridge University Press.

Nimmo R. (2010), *Milk, Modernity and the Making of the Human: Purifying the Social*. London: Routledge.

Pemberton T. (2022), *Make Hay While the Sun Shines: A Year on the Farm*. London: Radar.

Phelps T. (2011), *The British Milkman*. London: Shire Publications.

Phelps T. (2015), *Britain's Wartime Milkmen: From the Great War to the Second World War*. Gosport: Chaplin Books.

Roberts E.H.G. (2007), *The 9th King's (Liverpool Regiment) in the Great War, 1914–1918*. Yorkshire: Leonaur.

Scobie J. (2008), 'Cowkeepers from the Dales'. Article published in *Sedbergh Historian* Vol. V, No. 5. Sedbergh & District History Society.

Scott D. (2016), *Fields of Discovery: On the trail of Liverpool's Cowhouses*. DWS Publications.

Sharma B. (2019), *The Corner Shop*. London: Two Roads.

Spellerberg I. (2018), *Milk Cans: A Celebration of their History, Use and Design*. Apple Valley, Minnesota, USA: Astragal Press.

Stobart J. and Owens A. (2000), *Urban Fortunes: Property and Inheritance in the Town, 1700–1900*. Historical Urban Studies Series. London: Routledge.

Stout A. (1978), 'Three Centuries of London Cowkeeping'. Article published in *Farmers Weekly*. August 1978.

Stoner F. (1883), 'Management and Working of the Liverpool Town Dairies'. Essay published in the annual journal of the *Manchester, Liverpool and North Lancashire Agricultural Society*.

Bibliography

Struther J. (1932), *Sycamore Square & Other Verses*. London: Methuen.

Unwin F. (1984), *Reflections on the Mersey: Memoirs of the Twenties and Thirties*. County Meath, Ireland: The Gallery Press.

Valenze D. (2011), *Milk: A Local and Global History*. London: Yale University Press.

Walling P. (2018), *Till the Cows Come Home: The Story of Our Eternal Dependence*. London: Atlantic Books.

Ward A. (2016), *No Milk Today: The Vanishing World of the Milkman*. London: Robinson.

Whetham E.H. (1964), 'The London Milk Trade, 1860–1900'. *The Economic History Review,* Vol. 17, issue 2 (pp 369–380). London: A & C Black.

Winstanley M. (1996), 'Industrialization and the Small Farm: Family and Household Economy in Nineteenth-Century Lancashire'. *Past & Present,* No. 152 (pp 157–195). Oxford University Press on behalf of The Past and Present Society.

Wooding H. (1991), *Liverpool's Working Horses*. Liverpool: Print Origination (NW) Ltd.

Woollard M. (1998), 'The Classification of Occupations in the 1881 Census of England and Wales'. Article in *History and Computing*, October 1998.

Yorkshire Dales NPA (2018), *Every Barn (Cow 'Us) Tells a Story*. A pack of circular walk booklets for visitors. Yorkshire Dales National Park Authority.

Yorkshire Dales NPA (2020), *Dairy Days: The Story of Dairying in Wensleydale*. Yorkshire Dales National Park Authority.

Index

Abbey, Jean, 100
Adulteration, 28, 46, 75, 78–9
Agricultural Leave, 77
Aigburth (Liverpool district), 23, 82
Alan Godfrey Ordnance Survey Maps, 75
Almeroth-Williams, T., 3
Ancestry (website), 70, 83
Antique Bottle Collector magazine, 112
Argyle Dairy, Abingdon, 99
Arkengarthdale, 33
Armstrong, J., 88
Arnold, Nottinghamshire, 54
Ashbourne Heritage Society, 99
Atkins, Peter, 9, 25, 34, 41, 44, 65
Australia, 33, 37–9
Auty, Meryl, 118
Avenue Dairies, Brixton, 100

Baby Boom, 22, 58, 60
Bamforth & Co., 62
Banks, Steve, 107
Barham, George, 7, 104
Barn Gallon, 7
Barton-upon-Humber, 22, 99
Bartonsham Dairy, Hereford, 17, 99
Bartonsham History Group, 99
Baulks, 14
Belorussia, 40
Bishopdale, 33
Blackwell family, 17
Blitz (Blitzkrieg), 40, 50, 54
Bolton Bridge, 38
Boose, 13
Bowdin, Ralph, 11

Brewery Grain, 24, 70
British Agricultural History Society, 117
British Columbia, 38–9
British Dairy Farmers' Association, 22, 68
British Film Institute, 100, 138
British Genealogy, 70
British Newspaper Archive, 79, 135
Brockbank family, 100
Burnett, John, 3
Burnsall, Wharfedale, 35, 64

Callaghan, Jim, 13
Capstick, family, 97–8, 100, 107, 110, 138, 144–6
   Agnes, 94
   Edward, 78, 94
   Elizabeth, 139
   Janey, 21
   Joe, 56, 138
   Miles, 138
Cardiganshire, 73, 90, 97
Carpenter, R.S., 28
Casein, 28
Cattle Plague (Rinderpest), 10
Census enumerator, 83–9
Chain Migration, 34–5, 39, 89, 92, 139
Clipson, Terry, 22, 99
Collacott, Bert, 19, 96
Contagious Diseases (Animals) Act 1878, 14
Court Proceedings, 45, 78–9
Coventry, 51
Cow with the iron tail, 78–9

Index

Cowhouse (shippon), 10, 12–17, 21–4, 26, 32, 43, 64–5, 70, 72, 74, 83, 87, 89, 92, 95, 97, 101, 107, 121–6, 132, 154
Cowkeeperess, 88
Cowley family, 100
Croydon Dairymen and Cowkeepers' Association, 36
Cumbria, 36, 82, 98
Curtis family, 101
Curtler, William Henry Ricketts, 10

Dairy Farmers' Creamery (Liverpool) Ltd., 56
Dairy Workers' Charter (1924), 47
Dales Countryside Museum, Hawes, 107
Dickens, Charles, 78
Dictionary of Occupational Terms, 87
Dorset Dairies, 61
Dover (Dworetski) family, 40
Drewell family, 100
Drover, 30, 90, 97, 104

East Yorkshire Local History Society, 97
English Agricultural Society, 67
Enock, Arthur Guy, 45, 49
Evans, E. & Son, 108
Express Dairy Company, 7, 59, 112

Family Tree Forum, 70
Find A Will, 84
Finegan, Faith, 39, 96
Firmin family, 99
Fitzhenry family, 101
Flying Herd, 17, 67, 122
Fodder, 21–5, 43, 83
Foddergang, 14
Fore Milk, 134
Forkinghole, 14
Fothergill family, 91–2
Frost, John, 59
Fussell, George Edward, 4, 7

Gaddas, Mary, 29, 35
Garget, 134
Garston (Liverpool district), 11, 17, 22, 30, 38, 58, 64, 68, 72, 74, 76, 80
Genes Reunited, 70
Gilpin, Bernard, 17
Ginn and Goodman, 17, 44
Graham family, 105
Greenwood family, 139–42, 146–7
Groop, 14
Grundy, Joan Elizabeth, 34

Hall family, 99, 107
Hallas, Christine, 6
Handcan, 20, 47, 120
Handley family, 33
Handley, Tommy, 61
Hann family, 108
Hanson, James, 50, 56, 64
Harper family, 43, 97, 107, 139–50, 152
Harris, Alan, 97
Hayes, Megan, 29, 35, 58, 96–7
Hearfield, John and Marion, 103
Hearn, Marcus, 62
Hebden, Yorkshire, 11, 68, 72
Hereford, 17, 97, 99
Herefordshire Lore, 17, 97
Hill, Benny, 61, 100
Hill, H., 56
Hindley, C., 9
Hinshelwood, John, 97
Historical Directories project, 82
Hitchman's Dairies, 108
Hogg, family, 23–5
 Thomas, 56, 131
Hope, Edward William, 27
Horn, Adrian, 59
Hornsey Historical Society, 97
Howell, J.B., 46
Hudson, Ernie, 47
Hudson, Mark, 46, 112–14
Hughes, Ronnie, 107
Hull Cowkeepers and Farmers' Association, 71

Hull History Centre, 71
'Humphreys', 61

Inspection, 26–32, 123–24, 131–33
Irving, Mary, 82
Ives, Susanna, 108

Jenkins, Alan, 6, 45, 62
Jenkins, Stephanie, 102
Johnson, P., 6
Jones Dairy, Spitalfields, 107
Jones, T. Eaton, 134–35
Joy, family, 20, 22, 58, 72,
    Anthony, 74, 87
    Anthony Eric, 62, 76, 80
    Anthony Percival, 76
    Augustus Bowdin, 37
    Daniel, 11, 22, 68, 72–3,
    Dave, 20, 22, 28, 34, 39, 58, 65, 68, 74, 97, 101
    Hilda Mary, 37–8
    William Cecil, 30

Kenning family, 99
King's Liverpool Regiment, 76
Kirby and West Dairy Company, 103
Koch, Robert, 44, 65
Kosher milk, 29

Labour Corps, 76
Lancashire, 3, 8, 34, 56, 60, 91–3, 128
Langstrothdale, 33
Laycock's Dairy, London, 102
Leicester, 51
Leigh, S., 17
Licensing, 26, 74, 124, 132
Liverpool, 2, 17–18, 25–7, 31–42, 47, 50, 55–6, 59, 61, 66, 68, 70, 72, 74, 79, 86, 88, 91–109, 114, 119, 131–38, 139–53
Liverpool and District Cowkeepers' Association, 32, 56, 74, 78, 131, 135, 137
Liverpool-Manchester Railway, 6

Llanfihangel Y Creuddyn, 90
Llewellin, Colonel J., 54
London, 2–10, 24–5, 29, 34–6, 40–2, 44, 47, 51, 55, 57, 59, 65, 73–4, 90, 96–7, 99–100, 102–108
London Metropolitan Archives, 74
London, Midland and Scottish (LMS) Railway Company, 107
Lusitania, RMS, 38

Mackenzie, K.J., 16
Manchester Regiment, 76
Mansergh, Thomas Read, 104
Marriott, G., 33
Mason, family, 48, 90, 140, 148, 150, 152
    Edward Eubank, 26, 43, 48–9
    Thomas, 139
    William, 90
Mathias, P., 24
Matthews family, 17, 99
Maypole Dairy Co., 46, 57
McMullin, Eric and Hazel, 107
Medical Officer of Health, 41, 46, 75, 135
Mellor, Patsy, 19, 33, 35, 58, 72, 97
Metcalfe, family, 139–43
    Simon, 131
    William, 34, 74
Mew, 14
Midden, 12–14, 24–6, 124, 126, 134
Midland Counties Dairy, Wolverhampton, 109
Milk and Dairies Order of 1926, 134–5
Milk Bar, 48
Milk Bottle News, 84, 106, 114
Milk Churn (Milk Can), 6–7, 9, 21, 44, 46–7, 70, 87, 120
Milk Float, 19–20, 32, 42, 59–61, 70, 80, 87, 91, 110, 112
Milk Industry, The, magazine, 49
Milk Kit, 20, 45, 47, 120
Milk Marketing Board, 48–50, 59–60
Milk Ponies, The (poem), 48

Index

Milk Rationalisation, 50–1, 54
Milk Shop, 2, 6, 12, 14, 89
Milk (Special Designations) Order 1917, 44
Milk Vessels Recovery Ltd., 45
Milkhouse, 2, 11–13, 17, 22–6, 34, 37, 61, 82–3, 89, 94, 100, 121–6, 132–3
Milking Stool, 116, 134
Mingay, G.E., 2, 21
Molasses, 24
Morrison family, 100
Mr Seel's Garden, 106
Muck (cow), 12, 14, 21, 24–6, 30, 67–8, 85, 116, 126
Muckhole, 14, 126
Museum of English Rural Life, 66
Museum of Liverpool Life, 112
Museum of Soho, 106

National Archives, 68, 75, 82, 90, 101, 127–8
National Clean Milk Society, 44
National Library of Scotland, 75, 154
National Milk Publicity Council of England and Wales, 45
Nelson, family, 94, 139–45
    Ann, 74
    George, 140
    James, 139
Newspapers, 135
    Aberdeen Press and Journal, 51
    Coventry Evening Telegraph, 51
    Croydon Chronicle and East Surrey Advertiser, 36
    Daily Express, 61
    East Kent Times and Mail, 51
    Lancashire Evening Post, 137
    Leicester Evening Mail, 51
    Liverpool Daily Post, 136–8
    Liverpool Echo, 55, 65, 113, 137–8
    Liverpool Evening Express, 137
    Liverpool Mercury, 36, 65, 78–9, 119, 136–7
    Liverpool Weekly Courier, 8
    London Gazette, 56
    News Review, 48
    Nottingham Journal, 54
    Trowbridge Advertiser, 51
    Western Gazette, 42
    Western Mail, 51
New Zealand, 37
Nimmo, Richie, 7

Oilseed Cake, 24, 87
Old Dairy, Friern Manor, Stroud Green, 97, 103
Oral history, 80, 100
Ormskirk, Southport and Bootle Agricultural Society, 118

Parker family, 93
Pasteurisation, 44, 54, 56, 65
Pawson family, 106
Peel family, 91
Pemberton, Tom, 60
Pennine Dales, 34, 72
Phelps, Tom, 50, 61, 96
Pickering Brothers Ltd., 112
Postcards, 51, 62, 80–2
Poynter, Anne, 17
Pozieres, Battle of, 39
Prescott family, 92
Price, Edward (Eddie), 61
Primrose Dairy, Primrose Hill, 107
Provender, 43, 67, 136
Pudding Round, 19, 48

Rabinowitz, Mr I., 31
Railway Milk, 6–10, 107, 119
Ramsgate, 51–3
Rancher, 37–8
Refrigeration, 9, 54, 60
Roberts, E.H.G., 42
Roberts family, 106
Rootschat, 70
Royal Army Veterinary Corps, 76
Royal Borough of Kensington and Chelsea, 103

Royal Mail, 80
Royal Manchester, Liverpool and North Lancashire Agricultural Society, 15, 128
Rudstake, 14

Sainsbury family, 107
School Milk, 113
Scobie, Joyce, 35
Scott, Duncan, 26, 97–8, 107
Sedbergh, 74, 139–52
Settlestones, 14
Sharma, Babita, 58
Shinkfield family, 18
Shorthorn, 16
Skelbus, 14
Sloper's Dairy, Laindon, South Essex, 46, 103
Smith, Bruce, 104
South Africa, 37
Sowerby, T. & Sons, 66
Spellerberg, Ian, 119
St James's Park, London, 4
St Michael-in-the-Hamlet (Liverpool district), 11, 82
Stewardson, Isabel, 82
Stobart, J and Owens, A., 37
Stoner, Frederick, 15, 25, 130
Stones, Norman, 38
Stout, A., 24, 55
Stout, Janis, 40
Struther, Jan, 48
Sunter family, 88
Super Cream Line, 61
Swaledale, 13, 33, 101, 103

Taffy The Milk, 104
Taylor, Richard, 11, 82
TheGenealogist, 75–6, 154
Thornton, Gail, 101
Titterton family, 99
Transport Museum, Wythall, 112
Trowbridge, 51

Tuberculosis (TB), 27, 44, 65
Tynemouth, 53

Unigate, 56, 61
United Dairies, 50, 55, 57
Unwin, Frank, 18

Valenze, Deborah, 44
Veale family, 100
Verity, John, 79, 137

W. Sinclair of Otley, 68
Wales, 2, 8, 34–6, 45, 48, 82, 89, 97, 106, 113
Walker's Dairy, 103
Walling Philip, 24
Ward, Andrew, 60, 97
Warwick Farm Dairies, 107
Welford, J. & Sons Ltd., 108
Welford, Richard & Sons, 107
Wellington Dairy, Garston, 12, 30, 76–7, 80
Wenlock Committee, 28
Wensleydale, 6, 22, 33, 100, 106
Wharfedale, 33, 35, 64, 106
Whetham E. H., 4, 7, 10
Whitewash (quick-lime), 12, 15, 124
Whitfield, Matthew, 78
Windsor Carriage Works, Liverpool, 112
Winn, Henry, 132
Winstanley, Mike, 3
Wolfenden family, 11, 39, 96, 118
Wooding, Harry, 47
Woollard, M., 88
Wrathall family, 109
Wright family, 52–3, 58
Wright's Dairy, Chelsea, 105

Yorkshire, 3, 11, 13, 33–8, 61–2, 68, 72, 74, 86, 91, 95–101, 106, 109
Yorkshire Dales National Park Authority, 13, 100–101, 106